ALSO BY
DUSKO DODER

The Yugoslavs
U.S.-Soviet Summits: An Account of
East-West Diplomacy at the Top, 1955–1985
(with Gordon R. Weihmiller and David D. Newsom)

SHADOWS AND WHISPERS

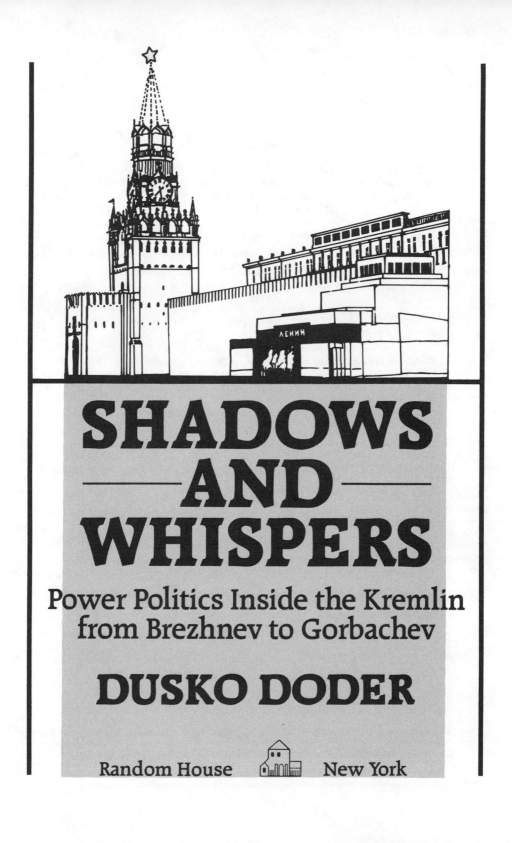

SHADOWS
——AND——
WHISPERS

Power Politics Inside the Kremlin
from Brezhnev to Gorbachev

DUSKO DODER

Random House   New York

Library of Congress Cataloging-in-Publication Data

Doder, Dusko.
Shadows and whispers.

1. Soviet Union—Politics and government—1982– .
I. Title.
DK288.D63 1986   947.085′4   86-10135
ISBN 0-394-54998-8

This publication was prepared in part under a grant from the
Woodrow Wilson International Center for Scholars, Washington, D.C.
The statements and views expressed herein are those of the author
and are not necessarily those of the Wilson Center.

Manufactured in the United States of America

24689753

FIRST EDITION

Book design by Carole Lowenstein

To my son, Peter

ACKNOWLEDGMENTS

Many helpful people and institutions have contributed to this book. The Washington *Post* deserves my deepest gratitude. I want to thank Benjamin C. Bradlee, Leonard Downie, Jr., Howard Simons, Philip Foisie, Jim Hoagland, Peter Osnos, Karen DeYoung, Michael Getler, and other *Post* editors for sending me to the Soviet Union on several occasions and for granting me a year's sabbatical to write this book.

It was completed at the Woodrow Wilson International Center for Scholars in Washington, D.C., where I was a fellow in the Kennan Institute for Advanced Russian Studies. My thanks go to James H. Billington, director of the Wilson Center, and Peter Reddaway, secretary of the Kennan Institute, for making my fellowship possible.

A substantial portion of the book was written at the Institute for Diplomacy, the School of Foreign Service, Georgetown University, in Washington, D.C., where I was a research associate. I want to thank Dean Peter Krogh and David D. Newsom, the institute's director, for their support. I also want to thank Nadja Krylov of the Intercultural Project of the Werner Erhard Foundation.

I owe a debt of gratitude to scores of Soviet citizens, many of them holding official positions, who shared their insights with me. They spoke candidly on the condition that they not be identified.

I have benefited from contacts with numerous diplomats but I want to mention Raymond E. Benson, Geoffrey Pearson, Guy de Muyser, Dagfinn Stenseth, R. M. Mohamad Choesin, Ercument Yavuzalp, Vahit Halefoglu, David J. E. Ratford, Dusan Strbac, Joachim von Arnim, Iftikhar Ali, and Hani Khasawneh. I am particularly indebted to Kemal Siddique, ambassador of Singapore in Moscow from 1984 to 1986, for his friendship and generosity in sharing his ideas.

Many persons have read portions of the manuscript and commented on them. I would especially like to mention my son, Peter, who was my first and severest critic, my wife, Karin, Ricky Silberman, Nancy Lieber, Robert E. Bartos, Paul K. Cook, Raymond Garthoff, Nicholas Gage, Michael Getler, Andrea Hamilton, Jan Otto Johansen, Robert G. Kaiser, Robert Lieber, Arkady Lvov, Murrey Marder, Don Oberdorfer, Leo Pappas, John Perazich, Elaine Rivera, Stephen Rosenfeld, Peter Silberman, Richard Stites, Svetozar Stojanovic, Branko Stosic, Richard M. Weintraub, and Bob Woodward. I alone bear responsibility for the facts and judgments in this book.

Peter Osnos, who served as the *Post*'s Moscow correspondent in the 1970s and who has since become associate publisher of Random House's Trade Books division, was the intellectual mentor of this book. Long before I finished my tour in Moscow, he urged me to write it, and subsequently he provided wise counsel and encouragement.

Michelle Maynard and Vivian Chakarian were my research assistants, eagle-eyed editors, and shrewd critics of the entire draft. Their help was invaluable. And I would also like to thank my colleague Patrick Tyler, who initiated me into the mysteries of word processing.

D. D.

Washington, D.C.
August 1986

CONTENTS

SHADOWS AND WHISPERS

INTRODUCTION

This is a book about one of the most dramatic periods in postwar Soviet history—a time encompassing the deaths, in rapid succession, of three aged Soviet leaders and the emergence of a younger man, Mikhail Gorbachev, representing a new generation of Kremlin power. I arrived in Moscow as correspondent for the Washington *Post* in the waning period of Leonid Brezhnev's long rule and was able to observe at first hand the Kremlin transitions from Brezhnev to Yuri Andropov to Konstantin Chernenko and, finally, to Gorbachev. This is not a comprehensive history but rather a journalist's account of a time that offered unique glimpses into the secret world of Soviet power.

I have been preparing to write a book like this for almost two decades, starting in the early summer of 1968, when I arrived in Moscow as a correspondent for United Press International. I kept notes in those years and continued to do so later. I joined the Washington *Post* in December 1970 and had the good fortune to be sent back to Moscow four times—on temporary duty in 1978 and again in 1980, for a full four-year stint from 1981 to 1985, and again in the winter of 1986. I also reported on Soviet affairs from Washington and served as the *Post*'s correspondent in Eastern Europe from 1973 to 1976, covering all Soviet-bloc countries from Poland in the north to Bulgaria in the south.

A journalist tends to assign greater importance to things he knows about than to those he cannot see. It is an occupational hazard all the more pronounced in Moscow, where there is very little information to be had beyond what the Soviet government chooses to make public. What I have done here is to consider the available evidence and to draw conclusions from it as best I can. I have made use of the reports and rumors that circulated among the Soviet elite if I judged them to be reliable, as well as information I obtained directly from knowledgeable sources. I was lucky enough to talk with several people who were close to the four Soviet leaders. They agreed to speak frankly on the condition that they not be identified. It is only natural that relatives and friends in such situations tend to have selective memories.

It is not my purpose in this book to draw comparisons or dwell on moral issues to prove the superiority of the Western way of life. This, to me at least, is self-evident. Rather, I sought to look at the Soviet Union on its own terms, in its own historical place and cultural and political environment, which are vastly different from our own. What I witnessed was the transition from entrenched power to a new generation favoring reform. Gorbachev has set out to modernize his country and de-Stalinize its political and economic system. It remains to be seen whether he will be able to subordinate the system to his purposes.

CHAPTER ONE

SCOOP

THE WEATHER IN MOSCOW had been frigid for weeks. A
dome of smog and vapor hanging over the city made breathing difficult. February is the cruelest month of the Russian winter,
and Muscovites struggled silently home after work through snow-
swept streets and into crowded subways. It was dark outside by
four in the afternoon. During the second week of February, the
city's vast avenues and squares were deserted by early evening.
People hurried home to watch the 1984 Winter Olympics, which
were in progress at Sarajevo. Soviet skaters had already collected
a host of medals, and the entire country seemed glued to their
television sets each night to follow the progress of their national
hockey team, the finest jewel in Russia's sports crown. Lovers
adjusted their rendezvous times; movie houses and restaurants
were empty; people sat around their screens to watch their team
move toward Olympic gold. In Russia, ice hockey invariably takes
precedence over politics, except in grave emergencies. On that

Thursday, February 9, 1984, there was no evidence of any dramatic event in the political sphere.

There had been rumors for several days about the health of Yuri V. Andropov, the Soviet leader for fifteen months, who had been hospitalized the previous fall and had been absent from public view for the past 173 days. It was reported that his condition had deteriorated. Life in Moscow that Thursday was calm, however; I doubt whether anyone in the city outside the charmed circle of power brokers knew what was happening.

It is commonplace in the West to describe the Kremlin, in Winston Churchill's memorable phrase, as a "riddle wrapped in a mystery inside an enigma"—and never was the description more apt than on that February night when, somewhat by accident, I noted that something was amiss. In retrospect, the events of that night capture the excitement, the frustration, the risks, and the realities of figuring out what is going on inside the Kremlin, not only for journalists but also for foreign governments.

I had decided to watch Soviet television, a stroke of luck as it turned out. The country was in the midst of a parliamentary election campaign and on that Thursday the newest member of the Soviet leadership, Yegor K. Ligachev, made his first nationally televised speech. I regard Soviet political rallies as exercises designed to induce mental lethargy through their mindless repetitiveness, and I felt reasonably sure that Ligachev would not break any new ground in his speech from Tomsk, in Siberia. But I wondered what had prompted Andropov to pluck a provincial official from Siberia, where he had served for eighteen years, and bring him into a key Kremlin position of power as the man in charge of party personnel. Despite his long illness, Andropov retained the mystique of a compelling leader with a talent for attracting dynamic and capable people. He had pushed Mikhail S. Gorbachev, the youngest member of the leadership, into the forefront of political life. Gorbachev and other Andropov protégés were different from the stereotype of Soviet politicians. All of them were young, self-possessed, urbane, tough, and seemingly imbued with a sense of purpose. I had never before seen Ligachev, who had become a Central Committee secretary only six weeks earlier, and I was interested to learn whether he, too, fit into the "new breed." But as I watched him on television that evening and tried to assess his personality, I was struck by his omission of a banal phrase that is almost mandatory in Soviet speeches: He did not convey Andropov's greetings to the people of Tomsk.

"Maybe Andropov is dead," I remarked casually to my wife. Based on so little, the idea sounded farfetched. Yet the omission was significant; it is far more likely that an American vice president or cabinet member campaigning in a presidential election would forget to extend the president's greetings to the voters of a midwestern town than that a senior Soviet official would fail to convey the Kremlin chief's customary greetings. Was it possible that the phrase was inadvertently cut by a technician? Highly unlikely. Or cut deliberately by the censor? But why? On whose authority?

What followed Ligachev's speech reinforced my suspicions. Without explanation, Soviet television changed its scheduled programming and instead of the Swedish pop group Abba, which my wife wanted to hear, presented musicians in tails playing classical music. It was a change similar to that on the day of Leonid I. Brezhnev's death fifteen months earlier, prior to the formal announcement the next morning. National mourning seemed to be starting in the same unobtrusive but unmistakable fashion.

Soviet politics has no other occasion as important as a Kremlin transition, none that could have a greater and more direct bearing on the life of the country and its people. The historic record of successions has been too fluid, their intervals too irregular, for an observer to discern an orderly pattern. Only one Kremlin leader, Nikita S. Khrushchev, was ousted in a palace coup. All the others died in office, lionized and venerated like the tsars until their last breath. Before the leader's death, deals on the succession may be discussed and plotted only in the greatest privacy among groups of like-minded politicians. Until the leader's heart stops beating there can be no public discussion, no decisions. This ensures that nobody can be absolutely certain until the last moment who the next general secretary of the Soviet Communist Party will be. I felt a surge of excitement, thinking that this was the day we had been expecting for weeks, a climactic day of hectic meetings, deals, and intrigues. But I had, of course, no information.

Since Andropov's disappearance from public view the previous September, diplomats and journalists had speculated about his health and who might follow him. The prevailing views on succession favored Gorbachev, Andropov's clear favorite, and Konstantin U. Chernenko, the choice of the older Brezhnev faction in the leadership. For months I had been adding long hours at night to my regular workday, wanting to be within the reach of a telephone, always having either a television or a radio turned on. Now I turned on both radios in the apartment, but the programs did not reveal anything. We ate dinner and watched the main evening news program, "Vremya" (Time), at 9:00 P.M. The broadcast turned out to be extremely thin on news, but that was not unusual. Ligachev's speech was barely mentioned. Then the picture shifted to Sarajevo, and the excitement, the gaiety, the colors, and the sounds of the Olympic Games, an indication of normalcy.

As I walked to my office across the courtyard, I decided that in analyzing the situation I should ignore the continuing Olympic coverage. The main purpose of the secrecy surrounding the death of a Soviet leader is to avoid disruptions or public confusion before the leadership settles the succession question, and canceling scheduled television coverage of a game by the national ice hockey team would guarantee public dismay. It would also alert Western embassies in Moscow to the crisis, the most vulnerable moment in the Kremlin's life. My job was to concentrate, to look for evidence and assess it. Alas, there was little to assess at that point.

Evidence? Such things are relative. In Moscow, one tends to assemble evidence through analysis of signs and portents, rather than from firsthand information. One thing that never ceases to amaze a foreigner, even after some years in the Soviet capital, is that it has no phone book—important denizens of Moscow do not give out their home phone numbers. However, I did have the numbers of several officials and could reach them at home in an emergency. But I knew that these men were confident that I would not bother them with questions on subjects they would not discuss over the telephone. As I had precisely such a question that night, I felt it would be a needless expenditure of hard-earned journalistic capital to phone them. So I sat in the office, staring at the charts of Soviet leaders adorning my walls, as I had been doing every day for months, and posing the hard queries to myself. Who's next? Would it be the youthful Gorbachev, who represented a new generation of Russians? Or would the old guard give the top job to Chernenko? Or was there another alternative?

The question was crucial because Andropov's tenure, however brief, had offered the hope that the ossified Soviet system might move into a new era. Virtually all indications pointed to Gorbachev as the heir and executor of Andropov's legacy. But the conservative forces were still strong and were expected to put forward Chernenko's candidacy, which many feared would mean an irretrievable loss for the reformist policy. Only in retrospect did it become clear that Andropov's tenure had had a lasting impact, which Chernenko could not undo and which ultimately created the basis for Gorbachev's drive for national reconstruction. But at that hour it was still unclear whether the country was about to undergo any transition at all.

It was ten in the evening. I was swept with a feeling of frustration and the urge to do something. I had only one realistic option: to call an acquaintance who was well positioned in the system, although he was not a senior official. Vasya had indirect access to sensitive information. We usually met at large receptions, where he felt at ease talking with me. I had run into him only two days earlier, at a function I had attended in the hope he would be present. He told me then that Andropov's health had taken a sharp turn for the worse. "That's all I know," he said. The next day I learned a few other tidbits along the same lines and wrote a story saying that the Soviet leader's condition had worsened and that he was unable to talk.

Although Vasya had discouraged me from meeting him alone, we had agreed on a telephone signal for emergencies. Such signals, he insisted, had to be sent from a public phone. If a meeting was possible, I would get a return call with a prearranged signal at my office in exactly twenty minutes.

There was an eerie muteness in the city as I drove toward the Lenin Library metro station, where I usually made calls from the ground-floor public phones. At night, the whole excursion took about ten minutes. As I passed the Armed Forces General Staff building, I noticed that it was fully lit. Outside the Lenin Library station I saw a military patrol, two soldiers and a noncommissioned officer. I noted these unusual signs, made the call, and rushed back to the bureau to await the return signal.

It never came. That night there was no official for me to consult. Vasya either was not home or had chosen to ignore my signal.

I went to the wire room in my office, which the *Post* shared with the daily newspaper *Mainichi* of Tokyo. The Tass machine smoothly emitted its daily diet of news but not the full text of Ligachev's speech. The Reuters wire concentrated on events in the Middle East, where there had been gunfire exchanges near Beirut involving United States naval forces. The *Mainichi* correspondent, Masai Egawa, who was a friend, came into the room to fetch his copy of the Tass material and told me that Andropov's son, Igor, had left Stockholm suddenly earlier in the day, according to an Agence France Presse dispatch from the Swedish capital, where Igor was a member of the Soviet delegation to an East-West disarmament conference.

I called the Agence France Presse Moscow bureau, but they said they had no additional information. Nevertheless, my earlier hunch had been reinforced by the news. Ligachev's speech, the canceled pop concert, Igor's departure from Stockholm—surely these were not coincidental happenings. More and more they were fusing into a composite picture. I also knew that the General Staff was at work this night, as on the night of Brezhnev's death, and what I needed to do now was to check other strategic locations in the city for signs of unusual nighttime activity.

It was past eleven and Moscow radio and television were still carrying reports from the Sarajevo games. I reasoned that television would end its broadcasts after the Olympic program was over, and this meant that the broadcast of Moscow Radio would be my only source of information. I checked the newspapers for radio programs. One of the main frequencies had a program of jazz scheduled for 11:35 P.M. That, I thought, should be decisive.

I wanted to consult with a trusted colleague. Possibly, I thought, my mind had wandered into a world of illusion. Big stories in Moscow invariably broke at night, when I tended to feel disconnected from the world. Slavko Stanic, correspondent for the Yugoslav news agency Tanjug, was an astute observer and a good friend. Not being competitors, we frequently discussed stories late at night, a practice that probably benefited me more than it did him. When I worked on stories with Stanic and other Yugoslav correspondents, I found communication with Russians easier— we did not have to go through the political fencing that Americans normally did, nor could the Russians easily fool us. The fact that I was an American of Yugoslav background worked to my advantage in Russia. I spoke the language and intuitively understood Russian anxieties, the country's secret fears and dissimulations, its difficulties in coping with the complexities of the modern world. Moreover, the Yugoslavs in Moscow were generally well informed. They and the Chinese followed domestic and ideological developments that were largely ignored by most others, and

11

they were willing to share their views with colleagues—unlike most journalists and diplomats from Soviet-bloc countries. I phoned Stanic to tell him I would stop by his office after midnight.

Driving toward the Kremlin I listened to the excited voice of the Soviet sportscaster. The gleaming white-marble General Staff building was still fully lit. I swung by the building and turned right, toward the river and the Ministry of Defense, a massive Stalinesque structure on the embankment. In my mind I could picture precisely the areas where the reception rooms were located; under normal conditions, only four reception-area windows would be lit at this hour of the night.

The embankment was almost empty. The Gorki Park Ferris wheel loomed high over the frozen river. The snowflakes began to wander down in front of my headlights. When I came upon the Ministry of Defense building, I saw that hundreds of its windows were lit. The fact that so many defense people were at work after eleven at night left no doubt that something extraordinary was happening. If it was not the leader's death, what else could it be? I got out of the car and crossed the street, beginning to count the windows; but I soon gave up. I remembered the latest Reuter reports on the fighting in the Middle East—possibly all that activity in the Defense Ministry was caused by the unusually dangerous situation in Beirut, I thought.

Driving back along the river toward the city's center, I heard the end of the Olympic broadcast on my car radio, followed by a brief news summary. I held my breath. It was 11:35 P.M. The scheduled jazz program was dropped without any explanation. The sounds of classical music came over the airwaves, soothingly, sweetly. Well, I said, there is only one explanation: Andropov surely has died. The conclave of the Soviet leadership to choose his successor must have begun in the early evening, with military aircraft dispatched to various parts of the country, which is spread over ten time zones, to bring regional party barons and all members of the policy-making Central Committee to Moscow. That was why

Andropov's son Igor had been summoned from Stockholm. I knew that other members of the family lived in Moscow, except for the dead leader's half sister, Valentina, who lived in Voronezh, about three hundred miles south of the capital. I also fitted the other telltale signs of the night into this picture. The country had clearly been placed on an emergency footing. By midnight, the radio-transmitting facilities of the Soviet armed forces and the KGB, the political police, would be relaying orders and messages throughout the country and the world.

For the first time that evening I felt really excited; I knew I was on to a very big story. Around me sprawled a cold and inhospitable city, by now asleep and unaware of the secret I had stumbled upon. After a bend in the river, there was the Kremlin, tower upon tower, dome upon dome, aglow with lights from red ramparts to the big golden onion tower of Ivan the Great 450 feet above the river, an enchanting fairytale sight on a snowy night. That I could feel so elated over the death of a man disturbed me, in all honesty. But in an obsessively secretive country I had discovered the most closely guarded secret. Nonetheless, I had to chase away this pleasantly exaggerated sense of accomplishment.

I parked the car near the vast Rossiya Hotel, not far from the ancestral home of the Romanovs, and sauntered into Red Square and toward the Central Committee building complex. The ruby stars atop Kremlin towers shone like jewels. The golden hands of the Spassky Tower clock had moved to midnight and the bell chimed the hour. The changing of the Kremlin honor guards took place in front of the Lenin Mausoleum. How many hundreds of times had I walked through this part of Moscow? How many times had I pondered the architecture of Saint Basil's Church?

The wind whipped the snow down Kuybishev Street. At each access road to the Central Committee complex, at each corner, I noticed two young men wearing woolen overcoats and fur hats, and I knew they were security officers. Fifteen months earlier, when I made an identical tour of the city at the time of Brezhnev's death, the same men were idling their time away after midnight. Who else would be hanging around the Old Square at this hour and in such inclement weather?

From the Old Square one can see the left wing of the KGB headquarters, built of granite and positioned next to Lubyanka, the prison and office building where Andropov had his office while he served as chairman of the secret police organization. The lights were on.

As I hurried back to the car, I felt certain that Andropov was dead. But could I write the story yet? Doubts rekindled as I recalled the firm statements of Soviet spokesmen that Andropov was recovering and that he was expected to deliver an election speech at the end of February. Rumors of an impending Kremlin transition had been circulating for weeks, yet so far they remained without substance.

For several days I had thought about Süleyman the Magnificent, the great sixteenth-century Turkish emperor, who took his army all the way to Vienna and died later at his camp in Hungary. Süleyman had scores of sons, and his grand vizier, trying to avoid an open power struggle over the succession, decided to keep the emperor's death a secret. The grand vizier, Mehmet Pasha, announced that the emperor had decided to return to his capital. He placed Süleyman's body in the royal coach and headed for Istanbul, but sent his best messenger ahead to alert one of Süleyman's sons, whom the vizier regarded as a worthy successor. The dead emperor's coach got a tumultuous reception when it rolled into the capital. The next day it was announced that the emperor had suddenly died and his son, the one favored by Mehmet Pasha, had succeeded him. I felt certain that something similar was under way at the Kremlin.

When I arrived at the Tanjug office and found Stanic seated gravely by his radio, I knew that he also must be aware of extraordinary conditions in the city. It turned out that he did not know about the change in TV programming nor about the lights at the four strategic buildings in the city, but his instincts and the classical music filling the austere room had led him to conclude that something highly unusual was happening. "Probably the boss," he said even before I told him about my findings. He used the word *hozyayin,* "the proprietor," the way the Russians use it to describe their leader.

Together we analyzed each piece of the puzzle, searching for any alternative to the obvious conclusion, for some flaw in our reasoning. In thirty minutes, I said, the radio is to begin its broadcast for the young people in Siberia who are building the Baikal-Amur railway, six or eight time zones away. If that program drops five minutes of humor and continues with classical music, then things will be clear. "Then there will be no doubt," Stanic said. "Andropov is definitely dead."

I felt that Stanic was summoning the resolve to file a story. For a journalist from a socialist country, this was exceptionally sensitive news. But he was a straight shooter, and for him as for me, Moscow life was made endurable by the challenge of the job; he was as delighted as a child each time he managed to pierce the wall of secrecy. Before coming to Moscow, Stanic had served as deputy editor in chief of Tanjug, a position of considerable responsibility in his country. Earlier he had spent seven years in Paris, first studying and then working. I had come to admire his integrity and his incisive mind as well as his brisk humor. He understood the essence of reporting in a society where virtually everything is a state secret. Normal reporting involves collecting facts, then drawing conclusions; but reporting from Moscow is almost 180 degrees different—one pieces clues and signs into a pattern to form a hypothesis and then goes about testing it.

Stanic was fastidious about facts, and even at that hour he decided to check the story by going to see a Soviet friend who lived within walking distance of his office. The source was not in a position to have access to matters dealing with the top leadership, he said, but it was still worth a try.

I was now under some time pressure to let my editors know about the story I would file. Driving back to my office across town would give me another chance to make a swing past the strategic points. The lights were still burning in the KGB headquarters, the Defense Ministry, and the General Staff building, but I noticed the complete absence of uniformed police, which was odd. I thought they must have been called in for instructions.

Back at my office, I turned on the radio and waited for the beginning of the program for young people in Siberia. When I heard the sounds of classical guitar I felt confident about dialing my office in Washington directly on telex and telling them the story. Rick Weintraub, the deputy foreign editor, came to chat with me on telex. In a slightly cryptic way, I told him that I planned to file a story that would be almost identical with the one I filed on November 10, 1982—the day of Brezhnev's death.

I typed with difficulty, making a lot of spelling errors, now running purely on nervous energy and suddenly aware of the great mental strain I had been under for some hours. Knowing that our telex exchange was being read simultaneously in some KGB office and fearing that my editors in Washington might ask questions about sources or require explanations that I did not want to share on an open line, I became somewhat testy. But Weintraub, a thoughtful man with extensive knowledge of foreign affairs, was soothing and low-key, grasping instantly the situation and the point I was making. I had been working on an obituary, I said, but now I was overtaken by events and would not be able to finish it. I suggested that it be done in Washington, as I had other work to do. "Don't worry," he said. "just go to it." I had two hours until the paper's first deadline.

I felt relieved when we ended the telex conversation. Driving back to Stanic's office, I noticed that the uniformed police were deployed again. Waiting at a traffic light, I was passed by an official black limousine roaring through the red light at eighty or ninety miles per hour; two other black Volgas hurried in the opposite direction.

I found Stanic even more determined to file a story, although his night visit had yielded only one new element—the exceptional nervousness of police. The guard in the compound where the Tanjug office is located rushed to the phone when he saw Stanic leaving the house, and two plainclothesmen materialized from nowhere to tail him. "They were five steps behind me all the time," Stanic said.

We discussed details now. Stanic said that he would focus his story entirely on the changes in television and radio programming, without mentioning anything else we had discovered, or even Andropov's name. His readers, he said, would be able to draw their own conclusions. As an afterthought he added somewhat sheepishly, "I have to call my ambassador and inform him about it." Tanjug, after all, was a government news agency. I thought how lucky I was not to have to consult anyone except my editors. It did occur to me, however, that the Yugoslav ambassador, Milojko Drulovic, enjoyed considerable access to the top Kremlin leadership and might be helpful.

It was past two in the morning as I listened to Stanic outline his story to the presumably sleepy ambassador. The ambassador was highly skeptical. I understood from the conversation that the ambassador was urging Stanic not to file. "Comrade ambassador, I work for Tanjug and it's my judgment that Tanjug should have this story," Stanic replied firmly. "I just thought I should inform you." After he placed the receiver in the cradle, Stanic relayed the substance of the ambassador's objections. He said his deputy had been in the company of some senior Soviet officials that very evening and had reported that everything was normal.

Despite my admiration for my friend's resolve, I was perturbed by the ambassador's comment. He was an experienced and cautious diplomat who previously had served as ambassador to Peking. We were still discussing the ambassador's view when he

17

called back. Stanic listened to the ambassador for several minutes, then repeated his intention to file the story. After hanging up, Stanic said, "He has checked around and said flat out that I am wrong and that Andropov is alive."

But my mind was made up too. The radio music was gradually shifting from classical to funereal, and the story took shape in my mind as I drove back to my office. I felt certain that by now my editors had contacted the CIA, the State Department, and other agencies in Washington that monitor Soviet radio transmissions, and that my factual reporting would be confirmed. The huge intelligence machinery of the U.S. government must have picked up the telltale signs, or so I thought.

I wrote the story conservatively, but after I finished transmitting it I felt anxious. I hoped that Tanjug would use Stanic's story— if we were wrong we could at least share the embarrassment. And yet, I thought, everything I wrote was factually correct. I started by saying that Soviet television had unexpectedly changed its scheduled program to classical music shortly after 8:00 P.M., and that the state radio followed with similar unexplained shifts later in the evening. I added that this came against the background of Andropov's long illness and suggested that the country had been placed on an emergency footing. The situation was identical, I said, with that on the night of November 9, 1982, just before the formal announcement of Brezhnev's death. Then I reported in detail all the signs that I had noticed and all the evidence to support the unmistakable conclusion that Andropov had died on that Thursday.

As I prepared to sleep in the predawn hours, I listened to mournful music emanating from the earphone of my transistor radio. I remembered that I was supposed to host a sit-down dinner party for fifty on that Friday evening; this was something we did once a year to pay off social obligations, and we had set the date weeks in advance for February 10. Invitation cards had been sent a week earlier. I had even hired two Gypsy musicians to entertain the guests, among them various Soviet figures and senior diplomats. So I left a note for my wife, who would be getting up in a couple of hours, saying that Andropov was dead and that we might have to cancel the party. I took a pill and sank into an uneasy sleep to the soothing, sad sounds of music.

While I slept, a separate story was unfolding in Washington.

After Weintraub received my initial advisory, *Post* editors and reporters, as I expected, immediately contacted the White House, the CIA, the State Department, and other agencies, giving them the details of my story and asking if more information had reached the U.S. government through its channels. Everyone said they had seen no such reports. After checking further, the officials called back to reaffirm that they had no information about any program changes or other telltale signs. Nevertheless, the *Post* editors decided to put my story on the front page.

Later that evening, several *Post* editors and reporters attended a gala State Department dinner. Among the luminaries present were Secretary of State George Shultz, Undersecretary Lawrence Eagleburger, and Soviet Ambassador Anatoly Dobrynin. An editor confronted Dobrynin with the story that was to appear the next morning, but the veteran diplomat laughed it off. "Come, come, come! He'll drop dead with these rumors." Eagleburger, however, said he would check the story. By the end of the dinner, he informed a *Post* executive that the story was wrong. "It's bullshit," Eagleburger said. "There's nothing to it." When the story was played back to the American embassy in Moscow that night, he added, U.S. diplomats joked, "Doder must be on pot."

Faced with such unequivocal denials, the *Post* editors decided to move the story off page 1 to page 28 and to slightly soften the language.

I was blissfully unaware of all this. When I woke up in mid-morning, I felt jubilant. I promptly learned from our Russian maid that the signals of an impending announcement of Andropov's death were unmistakable. The word had already spread through the establishment. I phoned Stanic. His agency had not used his file. "You are all alone," he said, congratulating me.

I walked over to the bureau and discovered to my chagrin in the routine daily cable from my home office that my story was not on page 1. I was baffled and angry. Front page, to a journalist, is the key objective. Seldom had I filed a story that I felt was more surefire front-page material. Then the official announcement came over Moscow television, saying that Andropov had died at 5:25 P.M. on Thursday. I plunged into reporting, driving down to the city's center, walking around in the crowds of people bundled up against the ravages of winter. At the Hall of Columns, workers were hoisting an enormous portrait of Andropov and stringing red-and-black bunting. Here, in the eighteenth-century Noblemen's Club, Andropov's body would lie at rest for the formal mourning, in the elegant hall of massive white columns and huge chandeliers. Throughout the city, men and women were putting up black rosettes, draping buildings in red, and placing black-bordered Soviet flags in the stanchions.

As I walked around the city canvassing opinion and looking for contacts, I realized that the mood of the capital—to the extent one could draw such conclusions on the basis of a dozen or so conversations—was for Gorbachev.

When I returned to my office hours later, I learned what had transpired in Washington and why my story was bumped from page 1. The explanation arrived in the form of a story set to appear in Saturday's paper and written by my colleague Michael Getler in Washington. As I read all the details of government denials, I felt a kind of perverse pleasure in having beaten the U.S. government.

By Friday evening, I had learned from a senior Soviet commentator that Chernenko had been selected chairman of the funeral commission, a clear sign that he had an edge over Gorbachev, despite the pro-Gorbachev sentiment I had detected earlier. The official announcement was to be made on television at nine in the evening. I took a cold shower before our dinner party, dressed, and stood near the door to greet the guests. I had thought before the party that most people, and particularly diplomats, would not turn up on such a busy day. This would have made it easier for me to leave and get back to work. But I underestimated how quickly word had spread about my exclusive story. With the exception of four important Soviet officials, everybody turned up at eight o'clock, including Sasha and Yasha Akulov, the father-and-son Gypsy duo who were occasionally hired by Foreign Minister Andrei Gromyko when he entertained at home. I was not to hear them play that night. I had already decided that after I had a chance to mingle during cocktails, I would leave my wife, Karin, and Danish minister counselor Mary Dau, the cohost of the dinner, in charge and quietly slip out.

Chatting with a guest, the Indonesian ambassador, Mohamad Choesin, I mentioned the choice of Chernenko to head the funeral commission. "That's it," he replied, adding that the old guard was still strong and would make Chernenko general secretary. The American ambassador, Arthur Hartman, reached a different conclusion. "They will never turn to Chernenko," he said assuredly. His selection as head of the funeral commission—"if that is true," Hartman added—"is most likely a move to pacify the old guard. It will be Gorbachev or [Politburo member Grigori] Romanov."

At nine o'clock, most of us moved into the study to watch the main television news show. The lead item was the announcement of Chernenko's appointment as head of the funeral commission. I left the room, quickly slipped into a sweatshirt, put on my sheepskin coat, and sneaked out of the house.

It was a frigid night. I checked my telex. It had a string of congratulatory cables, including one from Katharine Graham, the Post Company's chairman of the board. Needless to say, I was pleased.

I left the compound and drove down Kutuzovsky Prospect toward the Triumphal Arch, which commemorates the victory over Napoleon. Everything seemed normal; I did not sense that I was being followed. I slipped out of the car by a phone booth and dialed the number of a Soviet journalist I knew well. Like most of my Soviet contacts, he tended to talk with me in an oblique way, encumbered by formulations so full of double negatives and triple-dyed reservations as to constitute another language. But tonight he was brief. He did not know who was going to be the next leader nor did he know when the Central Committee meeting would be held. But, he said, he did not believe that it would be the next day, as was the case after Brezhnev's death. That meant that it would be another day or two before the situation could be cleared up.

I wrote the story with ease, for big stories write themselves. I also enjoyed one of the luxuries of a major event—I could write as much as I wanted; there are no space limitations on such stories. When I finished transmitting the file, I left the compound for the second time that night for a short drive to *Pravda*'s office to pick up the next day's edition; but it added nothing.

Back in my living room, trying to absorb the events of the past two days, I realized that I had hardly slept for forty-eight hours and that I was not going to fall asleep now before four in the morning. But long days were the norm during my tours in Moscow. I arrived in the last years of Brezhnev's life, when the country seemed weighed down by the inertia of a spent ideology. In the years that followed his death in 1982, the country was plugged in to alternating currents of hope and disappointment. A dispirited nation suddenly came alive as it felt the vitality and purpose that radiated out of Andropov's Kremlin, only to plunge into despondency again when he was succeeded by Chernenko. The eventual emergence of Gorbachev again held promise of new departures. As these events unfolded, one had to look for subtle signs, nuances of emphasis, and even silence to get a glimpse into the closed world of Kremlin power. So a journalist's job was to work not the way I had been taught—by covering the news through interviews, press conferences, and briefings—but through instinct, deduction, educated guesses, a little luck, willingness to stay up late—and the basic understanding that the Kremlin, impenetrable as it is, is made up of human beings.

CHAPTER TWO

GATHERING CRISIS

Empire in Flux

AN IMPORTANT MEETING took place in the evening of September 19, 1978, at the railway station of Mineralnyye Vody in the northern Caucasus. Leonid Brezhnev was traveling by train through southern Russia and decided to stop at one of the principal resort areas of the Stavropol region. He was at the height of his power. Two years earlier he had named himself marshal of the Soviet Union, an action disturbing to most professional soldiers but welcomed by the Defense Ministry chiefs as a sign of the leader's identification with the military, which seemed to guarantee his greater support of military outlays in the future. In 1977, he had ousted Nikolai Podgorny from the presidency and assumed that ceremonial post as well. These significant titles, added to his position as general secretary of the party, which he had held for more than a decade, symbolized his complete preeminence in the leadership.

Accompanied by his closest aide, Konstantin Chernenko,

Brezhnev was on his way to Baku, the capital of Soviet Azerbaijan. Since his health had begun to deteriorate, Brezhnev avoided airplanes whenever possible. When Brezhnev and Chernenko arrived in the Mineralnyye Vody railway station, they were greeted by Yuri Andropov, a member of the Politburo and chairman of the KGB, the secret police, who was vacationing in the area, and a young local politician, Mikhail Gorbachev, who was the party's top man in Stavropol. The four participants at this meeting could not possibly have imagined how their lives would be linked over the next seven years. And it would have required preternatural powers for anyone reading about it in *Pravda* two days later to divine that the general secretary had met and conferred with his three successors.

One could have entertained the theoretical possibility of Andropov as a future contender for Brezhnev's job, but it would have been much harder to consider Chernenko as a potential future leader. He had been running Brezhnev's office for more than two decades, as a professional party bureaucrat who prepared documents, controlled access to the boss, handled sensitive political and personal issues for him, and was known in the hierarchy, particularly as Brezhnev grew older, as the chief's alter ego. As Brezhnev consolidated his power, he brought Chernenko into the leadership, first as a secretary of the Central Committee in 1976, then as an alternate Politburo member in 1977, and finally as a full member of the ruling council in 1978. These promotions reflected Chernenko's power position not as an independent force but rather as a Brezhnev acolyte. To Central Committee *aparatchiks* they seemed personal gifts of the leader to a faithful aide, a show of Brezhnev's largesse. In Brezhnev's world no greater personal reward was possible than the gift of an important position. His son, Yuri, was deputy foreign trade minister. His son-in-law, Yuri Churbanov, was made a general and deputy minister of interior. His brother-in-law, Semyon Tsvigun, was deputy KGB chairman. How could he adequately thank his personal physician, Yevgeny

Chazov? Brezhnev made him a member of the Central Committee. Chernenko's long service obviously deserved a weighty political prize.

Nobody even gave any thought to Gorbachev, who was forty-seven years old at the time. True, the *Pravda* account of the meeting singled out the record harvest in the Stavropol region that summer and the success of local leaders in exceeding their planned production quotas by a wide margin. But Gorbachev was just a provincial politician, like hundreds of others who ran remote provinces in the huge empire and who came to Moscow twice a year for three days to attend the meetings of the Central Committee and Supreme Soviet. Nobody knew much about him. Even after he was transferred to Moscow, I never met anyone during Brezhnev's rule who considered Gorbachev a possible contender for a top position. His entire career was linked to Stavropol, an area equal in size to the state of Colorado and with a population of about 2.6 million, hardly the kind of power base normally required to reach the top. He became the region's party leader in 1970 and the next year was automatically made a full Central Committee member. Moreover, when he was brought to Moscow at the end of 1978 his position was not enviable; he was made responsible for one of the most troubled sectors of the Soviet economy—agriculture—which was obviously in serious and ever-deepening difficulties.

Both Andropov and Gorbachev were born in the Stavropol region, an area of the southern Russian steppes at the edge of the Caucasus Mountain Range, an exotic and stunningly beautiful landscape where the subtropical richness of the river valleys is set off by high mountains with everlasting snow. The range consists of two parallel massive walls, the higher one to the south, the lower one to the north. Gorbachev's native village, Privolnoe, lies in an area where the northern range drops away and the river Yegorlyk flows down from the highlands into a fertile grain-growing plain. The road Gorbachev had to take to reach Mineralnyye

Vody from Stavropol climbs through the foothills, passing the small railway station of Negutskaya, a village with a few scattered houses, in one of which Andropov was born.

The Caucasus was not part of the old Russia. But beginning in the late sixteenth century, the Russians edged closer and closer to the area. Peter the Great went as far as Derbent, trying to seize control of one of the two passes that lead through the formidable range. Russians moved into the area later, during the rule of Catherine the Great in the second half of the eighteenth century, and Marshal Count Suvorov established a permanent military settlement at the site of what is now the city of Stavropol. Remnants of the fortress, which had served as headquarters for the tsarist military command of the Caucasus border region, can still be seen in the city. The lines of communication from here to Georgia and Azerbaijan were occasionally threatened even a century later by vengeful Moslem guerrillas and hot-blooded mountain tribesmen, incidents that inspired much great literature. For a romantic Russian the Caucasus was a world not only of magic beauty, of mighty torrents, jagged peaks, and inaccessible passes, but also of surprising freedom, where man could quickly prove himself against the elements. Pushkin, Lermontov, and Tolstoy were all captivated by the magic of the area and wrote about it.* Settlers on the land lived as frontiersmen in a world of swashbuckling warriors, honor, pride, and glory—far away from the Russian heartland with its venal clerks, sullen serfs, and sycophantic courtiers.

Near the Suvorov monument and the historic fortress, Gorbachev put up a large statue in 1977 honoring the Red Army soldiers killed in the postrevolutionary civil war. From this highest point in the area one sees, as far as the eye can reach, rolling hills and fertile valleys dotted by single-family homes and luscious private gardens. People in this agricultural section of southern Russia

---

*Pushkin, in *A Captive of the Caucasus;* Lermontov, in *A Hero of Our Time;* Tolstoy, in *The Cossacks, The Raid,* and *Hadji Murad.*

speak softly, with southern rolled *r*s. Their manners are spontaneous, and in temperament they seem closer to the neighboring Ukrainians to the west than to the northern Russians. Their forefathers were soldiers and peasants whom Catherine and her successors sent to colonize this distant outpost of the empire and to ward off Turkish and Tatar armies. Most colonizers who settled here were not serfs, as in the Russian heartland; they were cossacks, or free farmers, who paid for their freedom by rendering military service to the empire. That was an important psychological distinction at one time, but whether it has survived to this day to make a difference in the attitudes and makeup of the people of Stavropol is debatable; local residents believe it has.

The Caucasus retains a grip on the imagination of the Russians, and they flock to the region each year for their holidays. This was an important asset for the young Gorbachev. Had he been a party leader in Yakutia or Vladivostok, he would never have had the personal contacts with high officials that Stavropol afforded. Andropov, who vacationed alternately in Mineralnyye Vody and nearby Kislovodsk, got to know Gorbachev and took a liking to him; the two frequently walked in the woods and discussed politics. The older man liked the younger man's wit and intelligence, his energy and capacity for teamwork, and the fact that Gorbachev and his family were untouched by any whiff of corruption. His mother and numerous relatives continued to live as they always had in Privolnoe and to work on the local collective farm, although Gorbachev was the most influential political official in the area. (Gorbachev's mother, Maria Panteleyevna, did not change her way of life even when her son became the country's leader.)

In 1978, these qualities also impressed another senior member of the leadership, Mikhail Suslov.* With Suslov's concurrence,

---

*Suslov served as first secretary of Stavropol from 1939 to 1944, and he retained close political ties to the area.

Andropov wanted to bring the promising young politician to the capital, and the opportunity presented itself in 1978 when Fyodor Kulakov, a member of the leadership responsible for the country's agriculture, died unexpectedly. Nothing could be done without Brezhnev's approval, and the September 19 meeting had been set up by Andropov as an occasion for the leader to meet and assess the prospective replacement for Kulakov. It was, in effect, Gorbachev's job interview. That it went well for him became clear in November, when Gorbachev was summoned to Moscow to run the country's agriculture and was named secretary of the Central Committee. Two years later, he was also a full Politburo member.

The timing of Gorbachev's move to Moscow in 1978 proved highly significant, as Brezhnev's era was drawing to a close, and the ruling gerontocracy was preparing for a power transition. The Soviets had only three precedents for such a transfer since the Bolshevik Revolution—the transitions from Lenin to Stalin, from Stalin to Khrushchev, and from Khrushchev to Brezhnev (Brezhnev's succession in 1964 involved a coup against Khrushchev). In the USSR the death of a leader constitutes a particularly powerful shock, as a result of a major flaw in the system bequeathed by Lenin: the absence of a clearly defined mechanism for the election of a new leader. The road to leadership is sufficiently clear—one invariably begins in the provinces and climbs the ladder of the party bureaucracy until one reaches the Politburo, or the ruling council of about twelve top party figures. But the process of selecting the party's general secretary, the country's leader, remains mysterious, calling for endless maneuverings and power struggles at the top, especially if the leader becomes ill. Over the next few years Brezhnev, Chernenko, Andropov, and Gorbachev would all be engaged in such political maneuverings during a dramatically compressed series of transitions.

Gorbachev's promotion marked the only attempt to rejuvenate the leadership during the last years of Brezhnev's life, and it seemed to have questionable results, as the appointment was followed by several disastrous harvests. In the fall and winter of 1981, there were widespread food shortages, causing much popular discontent. As the man responsible for agriculture, Gorbachev came under pressure, and some people thought he could become the fall guy for a leadership incapable of securing sufficient food for the country. Fortunately for Gorbachev, the agricultural setbacks were only one facet of a much broader and more dismal picture of a stagnating country.

‹‹‹ 2 ›››

THE rhythm of Russian history is divided into uneven periods defined by the reigns of tsars and more recently of general secretaries. Brezhnev's era was one of stability and had a tranquilizing effect on the country. After years of upheavals, first under the tyrannical Stalin and then under the erratic and unpredictable Khrushchev, the Soviet Union settled into an uneventful, regular sort of life and enjoyed a modest economic boom, at least by Soviet standards. The seventies, in particular, were the best years the country has ever known. Living standards went up; there were more private cars, more shops, restaurants, and luxury goods. Clothes became more fashionable and brighter. People had more money and leisure. At the same time, under Brezhnev, Russia achieved strategic parity with the United States, becoming militarily stronger than ever before in its history and beginning to blunder about vigorously indeed in the murky territory of global strategy. Moscow's direct influence abroad extended beyond the wildest dreams of Brezhnev's predecessors. South Vietnam, Laos, Cambodia, Ethiopia, Angola, Mozambique, Nicaragua, South Yemen—all these countries fell into the hands of Communist or pro-Soviet regimes.

Ironically, however, a multitude of economic, social, and foreign-policy problems came together at a time when the Brezhnev era was drawing to a close. Moreover, Brezhnev became seriously ill in the late seventies, and in the early eighties his physical frailties were aggravated by the rapid degeneration of his mental faculties. Much of this was obscured by his staff, the government's propaganda machine, and its rigid protocol. He had been in power for so long that he could afford lengthy absences from his desk— his well-oiled bureaucratic *aparat* was firmly entrenched and knew what the chief wanted. They shielded him during periods of indisposition by structuring his schedule so that nobody would notice anything wrong—public ceremonies requiring his presence were arranged at short notice when he was feeling strong. The paralysis at the top had political and economic side effects; yet the government projected an image of stability and orderliness, so that it was difficult to detect these problems early on. The propaganda machine hummed smoothly, as if Brezhnev's reign would last forever.

When I arrived in Moscow on temporary duty in the summer of 1978, it was apparent that incremental changes had taken place over the past decade. In the eight years that had elapsed since my previous stay in Moscow, the city had become a more relaxed place, less regimented. Memories came back of tense days after the Soviet invasion of Czechoslovakia in the summer of 1968; of furtive, conspiratorial meetings with dissidents; of sitting up all night in smoke-filled rooms in communal apartments, discussing abstractions with the abandon of youth. Now my old acquaintances and friends lived in their own apartments, burdened with everyday concerns. Most of them were less afraid, yet they were also careful of what they said to me. In the narrow circle of my friends I found something that was new, or at least more pronounced than before—the quest for the comforts of middle-class life: a car, a place in the country, a tiled bathroom, a Japanese stereo, a chance to travel abroad, at least to Bulgaria. I listened attentively—a distasteful task, since I disliked using friends as sources of information, even in an indirect way. But since the country lacked any open clearinghouse for ideas, one had to listen to conversations at more humble levels to gain a sense of the mood of the place. By the end of the seventies even dissident *samizdat,* or self-published, material had largely disappeared as the government managed to suppress political dissent. That deprived us of at least the clandestine channels of information and insight into forthright views and debates at the subterranean plane.

The talk of Moscow that summer was the August wedding in the Soviet capital of Christina Onassis and a recently divorced Russian shipping clerk, Sergei Kauzov. Apart from the tremendous propaganda value to the Kremlin that this somewhat absurd event presented, there was something symbolic about it, for even the whim of a rich woman said something about changing times in the Soviet Union. Such a situation would have been inconceivable only a decade or two earlier. What was one to make of the marriage of Onassis, heir to one of the great private fortunes in the West and stepdaughter of Jacqueline Kennedy, and a shipping clerk who earned seventy dollars a week and was a member of the Communist Party—and of the Kremlin's blessing such a union? To add another bizarre quality to the event, Onassis talked about a honeymoon in Siberia and a happy future sharing her new mother-in-law's one-bedroom apartment in Moscow.

I had never covered a wedding before, but this one was news. Never had the neighborhood of the Palace of Weddings witnessed such an enormous crowd of journalists, photographers, and camermen. Women in red-and-white scarves working on a large construction site next to the palace dropped their tools and rushed to the main entrance. Old ladies in surrounding buildings leaned out of windows. The bride, twenty-seven at the time, wearing a long mauve gown with a design of purple flowers, arrived at the Palace of Weddings in a beat-up Chevrolet Nova belonging to a Greek diplomat. Her husband-to-be, Sergei Kauzov, was thirty-seven.

We watched the couple emerge from the eighteenth-century building into the gorgeous summer morning and drive off in Kauzov's Volga sedan, which he started with some difficulty.

During that summer, I met old friends at less exalted levels of society. The Onassis wedding prompted one of them, Yura, to talk about his life. When I knew him in Moscow in the late sixties, he was passionately in love with an English girl. They wanted to marry but he could not get permission. At the time he worked for an important institution, and his superior gave him a clear choice —you can either keep your job or marry a foreigner, but you can't do both. He lost both the girl and the job. I had missed the outcome of the story when my assignment came to an end, and now, as we talked in the woods on a balmy summer afternoon, he filled in the details. I knew that they used to meet in Leningrad for a few days of passion that made bearable their months of long separation as Yura awaited permission to marry. She came there from Finland on short Intourist tours. However, he never did receive permission, and after nearly three years, he recalled, both of them were desperate. He could not see any future in the relationship, nor could she. That was the end, after one last meeting in Leningrad. He added wistfully that if he had been able to hold out for a few more years, the thing probably would have worked out. You see, he said, "things are changing . . . slowly."

But, I thought, Yura is a romantic sort. Surely the Onassis wedding was an exception, a great propaganda coup that fell into Moscow's lap, a low-risk exercise. Yet other voices were also optimistic, pointing out small improvements in their lives. I spent several pleasant evenings at the home of Julia and Vadim Sidur. Vadim, probably the finest sculptor in Russia, was exuberant because some statues of his had been erected in West Germany. True, the sculptures had gone up without official Soviet permission; Vadim's German admirers and friends—among the latter was the novelist Heinrich Böll—had somehow transported small models of them to Bonn and Frankfurt. A heavy coffee-table book devoted to Vadim and his work had been published in West Germany, and my friends beamed with pride as they leafed through the glossy photographs depicting his magnificent works. There was another piece of good news—having waited almost thirty years, Sidur had finally seen one of his abstract monuments erected in Moscow. The sculpture in Moscow, a massive thirty-by-ten-foot concrete abstraction, was set on the grounds of a medical institute and therefore did not require the approval of the Ministry of Culture. That the ministry persisted in its unyielding opposition to contemporary art could be seen in its denial of a formal request by the city of Belgrade to have Vadim design a monument in the Yugoslav capital. Here was the contradiction of Soviet life: The leaders of the Soviet Academy of Medical Sciences had sufficient clout to commission an abstract sculpture by Sidur, whereas the government of a socialist country was denied permission to have Sidur design a monument for its capital. How come? Perhaps, I suggested, the Soviet cultural barons, now in their sixties and seventies, did not want to make enemies in the medical world? Vadim had no explanation, but he speculated that the inherent conservatism of the Russians had little to do with ideology. "Imagine," he said, recalling the first visit to his studio by Alexander Solzhenitsyn, before the novelist won the Nobel Prize and long before he was expelled from Russia. "Solzhenitsyn came in and immediately expressed his strong dislike of abstract art. He said, 'If I came from another planet to a country where monuments and sculptures looked like this'—and he pointed at things in my studio —'I would go back right away.' So you see even Solzhenitsyn would not allow my sculptures in Russia."

Another old friend, Joseph Goldin, was irrepressibly optimistic. A short and rubicund man with playful eyes of azure blue, he sported a large beard that framed his pink face. He was a man of action as well as of imagination, a charming oddity in Moscow— a free spirit with a razor-sharp mind and no definable job or vocation. He had fixed his sights on "building space bridges" between the peoples of America and Russia through direct communication via gigantic TV screens, a slightly vague and highly ambitious task, given the fact that he had no official position within the system and had not been asked to undertake such a project. Joseph's penchant for regarding new technologies as cure-alls for international problems reflected a national trait; it remained a puzzle to me why direct communications between the people of, say, San Francisco and Novosibirsk would eliminate political strains. Although Jewish, Joseph did not want to emigrate; although a free spirit, he was not anti-Soviet. Yet, authoritarian regimes do not like people who, while not dissidents, are outspoken and uncontrollable. Joe was like an unguided missile whose mind could range far and deep in any direction, often reaching heretical-sounding conclusions. I got to know him—and to like him a great deal—back in 1968. His intellectual curiosity had increased since then. As he had a lot of free time, we would go to the theaters and discuss cultural and social trends, even politics, analyzing whatever was public knowledge. Underlying his thoughts in the summer of 1978 was optimism, a conviction, as he put it, that the question was no longer whether systemic changes were going to take place but how they would shape the future. We went swimming that summer, and under the spell of warm sun and the kindness and good cheer of other friends, we agreed that things seemed to be moving slowly in the right direction. The authorities were confronting a wave of rising expectations, pressures for a better life, and that seemed a natural progression.

On my way to a theater, I bumped into a friend who, when I first met him a decade earlier, had lived in one room with his parents, his wife, and a child. Now he was the business manager of a theater, with an apartment of his own and a small dacha in the country. As we walked along the Tverskoi Boulevard, we recalled with pleasure and nostalgia my initiation rites in the sixties—night-long conversations around various kitchen tables, where brilliant intellectual arguments were lubricated by vodka. Now he complained a lot—about his inability to get a car and the fact that the apartment was too small, only one bedroom. But even his complaints were a sign of the changing times.

Not everyone shared in the optimism. With my *Post* colleague Kevin Klose, I had a long discussion over a sumptuous lunch at the apartment of Venyamin Levich. Levich was the most prominent Jewish scientist to apply for permission to emigrate to Israel, and the authorities did not seem inclined to grant it. He and his wife were embittered by the long wait and the uncertainties of their lives; spiritually, they were no longer living in Russia. As we discussed how they could achieve their goal, Levich suddenly launched into criticism of U.S. foreign policy, and specifically attacked Washington's willingness to negotiate limitations on strategic weapons with the Soviet Union. "You should not conclude SALT agreements with them," he said, apparently feeling that a refusal to negotiate would inflict some retribution on those who forced the refuseniks into limbo. I found such criticism so unexpected and uncalled-for that I adopted a decorous reserve for the rest of our visit.*

On the whole, however, fragments of conversation, visits to the homes of a few friends, chance meetings, all fused gradually into a composite picture of a more relaxed Moscow. Although the Jewish refuseniks were complaining bitterly, tens of thousands of Jews were being allowed to leave (emigration had not been an option in the past). Life in Russia, it seemed, was slowly changing and becoming better.

And yet I had a feeling that in some ways nothing had changed since I had lived there in the late sixties. On the day we moved into the *Post*'s apartment, in the same compound where I had lived before, I walked over to the office across the familiar court-

---

*The Leviches were allowed to leave a year later as a result of a private representation on their behalf made by Senator Edward M. Kennedy of Massachusetts.

yard with the feeling of having returned to the old surroundings after a week's visit to Helsinki, not after an absence of eight years. The same faces, the same gestures, the same guards, the same salesladies in the Beryozka shop (special hard-currency shop for foreigners), the same carbolic acid smells in the hallways. And the same obvious KGB surveillance, which even my son, Peter, who was then nine, could immediately spot.

Two years later, when I came once more on a temporary summer assignment, my impressions were again contradictory. Moscow was spruced up for the 1980 Summer Olympic Games, one of the major events on the official Soviet calendar for the decade. Few cities in the world can compare with Moscow when it comes to creating a dazzling effect—miles of roads were repaved and instantly lined with trees, thousands of peeling façades were repainted, stores were stocked with goods, long-neglected and deserted churches were hastily restored to their former glory. I discovered beautiful sights in places I had passed hundreds of times in the past—the magnificent eighteenth-century church of Metropolitan Philip, near a new Olympic stadium, and the Holy Trinity Church on the Garden Ring. Both added beauty and a sense of history to previously drab neighborhoods.

But the games were marred by the American boycott. Moscow had been chosen as the site for the 1980 Summer Olympics at the height of détente, but the Soviet invasion of Afghanistan in December 1979 led President Carter to boycott the games and to impose an embargo on American grain sales. The Russians put on a brave face. The games were a brilliant show even without the Americans, an almost perfect, if curiously joyless, spectacle. In a televised speech after the Olympics, Brezhnev spoke with contempt about the American action. "So what," he said, pointing out that the games were a great success and that Moscow could buy wheat elsewhere. He also underscored his commitment to the regime of Afghan Communist leader Babrak Karmal: "No one should have any doubts about it." Brezhnev made no mention of Poland, which was becoming the most pressing problem for the Soviet empire.

Afghanistan, although a major diplomatic burden, was not a serious domestic issue in 1980. Poland was. The creation of an independent trade union, Solidarity, in a major Soviet-bloc country seemed to shake the entire foundation of communism. The authority of the Polish Communists was disintegrating daily, and the extent of Soviet concern was revealed in the decision in late August 1980 to resume jamming of Western broadcasts in Russian. The action clearly reflected Moscow's assessment that the developments in Poland were as threatening to the Soviet bloc as was the 1968 crisis in Czechoslovakia, which was "resolved" when Warsaw Pact armies marched into Prague. On the very morning jamming was resumed I had a call from the sculptor Sidur, who informed me about it. Although a staunch Soviet patriot, Vadim, like numerous other Soviet citizens, was an avid listener to Western broadcasts.*

By the summer of 1981, the Polish turmoil had intensified and the position of the Communist authorities in Warsaw had deteriorated even further. The mood of Moscow was now different from that of 1978 or even 1980. Back again in our old apartment—this time for a four-year stint—I pondered the change. Perhaps the most striking feature at the beginning of the eighties was a negative one: Brezhnev's stable regime had produced an amazing proliferation of corruption, a cynicism that undermined all enterprise. An air of stagnation, the timeless inertia of the bureaucracy, a crisis of spirit—all characterized a system that seemed to have accompanied its aging leaders into exhaustion and debility. The

*The history of Soviet jamming is significant: It started in 1948 with the onset of the Cold War and was lifted by Nikita Khrushchev in 1963. It was resumed during the Czechoslovak crisis in 1968 and again lifted in 1973, at the time of détente.

old men were clinging to the rhetoric of the past, but their jargon was incongruous with reality; it was the language of leaders incapable of dealing with a whole range of new civic, social, and personal problems that agitated the new generation. The nation seemed, at least for the time being, to have lost its sense of direction. The most popular rock group in the country, Mashina Vremeny (Time Machine), whose songs of the trials of everyday Soviet life were a reflection of popular culture, seemed to capture the loss of faith in its song "Bluebird of Hope." Its refrain ran as follows:

> I do not believe in promises,
> and will not do so in the future.
> There's no sense in believing in promises.

What I did not grasp at the beginning of my four-year stint in 1981 would strike me with the force of a revelation when things began to unravel following Brezhnev's illness in early 1982. By then, all the Kremlin's troubles had been given a sharper focus by a new, more assertive, and more confrontational American president who wanted to bury the Soviet-American détente shaped in the seventies. But for a long time the Russians simply ignored President Reagan's challenge, as if it could be wished away. Indeed, the summer of 1981 saw the first full-scale rock opera staged in Moscow, with a message favoring détente and urging cooperation between the two superpowers. The author of the lyrics was poet Andrei Voznesenky, who took a nineteenth-century love story involving a dashing Russian naval officer and a beautiful San Francisco woman as the basis for his *Juno and Perchance.* The lovers had to overcome religious and other differences, just as the two countries now had to cope with ideological differences. But youthful audiences were more interested in the choreography, by Bolshoi dancer Vladimir Vasilyev, which was bold indeed for the prudish Soviet capital and involved simulated sex scenes, and in the use of profanities, and costumes resembling the gear of Hell's Angels.

─────────────────────── ⫷ *3* ⫸ ───────────────────────

THE Polish labor unrest had a direct practical impact on the Soviet Union, apart from the profound and disheartening psychological damage it inflicted on the Soviet Communist Party. It set off a chain reaction throughout the interlocking economies of the Soviet-bloc nations, disrupting planned deliveries of goods and spare parts and forcing the Russians in effect to feed the Poles and supply them with energy. The food shortages in Russia in the fall of 1981 were aggravated by extensive Soviet shipments of food to Poland, but that was politically difficult to admit, since the average Russian by and large disliked the Poles. I found most people behind their government and criticizing the Poles as lazy and ungrateful. A joke illuminated this deep-seated resentment: "The Poles want to be paid American wages but they work the way we do in Russia!" The popular view held that sharp action by Moscow would give the Poles a lesson and quell unrest. To the extent that the average Russian grasped the larger implications of the Polish crisis, his concern was about the role and intentions of the United States there. Most Russians believed Moscow's charges that Reagan was using Poland to undermine socialism in general and the Soviet Union in particular. The purpose of U.S. policy, according to a view held widely in Moscow, was to undermine Brezhnev's policy of détente and to complicate his battle for European public opinion.

All this was not, however, fully perceived at the time, and it was difficult to find officials willing to discuss the matter. Hence it was my good fortune that the managing editor of the Washington *Post,* Howard Simons, arrived to visit us that fall.

Howard is a gentleman of the old school, warm, wise, with an excellent mind and a passion not only for journalism but for the arts, history, and ornithology. Long before arriving in Moscow he had expressed interest in meeting local bird-watchers and going with them into the woods to do what all bird-watchers do. I spent countless hours on the phone trying to explain this to various Soviet officials. "A bird-watcher, eh? In the woods around Moscow! And he is using binoculars?" Eventually, after long negotiations, Howard was allowed to go birding, accompanied by a local bird-watcher and our office driver, Ivan Karezin.

Arranging appointments with top officials was equally difficult. Pyotr F. Alexeyev, editor in chief of *Izvestia* and an important Central Committee member, was not available, until I actually shamed him into receiving Simons. I got him on the phone, a miraculous thing in itself, and then reminded him that he had been Howard's guest at two *Post* luncheons in Washington. "I know, I know," he replied irritably, "but I am really busy that whole week." I was thoroughly annoyed. "Now look, Pyotr Fyodorovich," I said as firmly as I could, "even Russian peasants would be more decent than you are. When they accept someone's hospitality they know how to return it!" There was a long silence and then he barked at me, "Okay, okay, I will see him."

We also saw Georgi Arbatov, Brezhnev's adviser on U.S. affairs, and Nikolai Inozemtsev, who was once a senior aide to Khrushchev and who now headed the most prestigious of Moscow's think tanks, the Institute of International Economic Relations. Both were Central Committee members and I saw them frequently, never without profit.

One purpose of visits such as Howard's is to provide the local correspondent with access to senior figures. Contrary to the prevailing view that all Soviet officials are closemouthed and never reveal anything unless they are told to do so, senior officials, if one can reach them, do talk quite freely. During our meeting with Alexeyev, for example, we were suddenly provided with insights into the situation in Afghanistan when Alexeyev described to us the hostilities Russians were facing there. As he volunteered information, his two deputies began rolling their eyes and coughing to get his attention. But Alexeyev went on: "It's terrible there," he continued, without paying attention to his subordinates. "Imagine, the other day crazy Moslem women marched to the house of our correspondent in Kabul . . . almost killed him."

Alexeyev was more interesting to me than the better-known figures, such as Arbatov, Inozemtsev, Yevgeny Primakov, head of the Institute for Oriental Studies, and other officials Simons met in Moscow. I knew these men to be sophisticated and articulate representatives of the Soviet establishment. Alexeyev, on the other hand, like most members of the Central Committee, seemed suspicious of foreigners and surprisingly ignorant of foreign countries despite frequent trips abroad. There was a crude streak to him. When Howard, in response to Alexeyev's question, said we were having difficulties in seeing other top figures in the government, Alexeyev leaned forward and with a steely smile said, "I'll make you a deal. I will arrange for you to meet anyone you want to meet, provided that you, when you get back to Washington, arrange meetings for our man there." Howard politely declined the offer. "Well, you see," Alexeyev said, breaking into laughter.

What our conversations revealed was that the Russians were of two minds when it came to Poland: There were people in the Kremlin who wanted to crush the Polish revolt, but the prevailing hope was that the Poles themselves would manage to contain things in the end. On domestic issues there was an undertone of pessimism in all these talks; Inozemtsev alone was quite explicit about the need to "restructure" the system. The economy, he said, "cannot operate the way it used to operate ten or fifteen years ago."

An almost palpable sense of relief was felt in Moscow after General Wojtiech Jaruzelski imposed martial law in Poland on the morning of December 13, moving unexpectedly in order to gain complete tactical surprise. Even Soviet intellectuals were relieved; many of them regarded the Poles as unfortunate martyrs in a situation of their own making. The popular reaction was placid. After a bitterly cold spell, Moscow enjoyed almost spring-like weather on that Monday, and people flooded into the parks during the lunch hour to bask in the warm sun. I went to Gorki Park to sample views. The typical reaction was "Finally order is being restored in Poland."

But in the Kremlin the atmosphere was anything but placid. Behind the façade of normalcy, Monday was a long and grim day for the Soviet leadership—the longest and grimmest they had known during the Polish crisis. For the Russians had urged Jaru-zelski to make an extremely tough decision. Now a failure to maintain control would definitely mean direct Soviet intervention. Throughout the day members of the ruling elite pored over reports from Poland, as I learned later from senior sources who dealt with the crisis. By the time the news from Poland was announced to the public, the reports indicated that Jaruzelski was in full control. Yet I was surprised the next day to learn from friends and acquaint-ances that Soviet Army reservists had been put on alert and mobilized during the night. Men were summoned shortly before midnight to show up within thirty minutes at prescribed locations, usually neighborhood schools, in battle gear. They returned to their homes in the morning. A friend who was among those called up, a professional in his mid-thirties, refused to tell me even months later what that was all about. No mention was made of this in the press—although Soviet military maneuvers had been a nerve-jangling sideshow to the Polish crisis ever since the forma-tion of Solidarity fifteen months earlier.

⋘ 4 ⋙

As the year 1981 came to a close, the Soviet Union seemed at a standstill. Its establishment was riddled with cynicism and corruption; its ideology was no longer a force that could galvanize masses into action. The old conviction that Russia was riding the crest of history had been supplanted by a feeling within the elite that communism was everywhere in retreat and the Americans everywhere on the march. The party, throbbing with pessimism, prepared for the succession crisis as if for war. But that meant resorting to subterfuges and creating illusions to obscure the fact —widely felt and perceived—that the old guard was incapable of handling challenges, either from within, arising from the public discontent and economic setbacks, or from without, as the Americans began to counter the Kremlin across the board.

Many problems were obvious. Official figures showed steadily declining rates of industrial growth and labor productivity, and a series of disastrous harvests. Then there came a 70 percent increase in the cost of oil extraction as the country, the world's largest producer of oil, sought to maintain and slightly increase output by developing the Siberian oil fields. The higher energy costs affected other industries already plagued by labor shortages and increased real costs of new capital equipment. Although the official statistics may have been slightly doctored to obscure the real scope of decline, they nevertheless showed that the economy was slowing down, that it was riddled with corruption and inefficiency, that crime was soaring, and that alcoholism had reached epidemic proportions. The reformist economist Abel Aganbegian, writing in the newspaper *Trud,* provided an insight into the impact of alcoholism on labor productivity and discipline. He said he had visited fifty major industrial firms in the course of 1981 and was shocked by his findings. In some firms, he said, authorities had had to set up "special brigades" to find drunk workers each day, and to try to prevent industrial accidents and injuries.

The personal experience of an acquaintance of mine gave these cold statistics vivid life. We were friends of his wife, a well-known actress, who graciously supplied us with hard-to-get theater tickets. Her engineer husband, a Communist Party member, was in charge of 320 workers at a major Moscow machine tool plant and put in long hours trying to fulfill his production quotas. One afternoon, when I called at their apartment to pick up some theater tickets, I found him in bed. He had been beaten up by his workers the previous day, his wife said. Why? How? What followed was a depressing tale of endless frustrations. Each day, he said, roughly forty workers would simply not show up for work, while another forty came to work drunk. This meant that one quarter of his work force was missing, and he simply could not meet the planned quotas. He had tried to reason with the workers, he said, but to no avail, and when he had threatened the drunk workers on the previous day, they ganged up on him and beat him up on the shop floor. There was nothing he could do about it, he said.

The situation in agriculture was even more distressing. I managed to obtain a copy of an internal study conducted by the Soviet Academy of Sciences, which revealed a disastrous deterioration over the past decade. Despite enormous investments in agriculture, the Soviet Union's food imports had increased tenfold, from $700 million in 1970 to $7.2 billion in 1980. Direct losses due to negligence and lack of storage facilities were huge—one fifth of the grain harvest and one third of the country's potato crop were left to rot. The mishandling of agricultural equipment was staggering, as was illustrated, among other things, by the fact that the number of tractors servicing collective farms had remained constant between 1976 and 1981 although the country produced 550,000 tractors every year and added them its pool of agricultural machinery.

While a complacent Brezhnev government ignored the signs of a gathering economic crisis, ideas of reform and national reconstruction percolated beneath the surface, occasionally finding their way into the public debate through oblique scholarly articles and official studies and assessments. These diagnosed the problems without offering specific suggestions about cures; but they were significant because they brought new thinking into official circles, if not at the top level, then among the younger people who were poised to move into upper echelons of power.

It was clear in 1981 that no changes in either domestic or foreign policies could even be contemplated without a clear decision at the top and the personal blessing of the general secretary. But with Brezhnev's health deteriorating and in the absence of a clear mechanism of succession, the country was, in effect, run by his personal staff headed by Chernenko.

As Brezhnev grew older, one of his personal aides confided to me after the leader's death, he was increasingly reluctant to have new faces around him and felt comfortable only with the old, familiar people. Except for natural attrition, there were virtually no changes in the composition of the Central Committee for the last ten years of his life. So partly by design and partly by default, the hallmark of his eighteen years in power was stability. Initially, Brezhnev and his confederates who deposed Khrushchev had deliberately avoided the erratic policy shifts and personnel changes that so disturbed the bureaucratic elite during Khrushchev's years in power. But this policy, which neatly fitted into Brezhnev's political outlook, eventually became an irreversible trend. Top officials acquired lifetime job security under Brezhnev, and this meant almost automatic security for countless officials in the middle and lower levels of the party and government bureaucracy. Eventually inertia seemed the principal force at work.

Immobility also affected foreign policy. Here was a curious situation. Brezhnev had become so identified with the policy of arms control that he did not even consider the alternatives—not because he did not want to obtain military advantages for his country wherever possible, but because he became a prisoner of his own public image. At first he and his colleagues were suspicious of American arms-control ideas, but once they started negotiations with the Nixon administration, Brezhnev embraced arms control and détente as the cornerstone of his foreign policy. He liked his image as a man of peace and initially was projecting a studied imitation of someone better and more thoughtful than he actually was. Eventually, however, he became completely identified with his role, and his concern about nuclear weapons and ways to control them carried conviction, even in private conversations. This was how one of his speechwriters described Brezhnev to me after his death. He genuinely wanted to be remembered the way Chancellor Helmut Schmidt described him after his last visit to Bonn, as a man of peace.

Brezhnev did his best to sound reasonable and accommodating during his Bonn visit in November 1981, trying to stimulate opposition in West Germany to the scheduled deployments of new American medium-range nuclear missiles there. The trip was complicated by an incident created by Andrei Sakharov, the dissident physicist and winner of the Nobel Peace Prize, who had been exiled in 1980 to the industrial city of Gorki, about 250 miles east of Moscow. Sakharov started a hunger strike to press the authorities to allow his stepson's fiancée to emigrate to the United States. After several weeks, the Kremlin yielded to Sakharov's demand. But this reinforced an impression that Brezhnev was determined to salvage détente at all costs, which was a source of dismay to some elements in the Soviet elite and especially in the armed forces. The propaganda machine indirectly fueled such resentments. The Soviet media daily printed dire news from America, pouncing on Reagan's remarks about the possibility of a limited nuclear war to buttress its argument that the United States was seeking to attain strategic superiority. The argument was targeted at foreign audiences and was primarily designed to generate nervousness and doubts in Western Europe about Reagan's nuclear policy. Given the magnitude of the danger portrayed, Brezhnev's response appeared hopelessly limp to his own audiences.

There was another side to this policy. For a long time Brezhnev had been fascinated by American technology, and access to it was a principal motivation for détente. Ever since the time of Peter the Great, tsars and general secretaries have sought contacts with the West to obtain its trade and technology, while doing everything possible to insulate the Russian population from the possibly infectious cultural and political values of the West. But Brezhnev had opened up his country more than any of his predecessors; he had raised living standards while achieving strategic parity with the United States. That such achievements were threatened in his last years must have been a source of great frustration and disappointment for a man of his determination and will.

Brezhnev's seventy-fifth birthday on December 19 turned into a somber occasion despite the splendor of the Kremlin's Saint George's Hall. Once again, members of the Soviet leadership concealed their concern and anxiety under masks of composure and formal courtesies, watching their leaders mingle serenely with guests, including all the top East European leaders except Jaruzelski, who was busy administering martial law in Poland. Jaruzelski's congratulatory message, which was read on the occasion, expressed gratitude to Brezhnev for his understanding of the "dramatic and difficult" situation in Poland. Brezhnev seemed physically fit and moved about with an ease that surprised me. Only later did I find out that during the last year of his life he became animated and performed with ease any time klieg lights were on.

Among the outpouring of tributes Brezhnev received was yet another Order of Lenin with the gold star of a Hero of the Soviet Union—the country's highest decoration. About three fourths of all space in Soviet newspapers was devoted to the birthday celebrations, including eight-column headlines hailing him as "the planet's most widely read author" for his numerous books about his own career and the achievements of communism. Brezhnev had developed his literary ambition late in life, after he became ill, and had gone along with this aspect of his personality cult because the lie, a harmless one, appealed to his vanity. But it was widely known in Moscow that his books were ghostwritten by Alexander Chakovsky, a Jew and the editor of *Literaturnaya Gazeta,* the weekly journal of the Writers' Union. Because he spoke English, Chakovsky was known in the foreign community and was generally regarded as Moscow's consummate cynic. I once talked about Brezhnev's tolerance of the cult with a member of his family, who asserted—in his defense—that it was impossible to remain unaffected by the adulation with which he was surrounded. This was nothing compared with the almost incredible flattery of Stalin as the universal genuis. But the men who rule the Kremlin are in the direct line of descent from the tsars, who were worshipped to an even greater extent.

Brezhnev, as I was to learn later, had little sense of what was going on at that point. His capacity to work had diminished sharply. Official visitors who met him professed to have found him fit, but others, who had seen him in earlier days, were struck by the marked deterioration of his physique. One American who saw him that December and found him vigorous and "thoroughly at ease" was Armand Hammer, chairman of Occidental Petroleum Company and a frequent visitor to Moscow. But Hammer was nearly a decade older than Brezhnev.

⟨⟨⟨ **5** ⟩⟩⟩

IN late December, propaganda charges and countercharges were spread across the front pages of Western and Soviet newspapers. Reagan's economic sanctions against Moscow and Warsaw aroused Russian anger. The Kremlin accused the American president of conducting a "campaign of hatred" against the Soviet Union in an effort to curtail relations and, as *Tass* put it in an outburst of indignation, "hurl the world back to the dark ages of the Cold War." Already at that point I sensed the outline of a long propaganda struggle rooted in the old compost of ideological hatreds.

It was not a pleasant time for members of our small foreign colony in Moscow. I felt this unhappy season in another, more personal, way. We had placed our son, Peter, in a Russian school, and he was not flourishing. At times of serious international tensions, teachers in Soviet schools frequently discuss current topics to present the Kremlin line on key issues. Reagan's nuclear policy and the perceived American threat were the most burning issues of the day, and teachers had been instructed to talk about them in school. Following these instructions, Peter's teacher lambasted the Americans for contemplating the creation of immoral weapons to fight immoral wars. There is hardly any doubt that the issue was presented to the sixth graders in the simplest black-and-white terms and without any attempt to provide countervailing arguments. All the routine denunciations probably would not have had the impact that they did on Peter if he hadn't been the only American in class. To make things worse, the teacher happened to look at him while she was castigating the United States. I believe she did so because she was embarrassed. I knew the lady and she was a kind person and a fine teacher. But Peter felt he was being accused of crimes he did not even comprehend. He did not want to stay in a Russian school anymore, and in January we moved him to the Anglo-American School.

At times such as this, I found comfort in other Americans. Indeed, we were heartened on New Year's Eve by the arrival of the Louisiana Repertory Jazz Ensemble, which ordinarily held forth on Wednesday nights at the Maple Leaf Bar in New Orleans, and which was brought to Moscow by S. Frederick Starr, the president of Oberlin College, who was an avid jazz-clarinet player as well as a historian.

In the absence of a Soviet-American cultural agreement and with relations entering a frigid phase, Ambassador Hartman and his resourceful wife, Donna, used an unorthodox approach to maintain the American presence in Moscow and invited the Louisiana group to be their guests. In the midst of my daily reporting of calamities and poisonous problems, I was delighted to have a chance for some vestige of a personal life. Moreover, Fred was a friend, and we enjoyed his music. So we stole off for a night of gaiety—which was verging on extravagant behavior for me because, to meet deadlines for a morning newspaper, I had to work nights. We danced the whole evening at Spaso House, the elegant American residence, which by now represented an almost forgotten world of style and comfort, and greeted the New Year with champagne.

With the pressures and uncertainties of the Polish crisis over, Brezhnev entered the last year of his life tied hand and foot not only by his physical frailties but also by the rigidified machinery of his government. His era was drawing to a close. No one in his immediate political entourage grasped the urgency of the Kremlin's needs. The accumulated restlessness within the elite, which had been held in check as long as the situation in Poland was unclear, now began to seep into the open. For the first time, Brezhnev's preeminent position was chipped at and pared by shadowy forces within the system. Whispers of discontent were everywhere. The government of old men floated as in a void, without a leader capable of making fundamental decisions, and most matters continued to move along existing tracks. As long as he was around, time stood still for his country.

The harbinger of clandestine attacks on Brezhnev was an article published in the December issue of a Leningrad literary magazine named after the cruiser *Aurora,* whose salvos ushered in the Bolshevik Revolution. The issue was dedicated to Brezhnev's sev-

51

enty-fifth birthday and featured his photograph. On page 75, the magazine carried a three-hundred-word essay entitled "Jubilee Speech," which was widely perceived as a scathing satire on Brezhnev's public and literary activities and his continuance in office despite his advanced age. The sketched caricature of the fictitious author bore unmistakable features of Brezhnev; the essay made an allusion to the fact that the party chief had allowed himself a few months earlier to be awarded the Lenin Prize for Literature. "Most people think of him as long dead, so great is the veneration of his talent. One can hardly believe that this wonderful writer is still alive . . . that he walks the same streets as the rest of us. He should be dead, after writing so many books. Any human being who had written so many books would have been in his grave a long time ago. But this one—this one is truly inhuman. He lives on and does not even think of dying, to the consternation of all." The writer's place, it continued, is beside Dostoyevski, Balzac, and Tolstoy. "He deserves the honor. Here he sits, right in front of me, red-cheeked and chubby, and it is hard to believe that he will die. But he will, sure as taxes. We won't have to wait for long. He won't disappoint us. We all believe in him so much. Let's hope that he completes the work still in hand and gladdens our hearts by departing [from this world] as soon as possible."

Something had happened. How could this thinly veiled piece of malice have passed the very tough censorship? *Aurora*'s editors undoubtedly had support in high places—at least that of the Leningrad party chief, Grigori Romanov. I found the quasi-public discontent with the tsar a new experience. We were not yet into the transition crisis, but the portents were disquieting. The mood of sizable sections of the elite had apparently shifted against Brezhnev and the old guard. I sensed a revival of Russian nationalism of the sort that emerges periodically when the people begin to feel that they have entered a chaotic and uncertain interregnum.

CHAPTER THREE

LIGHTS AND SHADOWS

Brezhnev Under Attack

ALL THAT JANUARY OF **1982** dark rumors circulated about corruption in high places. Slowly the rumors began to implicate the leader's intimate circle, and this amounted to an attack on his personal power and authority. When, in March, Brezhnev's health became an issue, the real succession struggle was inaugurated.

A crackdown on corruption had started the previous November with daily press exposés of scandals implicating petty and middle-level officials. The corruption ranged from a whopping multimillion-dollar embezzlement in Georgia, involving top local officials and managers, to a racket in Byelorussia, where workers and security guards at a Minsk packing plant ganged up to steal large quantities of meat. From the glut of detail, one got the impression that bribery, extortion, and speculation had reached such proportions that it was virtually impossible for average citizens to go about their daily business without breaking the law.

As the campaign gained intensity in the new year, the word was spread that the corruption reached much higher, up to the very top level of the party and government bureaucracy, which meant the people around Brezhnev. Then, on January 20, Tass announced that Semyon K. Tsvigun, first deputy chairman of the KGB, had died in Moscow after a long but unspecified illness. The extraordinary thing about Tsvigun's obituary, printed in all newspapers the next day, was that it was not signed by his brother-in-law, Leonid Brezhnev. This raised many eyebrows in the diplomatic community, for Tsvigun was also a member of the Central Committee and a four-star general with an assortment of the country's highest decorations that fully covered his chest on ceremonial occasions. Kremlin routine was immutable: Why did Brezhnev violate it? Obviously there must have been a reason for the general secretary to refuse to append his signature to the obituary of a Central Committee member.

A few days later, whispers spread that Tsvigun had committed suicide.

Tsvigun had married Vera Petrovna, the younger sister of Brezhnev's wife, Viktoria Petrovna, while he was a young operative in the Ukraine before World War II and Brezhnev was a relatively obscure provincial official in the Ukrainian city of Dnepropetrovsk. After war service, Tsvigun resumed his career in the KGB and was sent to Moldavia. Five years later, in 1950, Brezhnev, whose political career was on an upswing, was sent to Moldavia as its party leader. Obviously, family ties were important in Tsvigun's subsequent career—a year later he was named deputy chairman of the Moldavian KGB, and he became its chairman in 1954, just as Brezhnev was moving on to run a far larger section of the country, Kazakhstan. Tsvigun subsequently served in similar KGB positions in two sensitive Moslem republics, Tadzhikistan and Azerbaijan, until his brother-in-law, who in the meantime had become the party's general secretary, summoned him to Moscow in 1967 and appointed him first deputy chairman of the KGB. Tsvigun's move into the headquarters at Dzerzhinski Square coincided with the appointment of Andropov, a career politician, as chairman of the state security and intelligence organization. Tsvigun was Brezhnev's insurance policy, his own trusted man at the very peak of a vast police establishment.

I had no way to check out the Tsvigun rumors, nor could I pinpoint their source. My contacts within the party and government could not provide any information. This did not mean that the suicide rumor was false. Such was the skepticism about all official information that rumor frequently took the place of news, spreading through the city with lightning speed and providing a way of assessing political currents within the politically alert segment of the population. Like rumors on Wall Street, whether true or false, they led people to act, to take positions. But it would be dangerous for a correspondent to write, without being on absolutely solid ground, that a prominent personality such as Tsvigun had committed suicide. Although there was no censorship of our dispatches, we learned very quickly that Brezhnev and other personalities had to be treated with great caution and respect. If Leonid Zamyatin, the abrasive chief of the Central Committee Information Department,* found a correspondent's work unacceptably irreverent or insulting, he had a way of making the writer's life miserable, or, in extreme cases, of having correspondents expelled.

Russians in general are an apolitical people. They gossip over drinks about their jobs, illicit love affairs, the latest black-market deals. They talk about sports or poetry or almost any subject except politics. But various elites do talk about politics, and much of our information about happenings in Moscow came from sources who whispered and traded in rumors. Since information is rationed according to rank, a foreign correspondent had to socialize with members of the establishment. Moreover, one had

---

*Zamyatin was recently sent to Great Britain as ambassador, a demotion.

to keep in mind that although rumors were generally based on genuine information leaked by persons in the know, the sources frequently garbled their message with outlandish and irrelevant details to obscure its origin and, I believe, to protect themselves. To assess such information properly one had, to the extent possible, to locate the origin of a rumor and to consider who stood to gain by it.

The spread of information among the elite was one function of such rumors; some of them served another purpose of equal significance—the preparation of the public mind for things to come. The report of Tsvigun's suicide was in this category; it was linked with rumors of corruption and therefore seemed aimed at the leader. It became apparent to me that while Brezhnev's men sought to keep things calm and to ameliorate discontent, their opponents sought to inflame it.

Frequently I heard rumors from dissidents—but here again one operated in the dark. I suspected that some sources were merely masquerading as dissidents, and I was especially wary of those who seemed excessively anti-Soviet. It was quite possible that, in the old Russian tradition, the authorities had infiltrated the dissident groups, and excessive anti-Sovietism might well be a ploy to gain my confidence.

Tsvigun was a well-established figure in Moscow. I knew more about him than about any other KGB official. He had spent more than four decades in the KGB and was apparently an efficient and competent officer with an interest in literature and film. When he moved into the upper tier of the KGB hierarchy, he indulged his passion for literature by writing a novel (later turned into a movie), and he also produced a series of articles dealing with security issues. At first he acted as a consultant to a film studio, Mosfilm—a lucrative and undemanding job advising directors who were making detective films—and later he wrote several movie scripts. Among filmmakers who had worked with him, he was regarded as an intelligent but cautious man, more aware of risks than of opportunities, somewhat prosaic and orthodox in his outlook. Yet he was generally described as being a fair and incorruptible man whose main weakness may have been his roving eye. We in the foreign press could see him only at a distance, at the rare ceremonial occasions he had to attend. His face was rather coarse. With age he had gained weight, and his balding pate made his head look almost completely round. His eyes were cold and piercing, the eyes of an inquisitor, meant to frighten and immobilize suspects.

While scrambling to learn more about so elusive a person as a KGB deputy chairman, I spoke with an actor who had played in one of Tsvigun's films. Yes, he said, confirming one part of the official announcement, Tsvigun was ill and had recently undergone lung surgery. No, he added, Tsvigun was not a depressive person, not the sort of man likely to shoot himself. He was sixty-four and in good shape.

In addition to Brezhnev's abstention from signing the obituary, there was another mysterious thing about the case. For the first time, by reading the obituary, we learned the names of all the top officers of the KGB. The men who had lived all their lives in the shadow of anonymity had gone public. Why? Was this affair part of a struggle for power, an attempt to undermine Brezhnev's position by exposing corruption in high places? If so, Tsvigun must have figured—in a way that was not entirely clear—in the bigger scandal that broke a week after his death and that heralded a period when sniping at Brezhnev began in earnest.

In late January, KGB agents arrested a senior Ministry of Culture official, Anatoly Kolevatov; his deputy, Viktor Gorsky; and Boris Buryatia, a man-about-town generally known as Boris the Gypsy, who was the longtime lover of Brezhnev's only daughter, Galina. When agents raided Kolevatov's apartment, they discovered diamonds worth more than $1 million and about $280,000 in foreign currency. Jewels from the tsarist era were reportedly found in the possesion of Boris the Gypsy. Simultaneously, the

KGB moved against a senior Ministry of Interior official, General Konstantin Zotov, who was accused of receiving bribes, and yanked from his post as head of the visa office.

The news of the arrest of Boris the Gypsy spread like wildfire through the city. He was the best known of all those detained, a tall, flamboyant, handsome man who had started as a circus performer, moved on to the Bolshoi Theater chorus, and was frequently seen driving a yellow Mercedes sedan that belonged to Galina Brezhnev. He liked flashy clothes, wore a diamond-encrusted Orthodox cross under his shirt, and enjoyed a reputation as a great lover.

Galina's liaisons with various circus performers over the years had been a source of continual gossip. Her first husband was a trapeze artist. She divorced him to elope to the Crimea with another circus performer, who was Jewish; but their marriage was immediately annulled on Brezhnev's order. Eventually she married—with her father's enthusiastic blessing—a lieutenant colonel in the uniformed militia, who had been assigned to her as a security guard. Yuri Churbanov was a few years younger than Galina. Galina's cousin, who, I thought, disliked her and was jealous of her, confided to me that she believed the handsome and youthful officer was assigned to guard Galina in the hope that she would be attracted to him. In any event, Brezhnev instantly promoted his new son-in-law to the rank of lieutenant general and made him first deputy minister of interior. The interior minister, Nikolai Shcholokov, was an old Brezhnev crony and he smoothed Churbanov's upward move.

But after a few years of quiet married life, Galina again ventured into the world of circus performers and artists, embarrassing both her husband and her father. A strong-willed woman already past fifty, she openly flaunted her liaison with Boris the Gypsy, a man twenty years her junior. Whether Galina was aware of the black-marketeering and diamond smuggling that was carried on by her friends remains an open question. Probably she was not. Boris the Gypsy, Kolevatov, and the others may simply have used the prestige of Galina's name and her father's position to carry on their work with impunity.

By early February, Moscow was abuzz with whispers. It was a spicy scandal with elements that ensured the wildest possible circulation—the leader's daughter, her young lover, a diamond-smuggling racket, huge amounts of confiscated money. Underlying all this was the notion that the leader, now a sick and helpless old man, was unable to control his corrupt family. New rumors had it that Galina had been hospitalized to avoid an interrogation. Her brother, Yuri, was also reported to be hospitalized because of his drinking problem, which had become widely known in the foreign community when he had served with the Soviet embassy in Stockholm. Rumors were circulating that his drunken escapades had made him incapable of doing his job as deputy foreign trade minister. Soon another rumor had it that Boris the Gypsy had died in prison under mysterious circumstances (two years later authoritative sources confirmed this to me).

This scandal gave credence to earlier reports that Tsvigun had committed suicide. As first deputy KGB chairman, he must have known about plans to move against Galina's friends. Might he have resorted to suicide as a way of resolving a conflict between his professional duties and his desire to protect his brother-in-law and patron? Only later did we hear from people in the establishment that Tsvigun *had* tried to cover up the scandal, but that Andropov had reportedly forwarded the file to Mikhail Suslov, the ascetic and incorruptible high priest of Soviet communism, who summoned Tsvigun. What transpired in that meeting is not known, although rumor had it that the two men clashed so vigorously that no compromise was possible. Two days after Tsvigun's death, Suslov suffered a coronary, and he died on January 25 at the age of seventy-nine. I have heard knowledgeable people say that the clash with Tsvigun may have so disturbed the frail Suslov that it led to his death.

Nothing, of course, was said officially. Stonewalling was the time-honored way to minimize damage. But the political elite familiar with the Byzantine maneuverings of the Soviet hierarchy understood the crucial point in the murky affair: Some elements in the party were beginning to question Brezhnev's fitness to continue as its head. On February 22, *Pravda* published an article ostensibly summarizing readers' letters about private morals. The paper's editor in chief, Viktor Afanasiyev, was a strong supporter of the reformist trend in the establishment. That he allowed the following sentence to appear in the paper was illuminating: "Children reveal, as if in a mirror, the psychological conditions and convictions that prevail in their families."

The stench of corruption was symptomatic of a more fundamental change. Disaffection was now widespread among the new generation of technocrats, educated men and women. Two powerful institutions in Soviet society—the KGB and the armed forces—were also concerned and unhappy about the course of events. A combination of setbacks and misjudgments had all too obviously damaged the party's claim to infallibility and raised doubts about the adequacy of its policies.

There was something else underneath, too, like the pressure of a wound. If my inquiries received any meaningful responses at all, they were gestures of sad resignation by my contacts: There was nothing to be done, for the political system was such that even if the leader was unfit, there was no way to remove him from office without incurring unacceptable political and psychological costs. The two previous transitions in Soviet history had produced ideological and social upheavals that prevented the party from developing civic and cultural resources that would foster respect for its own institutions.

After Stalin's death in 1953, Khrushchev denounced the dictator's entire career and turned him into a nonperson, an action that has left the party and the country deeply split on the issue of Stalin to this date. Brezhnev and his confederates took the same course after they ousted Khrushchev in a palace coup in 1964. The country seemed to its younger generations to have been almost leaderless for much of the time since the death of Lenin in 1924. History books were rewritten often, to gloss over the forty-year span between Lenin and Brezhnev; references to Stalin and Khrushchev were eliminated, and their images were cut from films, obliterated from photographs. A monument to this practice is the colossal mosaic adorning the ceiling of the Komsomolsky Square metro station in Moscow. A massive panorama depicts the momentous victory-day parade in 1945 in Red Square, when captured Nazi banners were thrown in a heap in front of the Lenin Mausoleum before the Soviet leadership, headed by Stalin. The features of most of the leaders—now long disgraced—have been whitewashed to render them unrecognizable.

The Soviet Union seemed a country without a real history. I vividly remember that when I read my son's history book while he was still attending the Russian school, I was struck by the fact that its account of the period between 1924 and 1964 was boring because it had few heroes and no leaders. Instead, the children saw their country's history in terms of gigantic building projects, factories, and dams; it was as if Russia was nothing but a mammoth construction company.

From conversations with middle-level officials and academics I gained the distinct impression that a substantial portion of the elite now sought a sense of continuity, without which the country could not expect to prosper. So the establishment had to wait for nature to take its course. Yet another Kremlin coup would only widen by Brezhnev's eighteen years the forty-year gap in Soviet history and further weaken the system by diminishing its ability to mobilize the population except by brute force. To what extent this argument penetrated the top echelon of the party was not clear. What I could deduce from people at the edges of power with whom I spoke was that Andropov shared this view.

2

BY March, political life seemed to have returned to its normal course—at least this was what reams of Tass copy led us to believe. Brezhnev hosted a visit by Jaruzelski in early March, then led a group of senior Politburo members to attend the premiere of a new play, *So We Shall Win,* a work openly critical of Stalin.

In retrospect, one event in March appears significant, for it foreshadowed what was to come later. On March 5, Alexei Shibayev, chairman of the Soviet Trade Unions and a Brezhnev protégé, was dismissed from his post and accused of corrupt practices and mismanagement of union funds. The decision seemed to have been taken hastily, only ten days before the scheduled congress of the Trade Unions and three days after the publication of a long article by Shibayev about future union plans. Immediately after his dismissal, juicy rumors about Shibayev's misconduct surfaced, depicting him as a man who had used union funds to build private dachas for his relatives and friends and who was involved in sexual orgies, together with another Brezhnev protégé, Sergei Medunov, the party chief of the Krasnodar region, which includes some of the finest Black Sea holiday resorts. Listening to these whispered revelations, one had to wonder how such a man could head an organization that counted 127 million citizens as members and that worked closely with the party. Who had spread these rumors so promptly and so widely? We assumed the KGB was behind this move and other anticorruption actions.

Almost every day I went to the modest snack bar of the U.S. Embassy, where a number of American colleagues gathered for lunch and conversation. We speculated endlessly. Had Tsvigun tried to suppress the diamond-racket investigation? Or had he, as a loyal KGB operative, faced a situation so difficult that it prompted him to take his own life? To what extent were other senior figures alarmed at the extent of the Brezhnev's clique's economic offenses? Everyone had a pet theory, and we had some heated debates. Undoubtedly we came close to the truth in these informal seminars, but we certainly did not know it—as far as solid information was concerned, all of us were on shaky grounds.

The snack bar became for me a haven from the daily strains of living in the world of Russian winter with its leaden skies, frigid winds, an endless string of days bereft of sun, and snow piling up ever higher and higher—an American oasis where I could have hamburgers and catsup and Pepsi and, on rare occasions, even some green salad. It was also the only genuine marketplace of ideas in the American community. Twice a month we gathered in the political section's library for press briefings with the ambassador or, when he was out of town, with his deputy. We correspondents contributed to the senselessly adversarial tenor of such occasions by seeking specific details on the issues of the day, information that, even if the ambassador knew it, he was not authorized to relay. But most of the time we were—all of us—in the dark. For a while I attended these meetings principally for social reasons, but eventually I stopped going altogether. The snack-bar speculation was far more nourishing.

⟪⟪ 3 ⟫⟫

On March 22, 1982, Brezhnev traveled to Tashkent, the capital of Soviet Uzbekistan in Central Asia. There, not far from the Chinese border, he issued his strongest appeal to date for a rapprochement with China.

Under pressure both at home and abroad, Brezhnev had an almost desperate need to do something. The emergence of China on the world stage—and particularly its growing links with the

United States—was watched with considerable alarm in Moscow. Brezhnev sought a way to counter the American challenge as well as to stem the rising dismay about his policies, particularly among the military. Any improvement in relations with China would relieve pressures on him. He hoped, one of his senior aides told me later, to check the Sino-American rapprochement by telling the Chinese that the Americans were fostering mistrust between Moscow and Peking so that Washington could play one Communist giant against the other. The minimum shift Brezhnev urged the Chinese to make was based on the concept of equidistance in the Moscow-Washington-Peking triangle; as *Pravda* spelled it out a few months later, this would be in Peking's as well as in Moscow's interest. An opening of Sino-Soviet political talks "without any preconditions" would clear the path in this direction, and this was what Brezhnev proposed in Tashkent. He made an additional gesture—a significant public concession in view of the past bitter propaganda war between the two nations: Offering an olive branch, he asserted that despite ideological differences, the Russians had always considered China to be a socialist country. Brezhnev had made oblique overtures to China before, but without giving an inch on ideological issues; and the Chinese leaders, better than any others, knew how to deprive even the most forthcoming diplomatic initiative of its momentum so that it died a natural death. Brezhnev's Tashkent speech suggested a course of action that would precipitate a modest degree of rapprochement between the two Communist neighbors.

The next day Brezhnev toured Tashkent industrial firms, accompanied by the local Communist chieftain, Sharaf Rashidov, who was a nonvoting member of the Politburo. When they arrived at the Chkalov Aircraft Factory, Brezhnev was greeted by thousands of workers, who had set up makeshift scaffolding from which they could better observe the proceedings. As Brezhnev and Rashidov were approaching that area, the scaffolding suddenly collapsed. In the pandemonium that ensued, Brezhnev was hurled to the ground by his security men, who protected him with their bodies, assuming that the episode was an attempt on the leader's life. Then they hastily removed Brezhnev to a safer place, firing their weapons in the air to clear the way. This only added to the panic. It is not known how many persons were hurt or killed in the fearful disaster. A few weeks later, Tass announced the "sudden" death of Rashidov, without providing any details.

I learned about this incident much later from a senior Kremlin official, who insisted that although Brezhnev collapsed right on the grounds of the Chkalov factory, he did not have a stroke but rather suffered from shock. Other sources insisted that he suffered both. Whatever the reason, members of Brezhnev's entourage decided that he should immediately be hospitalized. As they were on the way to a local hospital, two aides, Leonid Zamyatin and Anatoly Alexandrov-Agentov, and a doctor decided to take the leader directly to Moscow. Before the official aircraft landed at Vnukovo VIP airport, the authorities cleared the reception lounge of all personnel. Only members of the leadership and Brezhnev's relatives were present as the leader was taken on a stretcher into an ambulance and rushed into the Kuntsevo Hospital.

Correspondents were, of course, ignorant of this at the time. So were Soviet journalists, who routinely witness comings and goings of the top leaders.

The published account of Brezhnev's return to Moscow seemed routine. There was, I realize in retrospect, one curious thing: A member of the leader's family—Brezhnev's son-in-law, General Churbanov—was listed among the senior Kremlin figures who went to the airport to meet the leader. Only later did we learn that all members of the Brezhnev family were alerted about his condition and all rushed to the airport.

The government was not able to hide Brezhnev's hospitalization for long. The next day a short Tass dispatch announced the postponement of the scheduled visit on March 29 of President Ali Nasser Mohammed of South Yemen. No explanation was offered.

This gave strength to rumors that something was seriously wrong. They were further fueled by the unexpected cancelation of a trip to England by Evgeny Chazov, Brezhnev's personal physician and head of the Fourth Department of the Ministry of Health, the department responsible for the care of Soviet leaders. As cochairman of International Physicians for the Prevention of Nuclear War, Chazov was to have attended an antiwar conference at Cambridge, England.* The atmosphere in Moscow was not only tense but confused; it was obvious that something important was up.

Brezhnev's health had been a big story for some time. Already in 1980 we had heard that an Assyrian woman named Dzuna had been brought to Moscow from the Caucasus because of her miraculous healing powers, and that she was treating Brezhnev. I had gotten to know Dzuna, a charming and generous woman with a thin dark face, piercing black eyes, and long black hair. A number of distinguished foreigners among her patients had told me that she in fact possessed some power that made them feel better. Lord knows whether this was true or not. The fact is that they believed it to be true. Officials in the Soviet gerontocracy who patronized Dzuna had installed her in a luxurious apartment in the center of Moscow. But this was not the time to visit Dzuna, and I set out to collect information elsewhere. Several of my contacts were in positions to know about the leader's health, but all were undoubtedly under strict orders to keep silent. Such matters are state secrets. However, after two days of roaming around the city I did manage to gather some information. What I learned may now seem insignificant, but it was more than anyone else in the Western colony knew with any degree of assurance, and it was more than most Soviet officials knew. This latter point was important psychologically and was a big break for me that greatly helped me

*International Physicians for the Prevention of Nuclear War was awarded the 1985 Nobel Peace Prize. The American cochairman of the group is Bernard Lown, Harvard cardiologist.

in my subsequent work, for the mentality of Soviet officialdom is predictable: My having sources on a story of such importance must mean that I had contacts in high places, that important personages had given me details about Brezhnev's health that had been withheld from establishment members; for whatever reasons, I must be favored by someone of great political importance. Such illusions enhanced my reputation among my official contacts and elsewhere.

The facts were somewhat less impressive. After an afternoon of rebuffs—everybody was either out of town or in conference— I went the next morning to the studio of a well-known nationalist painter, Ilya Glazunov, with whom I had made an appointment several weeks earlier. Glazunov was an accomplished artist, known for his portraits of prominent personages, foreign and Soviet. Several members of the Politburo were among his clients, and I wanted to reestablish contact with him on the assumption that one could meet interesting persons in his studio. When I had last seen him, in 1970, he was eagerly courting Western correspondents in hopes of having stories written about him. Now that he was an almost official court painter, he did not show any interest in us, and it had been difficult to set up the appointment. As I was entering Glazunov's building I ran into Vasya, the acquaintance with good political connections whom I mentioned earlier. It had not occurred to me to seek a meeting with him to ask him about Brezhnev's illness. I had figured that he could not know much. But a brief chat in the hallway proved my assumption wrong.

Brezhnev, Vasya said, was taken on a stretcher from the airplane to a hospital upon his return from Tashkent. It seemed, he added cautiously, that he had suffered a mild stroke and that he would remain hospitalized for several weeks. A meeting of the Central Committee, which was scheduled for the end of March, had been postponed until May 24. "They" think, Vasya said, that Brezhnev will recover. That was the extent of his knowledge, he concluded.

I knew that there was no sense in probing more, and so our conversation moved to our wives and children. Yet all the while I mulled over the information. As we parted I asked, "Is that stuff about Brezhnev right?" Vasya shut his eyes slowly, opened them, smiled, and said, "You've not heard it from me. Understood?" What were Vasya's reasons for telling me things, as he did that morning? I had frequently pondered the question without coming up with a decent answer. What if the motives of this man were diabolical? It had occurred to me more than once that Vasya could be connected with the KGB, that I could be the object of KGB manipulation, or that some other elements in the elite wanted to float information in this peculiar way, with ulterior motives in mind. Yet I had known Vasya and his family for a long time and had seen him in a variety of settings, which allowed me to look at him through different lenses. I doubted that I could be fooled so completely. I must often have come into contact with KGB men who used covers such as journalists or diplomats or bureaucrats; but this situation was like the weather—there was nothing I could do about it. I was in the business of collecting news and had to start with whatever information I could get. With all the rumors about Brezhnev, now I had some specific details.

Needless to say, I was excited. I forgot about the appointment with Glazunov. At last I had something to work with.

In my experience, when Soviet officials were asked questions in a general, probing way, they occasionally responded, without batting an eye, that they did not know a thing about the subject. But when I had details about an event or a policy and raised them privately with those in positions of authority, I never knew them to lie deliberately. The quest for information was not hopeless, provided you approached the sources in the right way. That meant, of course, that you had known your contacts for some time and that you had managed to convince them that you would not betray them as the source. With only rare exceptions, I scrupulously resisted the temptation to extract information under false pretenses or deliberately mislead people about the exact nature of my inquiry. Those people I dealt with would either confirm the facts and provide some explanations or say right off that this was a subject they could not discuss with me.

I feared the latter response that afternoon when I managed to see a senior official at his office. To avoid a quick rebuff, I first told him, as nonchalantly as I could, that I was surprised that the Central Committee plenum was being put off until May 24.

He winced. I continued, "But what really interests me is the condition of the general secretary. How serious is it?"

The official looked at me with a puzzled expression. "Who told you about it?" he asked, which was already indirect confirmation. I could not tell him, I said, just as I would not tell others about my conversation with him. I told him all I knew, but in a way that suggested I knew more. "Well," he said somewhat irritably, putting down his glasses, "you are correct. The plenum is set for May twenty-four. But I can tell you that the doctors say that the general secretary will be in good shape in a few weeks." I asked him about the Tashkent incident, but he said he did not know exactly what had happened there, although he knew that Brezhnev's health had deteriorated and that he had had to be hospitalized. "But it's a minor matter, I'm told," he added.

Both my sources said that Brezhnev was expected to recover after a few weeks in the hospital, and I wondered, as I was sorting my thoughts before beginning to write a story, whether this was wishful thinking, real information, or misinformation. But what if Brezhnev had not been carried away on a stretcher upon his arrival in Moscow? After all, Vasya had not actually witnessed it. The image seemed important to me as the illustration not only of Brezhnev's enfeebled physical condition but also of the political paralysis of his regime. I also felt the symbolic importance of this image for the rest of Brezhnev's rule—it showed the shadow of death over the Kremlin and the beginning of the succession crisis.

The temptation to be exclusive with a story that would subsequently hit the front pages throughout the world was tempered by fear of being wrong, and if wrong, of having to confront the police and propaganda machinery of a powerful state. I never feared anything in Moscow when I knew that my information was accurate and my analysis reasonable. No matter how powerful the state was, it could do little if the story was correct. There was a peculiarly Russian angle to this, something that Turgenev phrased succinctly when he described his compatriots as "the most incorrigible liars" in the world, adding, however, that "there is nothing they respect so much as the truth."

I looked several times at the telex copy of my story, which was all ready to be sent. All I had to do was dial the number in Washington, press a button, and let the tape run through my rickety East German machine. I had already made the decision, yet I was procrastinating. The stakes this time were high; after all, I just might be wrong. Whenever I am gripped by anxiety or fear, I tend to make small mistakes. That night I made the mistake of writing the exact date of the next Central Committee plenum. There was no need to be so precise. Afterward I was to bite my nails over that piece of foolishness. Irrespective of how good the sources were, much could happen in two months to dictate a shift of the plenum date. I could have protected myself by simply saying that the plenum would be held in "late May." But I was worried more about the overall impact of the story.

In a moment of squeamishness before sending it, I did something I never did again. I was going to go through the same sequence of troubling questions many times over the next few years, but I would never again offer to share a major story with a colleague because I was afraid of its consequences. But that night I wanted to play it safe and I offered to share my information with Serge Schmemann of the New York *Times.*

Schmemann was an excellent correspondent, thoroughly at home in the language and deeply interested in his job. He had good contacts among Russians, but he gravitated toward the literary and artistic crowd rather than the politicians. He was an exceptionally fair and decent man and I liked him. But my offer was self-serving: I was looking for someone to share the blame, should there be blame the next day. That he turned down my offer late that night only increased my respect for Schmemann. "I can't do it," he said, thanking me. "I do not have the sources for it myself." I knew he was right. I could not imagine myself doing anything different in such a situation. So I dialed Washington and transmitted the story.

The next morning, for the first time, I confronted a strange problem with the American embassy. A political officer called me and in urgent tones demanded that I come to his office. He sounded the way I imagine a Soviet official sounds when he demands the presence of a minion. I told him that under normal circumstances, if he wanted to see me, he should come to my office, but since it was a Friday and I was going to attend the ambassador's regular briefing that afternoon, I would stop by his office afterward.

Frank Tonini, the press attaché, escorted me to the office of the political officer, who started right off by demanding to know the source for the story I filed the night before. It was not possible that I had the correct date for the next Central Committee plenum. The Soviets had never announced the plenum so much in advance, he said. "You've got to convince me that your sources are right." His abrasive attitude and tone of voice annoyed me. I had no intention of doing any such thing, I told him. "As far as I'm concerned, you pay twenty-five cents for a copy of the Washington *Post,* and if you have any problems write to the editor!" The conversation quickly deteriorated, and I stormed out of the office. Later, in Washington, a friend of mine at the Department of State told me that my name had appeared in a "negative context" in the dispatches of the Moscow embassy.

For almost two months I was on tenterhooks about the Central Committee plenum. By now the Brezhnev illness had been confirmed and for several weeks, until he appeared in late April, there were rumors that he was either dead or about to die. The date May 24 became a litmus test for the quality of my sources. Other American colleagues vowed to buy me a box of Cuban cigars if the date turned out to be correct. So did Tonini. When the plenum in fact met on May 24, only Tonini kept his word.

Brezhnev appeared in public on April 22 at the obligatory Lenin anniversary fete, but he looked frail and distinctly thinner. His face seemed immobile and his eyes unfocused. Yet I had never seen him preside over a more emotional reception. It was not known until the very last moment whether he would have enough strength to put in an appearance. He shuffled into the vast hall of the Kremlin Palace of Congresses—a solitary, sick old man performing the strenuous tasks demanded of him. The tremendous and sustained applause and an outpouring of emotion were a tribute to the brave old man, not to the leader.

While he was in the hospital, various factions were positioning themselves for the succession, and Andropov made his move toward the ultimate prize.

← CHAPTER FOUR →

ANDROPOV'S GAMBIT

LEONID BREZHNEV'S ILLNESS in March marked the beginning of a restless period in which it was clear to everyone that a power transition was approaching. There was a distinct sense of foreboding in the country as a whole, and in the political world, various constituencies looked for a strong leader to end the drift in policy and growing economic weakness.

The old guard's world had begun to unravel with the death on January 25 of Mikhail Suslov, the most powerful of all the men around Brezhnev. Suslov's death changed the balance of power in the leadership and removed from the scene the iron-willed custodian of the Revolution, whose long tenure had lent stability and consistency to Brezhnev's administration. Then, in early 1982, other old communists began to die one after another—such men as Marshal Vasily Chuikov, the victor of Stalingrad; Marshal Pavel Rotmistrov, the chief marshal of the armored forces; Colonel General Konstantin Grushevoy, the chief political commissar of the Moscow military district and Brezhnev's close personal friend. At Grushevoy's funeral, despite television cameras, Brezhnev openly wept—something the Soviet viewers had never seen before.

Suslov's departure left a gaping hole in the leadership. There was no obvious claimant to succeed him as the party's second secretary. Nor did it seem possible that anyone could simply step into Suslov's shoes and take over all his duties. No appointment of any significance had been made without his personal blessing; nothing controversial in the world of theater and the arts had seen the light of day without his approval. He played a decisive role in shaping Kremlin policies on issues ranging from the ideological disputes with Yugoslavia and China to the suppression of the Prague Spring. His last pronouncement on socialism was addressed to Poland—shortly before the imposition of martial law there—and included the warning that "any deviation from our revolutionary teaching brings with it fatal consequences." For the previous two decades it had been Suslov who had determined what was and what was not a deviation.

Six feet tall, gaunt, and nearsighted, Suslov was the éminence grise of the Kremlin. He knew no rival in the degree of his dogmatic belief in communism. This, and the fact that he did not aspire to become the leader, made him the kingmaker in the labyrinth of Kremlin power. He came from Russian peasant stock and had made a brilliant academic career in Moscow. Upon graduation from the Plekhanov Institute of Economics in 1928 at the top of his class, he joined the Institute of Red Professors, which was run by the Central Committee and taught Marxist political science. Simultaneously he held a professorship at Moscow University. Among his students were numerous prominent figures in Soviet history, from Nikita Khrushchev to Nadezhda Alliluyeva, Stalin's wife.

Although he possessed great intelligence and agility of mind,

Suslov made no outstanding theoretical contributions. What set him apart was his skill in providing ideological justifications for practical party policies, and an unusual gift for manipulating people and power. He was an utterly ruthless man when it came to any deviation from orthodoxy, as he had demonstrated in the 1930s when working directly under the notorious Internal Affairs commissar Nikolai Yezhov in one of the biggest internal bloodlettings of Stalin's regime. The scope of the purge was vast—70 percent of the members of the Central Committee were shot—and it opened the way for Suslov into the Central Committee in 1939, when he was made first secretary of the Stavropol region. He was called to Moscow at the war's end and was made a secretary of the Central Committee in 1947—a job he held until his death. In 1948 he was appointed editor in chief of *Pravda* but a year later was moved to a more important ideological task, that of leading the vicious and largely anti-Semitic campaign against those who were called the "cosmopolitans." He was elected a member of the Politburo in 1952. At that time Andropov was a junior official in the Foreign Ministry, Chernenko worked as a propagandist in the provinces, Gorbachev was a sophomore at Moscow University, and even Brezhnev was only a nonvoting member of the Politburo.

With Suslov gone and Brezhnev partially incapacitated, the reins of power were in the hands of an unsteady group of old-guard politicians who began to position themselves for the succession.

The obvious candidates for the helm—both Brezhnev protégés —were hardly inspiring. Andrei P. Kirilenko and Konstantin Chernenko both held the magic combination of jobs that qualified them for the succession sweepstakes—they were full members of the thirteen-man Politburo and secretaries of the Central Committee. We saw them only from a distance at ceremonial occasions or at formal receptions. Unlike Brezhnev, both lacked any charisma. Traces of their rustic background were evident in their features and mannerisms. Politically, neither man had qualities that would distinguish him from his mentor or suggest that he could bring the country something new.

For a long time Kirilenko had been regarded as Brezhnev's heir apparent. He presided at Politburo meetings when Brezhnev was traveling or indisposed and acted as his deputy when protocol demanded that the top party official be present. A short, white-haired man with a big round face and slightly oriental-looking eyes, he seemed, in private, as unimposing as a man of power could be. (This was how a leading Italian Communist described him.) But in public his demeanor changed; there was an air of arrogance about him that came from wielding great influence for a long time. After Brezhnev, Kirilenko had the longest tenure in the Politburo, and despite his advanced age—he was a year older than the leader—he could be expected to claim the top post as his right. Because of his training as an aircraft engineer, he supervised the military-industrial complex, a powerful constituency that, at an earlier point, could have made his claim almost irresistible. But age and health worked against him. For some time I had heard from well-informed foreign communists that Kirilenko's mental faculties had deteriorated and that he had difficulty mastering the details of position papers. That appeared to be one of the reasons that Brezhnev distanced himself from Kirilenko, as was revealed at Suslov's funeral. (It is possible that Brezhnev's personal preference for Chernenko also had something to do with it.)

At Suslov's funeral, the lineup of top politicians in the Hall of Columns revealed Brezhnev's choice—Chernenko was placed ahead of Kirilenko and Andropov, while Gorbachev was in the last position.

The prominence accorded to Chernenko was conspicuous—he had joined the Politburo in 1978 and was junior to all except Gorbachev and Premier Nikolai Tikhonov. But this testified to the closeness between Brezhnev and Chernenko. I had caught an unforgettable glimpse of this relationship on television the previous September, when Brezhnev awarded the Order of Lenin to

Chernenko on his seventieth birthday; there they were, two old men overcome with emotion, with Brezhnev forgetting protocol and addressing his faithful aide with the familiar personal pronoun *ti* when pinning a gold star on his chest. I had never before heard Brezhnev use this familiar form of address. On that occasion the two men seemed to be playacting like children, entranced by the gold star and completely oblivious of their surroundings—a scene so outlandish that it was hard to believe that both filled key roles in running a great and powerful country.

With Brezhnev's support, Chernenko stood to inherit his patron's constituency. Like Kirilenko, Chernenko was a sturdy man of medium height, slightly oriental features, and no magnetism. There was something wooden about him in public, but in private conversations the impression he made was a good one. His mind was sharp and logical and he possessed a command of technical detail that came from his long service as Brezhnev's key personal assistant. Moreover, he appeared to be one of the healthiest men in the leadership. Yet the elite had strong reservations about Chernenko. I recall a Soviet acquaintance of mine, who belonged to the upper echelon of the party bureaucracy, stating emphatically as we discussed the issue: "Mark my words! Chernenko will never become party leader. Never!" It was a strange thing to say, since I knew that following the death of Suslov it was Chernenko who, on an informal basis, took over most of his important duties. From all indications he was moving up and up.

In March the name of Yuri Andropov surfaced for the first time in my discussions with knowledgeable Soviet officials. Although a career politician and Politburo member, Andropov had served for the previous fifteen years as chairman of the KGB, the Committee on State Security. The stigma attached to that position, at least in the minds of foreigners, seemed to rule out his candidacy, as did the fact that he was not a secretary of the Central Committee. In addition, I suspected that Andropov was in poor health. During the last national elections, foreign correspondents had gone to a school near our compound on Kutuzovsky Prospect to watch Brezhnev vote. The ritual provided us with an opportunity to see the leader at close range and perhaps throw a question or two at him. While attention was focused on Brezhnev, I noticed a familiar stooping figure in the background. It was Andropov. He lived in the same building as Brezhnev and they voted at the same polling station near their home. I had not seen him for some time and was stunned at how fragile he appeared to be; he looked like an old retired college professor. A colleague, Jim Gallagher of the Chicago *Tribune,* also noticed Andropov's condition and remarked to me, "He looks worse than Brezhnev!"

Andropov was an enigmatic figure. He enjoyed the reputation of being a modern man, an intellectual who wanted to *do* things, but that reputation was based on his career in the 1960s, when he was a rising young star in the leadership, before he became KGB chairman and was engulfed in the mysterious world of the secret police. To the extent that national recognition was an important factor in Soviet politics—and its importance is debatable—he had a distinct edge. Most other leadership contenders suffered on this score; they might cut a towering figure in Moscow or in the regions under their control, but they cast only a blurry shadow in the rest of the country. But everybody knew Andropov's name. Moreover, as KGB chairman he had his agents everywhere, and those were important people wherever they were.

There was one other unique personality whose prestige in the party exceeded that of most. This was Dmitri Ustinov, the defense minister. Like Andropov, Ustinov was a Politburo member but not a Central Committee secretary. Also like Andropov, he was a nationally known figure whose standing was based on a perception that he was a man of great experience and sober judgment, without personal political ambitions. An engineer, he had held some of the most important jobs in the country during more than forty years of service, beginning as minister of armaments. In 1941, when all the men around Brezhnev, and the leader himself, were still provincial or Komsomol (Communist youth organization) officials, Ustinov, then thirty-two, was put in charge of the armaments industry. He successfully conducted the first and perhaps the most crucial Soviet operation in World War II, the evacuation of more than 350 factories from European Russia to the Urals before the rapidly advancing Nazi armies. An unknown figure, he presided over miracles. The success of this operation placed him in the pantheon of war heroes. Subsequently he organized the large-scale arms-production program under difficult conditions, and he remained directly in charge of the military-industrial complex and the space program until he was appointed defense minister in 1976. As minister, he donned the uniform of a marshal to placate the armed forces chiefs, who wanted one of their own in charge. That uniform now had become an impediment to a political career, especially after the imposition of martial law in Poland. To make a marshal—even a civilian marshal like Ustinov—head of the party could be seen as a proof that communism had to be rescued by the military everywhere, even in its citadel.

There were other men around Brezhnev, but they were not considered potential candidates for the leadership. I never heard any Soviet official or analyst seriously suggest as possibilities Moscow party chief Viktor Grishin, who had the appearance of a sleazy *aparatchik,* or the energetic and brutish Grigori Romanov, who was party chief in Leningrad. Given the nature of the Soviet political world, Chernenko, Kirilenko, Andropov, and Ustinov became focal points for the ambitious men and women, bureaucracies, and elites—a complex web of alliances and cross-alliances —who sensed that the Brezhnev period was drawing to its natural end.

Gorbachev, the youngest Politburo member, was completely in the shadows, and there were no other representatives of his generation preparing to claim national recognition. The notion that he could be a candidate for the top job seemed so outlandish to me, and I believe to most of my colleagues, that we entirely ignored

him. Gorbachev did nothing to draw attention to the fact, which
I overlooked in my dispatches, that, like Kirilenko and Chernenko,
he too was a member of the Politburo and also a secretary of the
Central Committee.

Nor did it seem likely that Andropov and Ustinov were in the
race. In an article I wrote on April 5, I summed up the conventional
wisdom in our community: While their influence was great, neither the armed forces nor the KGB was expected to provide the
new leader in the Kremlin.

But that was before Andropov made his move. On April 22, in
my story about Brezhnev's reappearance at the Lenin anniversary
fete, I included as paragraph six what was to my mind a significant piece of intelligence—namely that Andropov had already
been chosen to take over Suslov's job as second secretary, that he
had moved into the Central Committee, and that he would formally leave his KGB post at the forthcoming plenum in May.

⋘ 2 ⋙

I managed—much later, through arduous conversations with
several Kremlin officials and over many vodkas—to elicit some
details to piece together the events in the first half of 1982. Each
important shift in the Politburo produced nervousness and concern among members of the establishment at almost every level;
behind each personality vying for the top prize were countless
men and women whose careers were at stake.

After Suslov's death nobody made time for serious thought
about a new second secretary. Because of his closeness to the
leader, Chernenko took over some of Suslov's duties, and it
seemed that postponing a decision would give him the job by
default. But after the Tashkent incident and with Brezhnev hospitalized, the question could no longer be put off. The tense interna-

tional situation made it urgent to add a senior secretary to the Secretariat, and Andropov's supporters moved to claim Suslov's job for him. To mollify Brezhnevites in the Politburo, it was proposed that Chernenko retain some of the functions he had assumed, thereby expanding his responsibilities. A senior Kremlin official told me that this arrangement had the blessing of Brezhnev, who was still in the hospital.

Although most officials tended to skirt around Andropov's personal drive to power, the entire operation seemed marked by a characteristic Andropov touch—accurate information, good timing, intelligent planning, and quick execution to ensure success.

Politicians in other societies also have to learn to bide their time, but in the Soviet Union the demand for self-discipline is absolute. The leader and his team chart the course. Others are expected to be loyal and unquestioning, even when they are convinced that the course is wrong. It is amazing to consider the long years of self-discipline of men like Andropov or Gorbachev, even in matters of style. Take Gorbachev, for instance: His speeches were dull and droning while he was a Politburo member, yet only a month after his accession he displayed stunning oratorical skills. Obviously he had been willfully denying a natural gift for all the previous years. But a junior politician cannot deliver spellbinding speeches if his supreme boss is a turgid orator; a regional noble must not outshine the tsar.

To the outside world, such restraint gave a monochromatic tone to the Kremlin political landscape. But inside the Kremlin, self-discipline surely exacted its psychological price when it came to deeply felt issues. One would rarely hear about such matters, and then only obliquely from families of the men at the top. The private dramas, the anguish, and the intrigue surrounding the Afghan invasion, for example, are said to have been momentous, particularly for someone such as Alexei Kosygin, who opposed the venture and viewed it as potentially ruinous. Yet publicly he supported the invasion. Anyone who had reached the highest councils of Kremlin authority had to accept the system. Modern Russia, in fundamental ways, is a military empire, a state where strict protocol must be observed in public at all times, lest confusing signals be sent to the population and precipitate a disintegration of the civic or bureaucratic order. The system cannot allow any exceptions. To this tsarist inheritance the Soviets added the notion that the party is always right and that the role of the individual in history is marginal. The leader mattered because he was the symbol of the militarized governing style.

A corollary aspect of Soviet politics is the concept of collective leadership. After the Stalin era, the ruling elite clearly decided never to allow a recurrence of that kind of bloody tyranny. Hence the evolution of a process in which every important decision must be approved by a majority of Politburo members.

And yet, the mechanics of power give the general secretary of the Communist Party great authority. The pinnacle in the Kremlin is the Secretariat of the Central Committee, usually composed of nine to eleven persons, and chaired by the general secretary. It prepares the issues for decision by the Politburo, usually composed of about a dozen highest officials. The Politburo is also chaired by the general secretary.

The procedure, as explained to me by a number of officials, is as follows: On Monday, important issues coming up for decision are considered by secretaries of the Central Committee and their staff (officials familiar with the problems as well as expert advisers attend these meetings). On Tuesday, the Secretariat reaches tentative decisions and assembles relevant documentation to be forwarded to the general secretary. At this point the senior secretary—who is known as second secretary, although such a title does not formally exist—guides the flow of decisions. On Wednesday, the general secretary reviews the papers and his large personal staff goes over each item (at that point, the staff calls on various officials and experts to again testify or explain aspects of various issues). The general secretary's staff then prepares final documents, which are handed to each Politburo member on Thursday or Friday, depending on circumstances.

A great deal depends on the leader, his instincts and inclinations, his temperament. The process provides him with the capacity to dominate a sprawling government filled with metropolitan and regional barons seeking to expand their domains. Since he controls both the Secretariat and the Politburo, the leader can have his way whenever he sets his mind to it. Moreover, he is the symbol of the state, using the mystique of his Kremlin office much as the Romanov tsars used it. Those members of the leadership who are both secretaries and Politburo members also enjoy a distinct advantage. They first shape the issues, then vote on them when they come before the Politburo. Implicit in the mechanics is the fact that an ailing leader has to defend his personal authority against those seeking to limit the scope of his decisions. But only when he is unable to assert himself in physical terms, because of illness or for other reasons, does the process become confusing and complicated. And that was the case during the last year of Brezhnev's life, when the establishment moved into a period of waiting, a pretransitional limbo, when the ruling party bureaucracy focused a great deal of its time and energy on its own internal upheavals.

Andropov was able to move into the vacuum and position himself as second secretary of the party because of this disarray in the party. He was not the party bureaucracy's choice. Its machinery was still in the hands of Brezhnev and Chernenko. But during Brezhnev's eighteen years in power the political elite had grown in size and, naturally, disagreements and debates had multiplied, frequently generating ripples that spread to its fringes and beyond —ripples that were now turning into small waves of pressure for change. The lack of determined leadership and cohesion, the alarming economic indicators, and an assortment of other misfortunes had brought the country to a turning point. Technocrats and experts in institutes and research centers, new and younger elites in the provinces, the new generation in general, were dismayed with the course of events. These people looked to Andropov for leadership. More important, the coalition for change included Andropov's own organization, the KGB, and the armed forces. For some time the military chiefs had been showing uneasiness about policy drift and particularly about a complacent response to Reagan's rearmament drive.

In March a new book, *Always on Guard in Defense of the Fatherland,* written by Marshal Nikolai Ogarkov, the chief of general staff and the country's highest career officer, hit the bookstores. Ogarkov was concerned about the "fast pace" of the development of American military technology. He said measures must be taken to modernize Soviet strategic forces and enhance the performance of the Soviet economy. Then came a warning: "In these conditions, the failure to change views in time, and stagnation in the development and deployment of new kinds of military construction, are fraught with serious consequences." Who in the Kremlin was supposed to change his views?

<<< **3** >>>

ANDROPOV'S appointment as a secretary of the Central Committee was announced publicly on May 24, 1982. The speedy shedding of his KGB association left no doubt about his intentions.

By moving from the KGB headquarters in Dzerzhinski Square to the Central Committee in Old Square he became, almost overnight, a candidate for the top job. Physically, the two buildings are only about fifteen hundred feet apart; the psychological distance between them is enormous, however.

The move was a serious blow to Chernenko's ambitions. One thing that gave him some comfort was the appointment of Vitaly

Fedorchuk as new KGB chairman to succeed Andropov. A high official told me much later that Andropov had advanced the candidacy of Anatoly Dobrynin, the veteran Soviet ambassador to Washington, to become the new KGB chairman. But Chernenko, using his friendship with Brezhnev, arranged for the appointment of his ally Fedorchuk.

The new chairman was a no-nonsense career KGB officer who had spent most of his service in the Ukraine, which was Brezhnev's and Chernenko's power base. A tall, sturdy, and menacing-looking man well known for toughness and ruthlessness, he had no national standing. The choice caused genuine surprise in Moscow, since Fedorchuk was not a member of the Central Committee, and several other high KGB officials, who were, outranked him politically. Nobody knew just how such a man was selected for one of the key positions in the country, but the speculation within the official circles invariably was that Chernenko had brought Fedorchuk from Kiev, where he was chairman of the Ukrainian KGB, to Moscow in an effort to neutralize Andropov in his power base.*

Could Andropov have blocked Fedorchuk's appointment? "Of course," a knowledgeable Soviet official told me. "But in that case he would have had to advance strong reasons. And there were powerful reasons, given Fedorchuk's lack of experience in foreign affairs. After all, more than 50 percent of KGB business is foreign. But it would have been a serious tactical mistake; it would have made Andropov look as if he was trying to retain the control of KGB while moving over to the Central Committee." Such a move would not only have alarmed Chernenko but also have raised serious doubts among other leaders about Andropov's intentions.

---

*Later in the year Andropov, as general secretary, hastily replaced Fedorchuk with his own trusted lieutenant, Viktor Cherbikov, who had come to the KGB the same year as Andropov. Fedorchuk was moved to the far less important Ministry of Interior and was eventually retired by Gorbachev.

Nor was it necessary for Andropov to fight the appointment. After fifteen years as KGB chairman, Andropov had a stranglehold on the organization. He had reshaped it and imbued it with a new spirit. The KGB remained an instrument of oppression, but it was more sophisticated than before. Andropov had extended its operations and had brought in new men and women. Reversing the legacy of the Stalin years, when the secret police was a grotesque assortment of criminally inclined misfits and outright criminals, he had built a new KGB, which claimed the best graduates coming out of Soviet universities. A substantial number of its officers were scientists capable of carrying out industrial espionage and of analyzing Western scientific publications. Others had knowledge of foreign languages and foreign cultures, or had specialized in fields ranging from strategic weapons to international finance to mining. Andropov's people were generally younger, better educated, more worldly, serving an elite organization that was the guardian of the Soviet system and that provided them privileges and a good life. Above all, Andropov had worked to restore the domestic prestige of the KGB after a series of devastating blows, not only under Stalin but also under Khrushchev and Brezhnev.

To understand Andropov at that point one has to understand the KGB—yet it is impossible to write with certitude about that organization. Most of the information comes from defectors, the majority of them junior officers working abroad. The men who run the KGB and who know more than one compartment of its operations do not as a rule, I believe, travel abroad. What I knew from observation reinforced the image of the KGB as a huge police establishment, efficient, disciplined, and all-knowing. Yet such observation focused on the goon squad, the only KGB personnel we journalists encountered at the trials of dissidents and elsewhere—agents who controlled crowds, who masqueraded as street toughs and roughed up protesters, who hovered near important personalities and prevented us from approaching them, who intimidated our friends in the dissident community and among Jewish refuseniks, who sometimes followed us around the city, and who, when the spirit moved them, arranged unpleasantnesses for us, such as puncturing our tires in the middle of the night. These men, given to sporting leather coats and an air of arrogance, were the bullyboys we detested. Then there were agents in various Soviet institutions, about whom I heard from my friends. But in our accounts of the persecution of dissidents the bullyboys received more prominence than they deserved, it seems to me in retrospect, just as we attached more importance to those persecutions than we should have. Resistance to an authoritarian regime makes news, and I was tempted to play it up. Moreover, my heart was certainly on the side of those persecuted. What I failed to emphasize was that the dissidents never had much effect upon the vast majority of the population—and my omission tended to leave readers with the impression that an important internal struggle was under way in the Soviet Union when, in fact, we were talking about only perhaps a few hundred courageous people willing to risk imprisonment to fight for freedom of speech.

That May I had a chance to see a large assortment of KGB goons, all in their Sunday best, attending church to listen to American evangelist Billy Graham. They packed the churches—young clean-shaven men standing quietly and looking pious, as the occasion required. Graham was in Moscow attending a religious conference against nuclear weapons and also looking for the opportunity to bring his religious crusade to Russia. The KGB regarded Graham's scheduled sermons as risky and ordered hundreds of operatives to fill roughly one third of the available space; the remaining space was shared almost equally by foreigners and old women worshipers. Outside, uniformed police had put up barricades sealing off the streets. Graham made the occasion even more grotesque when he declared at a press conference that he had encountered no restrictions on religious freedom during his six-day visit. He found the churches in Moscow packed to capacity, he said, adding, "You would never get that in Charlotte, North Carolina." We were all outraged by his remarks, since the Soviets were so open about their opposition to religion. But the evangelist went on to say that he had discovered many "positive" things during his visit, which was, as he put it, "the most intensive period of time in my entire ministry." And, he added, "the meals I had are among the best I have ever had. In the United States you have to be a millionaire to have caviar and I have had caviar with almost every meal I've had here." The KGB operatives in the audience must have been delighted. This was at a time of food shortages so severe that Brezhnev proposed that same month a new "food program" to reassure the population that steps were being taken to alleviate the problem.

But there was another, more shadowy, side of the KGB, which we never saw: its sections dealing with technological spying, counterintelligence, and analysis. A responsible American official once described officers in these branches of the KGB as knowl-edgeable, often sophisticated, and generally matter-of-fact people who could be quite frank, forthright, and even critical in discuss-ing various aspects of Soviet life. These qualities were a sort of litmus test, he said, "for anyone behaving in this fashion while dealing with me must be KGB."

A few years later, in the summer of 1984, an extraordinary ten-part television series about KGB counterintelligence activities revealed a surprising level of analytical sophistication and tech-nological capability. The series, *Tass Is Authorized to State,* was written by Julian Semyonov, who said in a televised interview that he was given access to raw KGB files and that he had merely changed some names and added a few dramatic touches to hold the story together. This was a stunning admission, something I had never heard before in my years in Moscow. Several senior KGB officers were listed as having served as consultants for the production. The series purported to be a docudrama about a suc-cessful KGB effort to foil an American intelligence operation in

Moscow. The story was exciting, the acting superb. I could recall only one similar Soviet series, called *Seventeen Flashes of Spring,* which was shown in 1973 and described the exploits of a Soviet intelligence agent in Nazi Germany. But Semyonov's series showed the KGB's operation in Russia in the late 1970s. It took the viewers inside the KGB headquarters in Dzerzhinski Square and showed the most modern means of surveillance and communications. The CIA, according to the plot, had recruited a Soviet official during his tour of duty in an unnamed African country. Upon his return to Moscow, the official was given a responsible position in a government institute and began supplying the CIA with sensitive information. After a number of complex cloak-and-dagger operations, the KGB discovered the traitor but could not firmly link him to the American embassy, since he managed to commit suicide by swallowing poison. From that point on, an even more complex series of events and circumstances permitted the KGB to fool American operatives into believing their agent had not been detected and continued to function as before. The ruse worked so well that KGB agents managed to seize an American agent as he was about to pick up purportedly genuine pieces of intelligence at a secret drop.

The series, made while Andropov was general secretary, may have been designed to symbolize the complete rehabilitation of the KGB. It purported to depict the new spirit within the organization and its leaders' insistence on the legality of its procedures, as well as to demonstrate the ever-present threat to the security of the state posed by foreign, and particularly American, intelligence services.

To the extent that one believed the film represented the type of people who served in the secret police, one imagined that the real KGB men were staunch supporters of their chief not merely because he had managed to restore their standing in the country but also because they shared his concerns about the crisis of their society, the scope of which they, as intelligent and well-informed people, knew better than most other party members. So the KGB stood by Andropov during the power struggle of 1982; and Andropov, in parting with the senior KGB staff in May 1982, reminded them that he counted on their loyalty because, despite his moving into the Central Committee Secretariat, "fifteen years is fifteen years—you cannot hide them away, they will always be with me and it seems also that you will always be with me."*

⫸ 4 ⫷

BREZHNEV went on vacation in June, and domestic political life seemed to come to a standstill. The Kremlin's propaganda centered its attention on foreign affairs. Britain's war with Argentina over the Falkland Islands gave the Russians an opportunity to strengthen ties with Argentina, which they had established two years earlier with large purchases of grain following President Carter's embargo on U.S. grain sales to the Soviet Union. The Israeli invasion of Lebanon provoked empty Soviet gestures. American pressure was unrelenting and shifted from harsh anti-Communist rhetoric to specific punitive economic measures. The most tangible was the ban on sales of American technology for the construction of the Siberian gas pipeline, which was to carry Soviet natural gas to Western Europe. West European firms using U.S. technology were also affected. There was no question that the Russians could produce the needed equipment themselves, since the $10 billion pipeline had become not only an economic necessity but also an issue of national prestige. Yet the ban did cause some production mix-ups. There was other bad news. In late July it became clear that the country was heading toward its

---

*Andropov's speech to the collegium of the KGB was shown in a documentary film about his life in 1985.

fourth bad harvest in a row. Newspapers blamed the weather; official figures showed meat production in the first half of 1982 declining by 2 percent from the already poor level of the previous year, and newspapers reported that collective farmers were killing young cattle to meet state production quotas. *Pravda* gave a devastating account of losses due to transportation problems.

All these troubles shook up the establishment. The only bright spot was the emergence of a strong movement in Western Europe against the scheduled deployment of new American nuclear missiles. The Russians apparently calculated that West European politicians could be deterred by public opinion from going along with the American plan. There was a certain logic to this calculation at the time; the deployment date was more than a year away. Yet, considering that the missiles were eventually deployed, one might wonder how the Kremlin could have so misjudged the political, diplomatic, and propaganda struggle to be waged over the issue of Euromissiles. The Soviets evidently had no fallback position except all-out opposition.

There was a brief flicker of hope that summer that the appointment of George P. Shultz as secretary of state might signal a change for the better in Washington's policies. Both Foreign Minister Andrei Gromyko and Georgi Arbatov, director of the government think tank on American affairs, sounded hopeful. The foreign policy establishment knew Shultz from his years as Richard Nixon's secretary of the treasury and thought him a serious and reasonable man who might turn out to be a moderating influence on the Reagan administration.

But officials linked to the defense establishment were pessimistic. Oleg Bykov, the veteran arms-control expert, suggested to a group of experts from Washington's Institute for Policy Studies that Moscow might be forced to adopt a "launch on warning" posture in response to the scheduled deployment of new American missiles in Europe. This meant a strategy calling for quick firing of Soviet missiles at North America and Europe if Soviet intelligence monitoring facilities reported that an attack on Russia was under way. Marcus Raskin, leader of the American group, quoted Bykov as saying that this would almost eliminate the "human element" from calculations in emergencies. It was a chilling prospect that would undoubtedly increase the likelihood of an accidental war. The same ominous warning was repeated that summer by Marshal Ustinov. It was difficult to determine whether the Russians were seriously considering this option or were merely trying to frighten Western public opinion and thereby increase pressures on Reagan. In retrospect, such pronouncements seem to have been part of a massive propaganda battle over Euromissiles, the kind of talk that stimulated the antinuclear movement in the West, but it was difficult to conclude so at the time.

With its propaganda machine in full swing, the Kremlin had to swallow its traditional aversion to anything spontaneous and allow a group of about three hundred pacifist Scandinavian women to stage a peace march through the Soviet Union. As the march approached Moscow, the authorities arrested two Russian citizens and placed nine others under surveillance in an effort to keep them from making contact with the foreign pacifists. The eleven Soviets had organized a committee for peace and East-West understanding, in itself a dubious enterprise since a majority of its members were refuseniks trying to attract publicity as part of their effort to emigrate. Nevertheless the harassment by the authorities was an example of Soviet hypocrisy in encouraging pacifism in the West while suppressing it at home. Rarely, I wrote in the *Post,* has rhetoric had so strange an encounter with reality. I could not resist playing with a linguistic ambiguity when I questioned the meaning of the Kremlin's battle cry "the struggle for peace" *(borba za mir).* The Russian word *mir* means both "peace" and "world." What did the Russians have in mind while fighting for *mir?* I asked. This was a rather cheap shot. The displeasure the story evoked in high circles was translated into an editorial in *Izvestia* entitled "Lying, Lying," which publicly castigated me for "blackening" Moscow's peace policy. I was in Sicily at the time and I heard about the *Izvestia* blast from Howard Simons, the *Post*'s managing editor, and my colleague Robert Kaiser, who phoned me from Washington. The Russians succeeded in spoiling my vacation a bit; I wondered whether I would be expelled. I decided to ignore the entire episode. My reasoning was simple. While we were away from Moscow, the Kremlin had ordered the expulsion of my *Newsweek* colleague, Andrew Nagorski. I did not believe that they would so soon expel another American journalist.

5

I returned to Moscow at the end of August. September 1 was the opening day of Moscow's political season as well as the first day of school. Each year during August workers would resurface Kutuzovsky Prospect, one of the main thoroughfares, which was used daily by the leadership during the other eleven months. The job had to be done meticulously, for Brezhnev, Andropov, Kirilenko, and many other top officials had their apartments on this avenue. Moreover, virtually all high officials had their country homes on the western edges of the city and used Kutuzovsky Prospect to drive to and from work.

Since our compound was on Kutuzovsky Prospect, it was simple and painless to watch the happenings on September 1, when the city braced itself for another season. Police officers would suddenly reappear every five hundred yards or so, standing in the middle lane of the huge avenue—which at some points could comfortably accommodate seven lanes of traffic in each direction —and waving motorists away from the central lanes. This was the sign that the leader was back in town. I went for a walk on that

Wednesday morning to witness a stream of black limousines coming from the western suburbs and heading toward the Kremlin. It was like any other September 1.

I began making my rounds immediately and calling on my acquaintances and friends. They whispered that a power struggle between Chernenko and Andropov was under way. The bureaucracy, various elites, the entire political world of Moscow, were divided—it seemed down the middle—on the issue of succession. The Kremlin itself, rich with intrigue, was silent. But the most significant rumor involved Kirilenko. My contacts whispered that Kirilenko was in trouble, but nobody could say why. One account alleged that Kirilenko's stepson had been caught embezzling large amounts of money while working for the Soviet trade mission in Switzerland. He was seized by KGB agents, the story had it, as he prepared to defect. Another rumor had Kirilenko's son-in-law, who was a diplomat, defecting to the West. A singularly malicious rumor alleged that Kirilenko had tried to commit suicide and—perhaps worse—had failed. Later I learned that all these tales were false. Yet, at the time it was clear that the profusion of rumors testified to Kirilenko's political vulnerability.

I spent many late nights in my office speculating about all this with Abdel Malek Khalil, the veteran correspondent of the Cairo newspaper *Al Ahram.* After more than a decade in Moscow he had a perspective few other foreigners had. With his Arab penchant for speculative thought Malek continuously sought new answers. Who wanted Kirilenko discredited? It was clear to us that as the senior man after Brezhnev, Kirilenko stood in the way of the two main pretenders. Andropov and Chernenko, despite their intense rivalry, shared a common interest in seeing him removed from the scene. If this line of thinking was correct, we figured, then Kirilenko had no chance.

In early summer, Kirilenko had gone to Krasnodar to make a speech in support of Sergei Medunov, the local party baron, who was well known for his corruption. But Medunov was a personal friend of Brezhnev's and one of the most influential Central Committee members. His province included some of the most scenic parts of the Black Sea coast, a principal summer playground of a largely frigid land. Millions of citizens, from the permanently frozen stretches of Siberia in the east to the frigid areas of the Kola Peninsula in the west, each year flock to Krasnodar beaches and resorts. So do luminaries of the political and cultural world of Moscow and Leningrad. A majority of military personnel, many of whom serve long tours in the cold parts of the country, settle down, upon retirement, in and around the Sochi area to enjoy its balmy climate and its relative abundance of food. Medunov and his people controlled property and building permits. Huge extortionist schemes successfully implemented by Medunov became a part of the public record over the years, but letters and petitions against him signed by prominent personalities, particularly retired military officers, fell on deaf ears. When inspectors from Moscow came down to investigate the charges, Medunov treated them lavishly. One "hospitality" service was a discreet brothel outside the city of Krasnodar. It was set up by Medunov as a VIP "rest home" of twelve apartments, where his guests could sleep and enjoy themselves. Reliable informants told me that a group of retired officers had attempted in 1981 to hand a letter of complaint against Medunov directly to Brezhnev by blocking his motorcade. But they failed. No action could be taken against Brezhnev's personal friend.

It was not clear why Kirilenko went to Medunov's aid at a point when Brezhnev's health and authority were deteriorating and when the country, for all practical purposes, had entered a period of interregnum. The Krasnodar speech was Kirilenko's last public address. Shortly afterward, the KGB moved against Medunov on corruption charges, and soon he was replaced by Vitali Vorotnikov, who had been Soviet ambassador to Cuba. This was a double blow to Brezhnev: Not only did Andropov move against his personal friend; he replaced Medunov with a man whom Brezhnev and Chernenko had sent into diplomatic exile three years earlier.

Vorotnikov had made a career in the industrial town of Kuybyshev before he was made first secretary of the Voronezh region in 1971 and promoted to the post of first deputy premier of the Russian Federation in 1975. He was also a member of the Central Committee. What precipitated Vorotnikov's sudden demotion in 1979 was not generally known. Now Andropov brought him out of exile and placed him in a key regional job—the first step in one of the most spectacular political careers made in recent decades.

There was some question that fall whether Brezhnev was aware of these things and, if so, to what extent. After his summer break, he appeared in better physical condition. In mid-September he hosted the postponed visit of South Yemeni leader Ali Nasser Mohammed, the only Marxist ruler in the Arab world. But we could not learn anything from the Yemenis beyond what was published in a communiqué filled with denunciation of American and Israeli perfidy and promises of Russian assistance.

But then Brezhnev traveled to Baku, the capital of Azerbaijan, where he always got a warm reception, riding into the city like a Roman emperor and being given a *kindzhal,* or Islamic dagger, made of gold and encrusted with diamonds and other precious stones, and other gifts that symbolized extravagant Moslem hospitality. We watched in disbelief his address in Baku, which was carried live on national television; Brezhnev started out by actually reading the wrong speech! Members of the presidium, having the text of his speech in front of them, began to exchange nervous glances, and presently we saw Andrei Alexandrov-Agentov, Brezhnev's national security adviser, rushing toward the speaker's podium with a handful of papers, standing there for a minute, letting his chief finish a long sentence. The TV cameramen were still not aware that something was wrong. Then, on a cue from Azerbaijani leader Gaidar Aliyev, the audience began to applaud and the TV cameras shifted away from Brezhnev so that

Alexandrov could tell him what had happened and give him the text of the right speech. Brezhnev looked somewhat baffled when the cameras focused on him again. "It seems we will have to start all over again," he said in a rather disarming way. "It was not my mistake, comrades." This time the audience gave him truly warm and sustained applause.

Prime Minister Indira Gandhi of India arrived in Moscow a week later, after the year's first snow. Although Brezhnev appeared animated on television, Indian officials let it be known privately that his grasp of issues was shaky. Even the tactful Mrs. Gandhi said upon her return to New Delhi that she deliberately had not raised any difficult questions with Brezhnev during their tête-à-tête.

Intuitively I felt that the end was approaching, and I began to work on a series of three long articles that were to sum up Brezhnev's eighteen years in power, the crisis that had descended on his country in the twilight of his rule, and the problem of succession. The last issue was the most difficult to discuss. Kirilenko had vanished from sight. Andropov largely kept out of the public eye, presumably clearing paths and cementing alliances.* The most visible figure was Chernenko, aggressively cocky and always at Brezhnev's side, looking like the heir apparent.

In October, Chernenko delivered a major foreign policy speech at Tbilisi, in Georgia. He also published a book that was widely and favorably reviewed. I recall one instance when, before the country and the assembled ruling elite, Chernenko behaved with such confidence that I felt he had the ultimate prize in his pocket. The incident took place on November 5, two days before the anniversary of the Bolshevik Revolution, at the nationally tele-

---

*Since moving into the Secretariat, he had made only two high-profile appearances. In June he accepted a medal from the city of Kiev, which was celebrating its millennium, and did so as second secretary and in the name of the entire leadership. On the last day of August he headed the delegation that welcomed Brezhnev back to Moscow after his holidays.

vised Kremlin Palace of Congresses rally. Chernenko had apparently arranged for a demonstration of his authority. Three times during the meeting, his aides came with some official papers that had to be signed. Each time Chernenko was seen receiving and reading the documents, then passing them in front of Brezhnev to Ustinov, who read them and passed them to Andropov, who looked at them briefly and perfunctorily and returned them to Chernenko, who signed them and gave them back to the aides. The purpose of this exercise was to show everyone that Chernenko was running the show, for all practical purposes. I could not conceive of an issue important enough to demand the immediate attention of the top leaders on such a festive occasion as the sixty-fifth anniversary of Soviet power. The only time I had seen something similar was when the leaders were informed about the successful completion of a manned space flight that had been experiencing serious reentry difficulties.

Wang Chongjie, bureau chief of China's Xinhua News Agency, agreed with my view that Chernenko's gambit was an effort to head off Andropov and to show the whole party that he was the natural heir of Brezhnev. Wang was one of the most experienced foreign observers in Moscow, a graduate of Leningrad University who had spent more than ten years as Moscow correspondent. He was sure, he told me as we left the Palace of Congresses, that the leadership question remained unsettled. Such a critical decision could not crystallize before Brezhnev's death.

My series of articles, which I had finished in late October, was to begin appearing in the *Post* on November 7, the Soviet national holiday, which happened to be Brezhnev's last appearance. His death on November 10 made me look almost prescient in the eyes of my colleagues.

I could have done even better. Before the articles were published, I was asked in a telex message from Washington whether I would object to calling the series "The Final Days." I hastily said I did. I thought I had solid information suggesting that Brezhnev's

demise was not imminent. A week before, President Spiros Kyprianou of Cyprus had arrived in Moscow for talks with Brezhnev.
One of the senior Cypriot diplomats, a good friend of mine who
was also fluent in Russian, accompanied Kyprianou into the
Kremlin. Naturally, I sought an eyewitness assessment and my
friend advised me that Brezhnev was in good shape and that he
cracked jokes during the talks. This turned out to be a great lesson
for me in the perils of diplomatic reporting. A few months later,
during lunch, my Cypriot friend apologized for having deliberately
misinformed me. The interests of his country, he said, made it
incumbent upon him not to be the source of an adverse report on
the Kremlin chief's health—the Russians knew that we were
friends. Then he proceeded to describe the talks, which on the
Soviet side had been entirely conducted by Gromyko, with Brezhnev slumping in his seat and doodling on a piece of paper. At one
point, after Kyprianou mentioned the United Nations, Brezhnev
suddenly looked up, turned to Gromyko, and said, "Is he again
talking about Waldheim?" By that time Kurt Waldheim, the former U.N. secretary general, had been out of office for nearly a
year.

6

AT the end of October Brezhnev moved to allay growing uneasiness in the upper echelons of the armed forces by convening
extraordinary "consultations" in the Kremlin with the military
chiefs. All top Defense Ministry officials, all marshals, the commanders of all services, all regional commanders, as well as commanders of Soviet forces abroad—the entire political directorate
of the armed forces—and all key industrial and scientific leaders
of the military-industrial complex were present. Nobody could
recall a similar consultation between the military and civilian

leaders. Brezhnev's tone was defensive, apparently in response to behind-the-scenes criticism by the military chiefs that his policy failed to provide adequate countermeasures to Reagan's rearmament program. Georgi Arbatov told me a few days later that Brezhnev himself had come to the conclusion that his hopes of salvaging détente were illusory and that he was facing a major policy decision. Arbatov, who advised Brezhnev on American matters, quoted the leader as saying privately, "We are at a crossroads and we have to decide which way to go."

Brezhnev's speech to the military chiefs indicated the direction he had chosen. The leader promised to take measures "to meet all your needs." Continued deterioration in Soviet-American relations had raised unspecified "new" questions, he said, and these "must be solved without delay." The competition in military technology had acquired a "fundamentally new character," he said, appealing to the scientific establishment to move ahead at a faster clip. "Lagging in this competition is inadmissible," he added. The speech suggested a significant hardening. It was what the marshals and generals wanted to hear. They had been making warning signals for more than a year, though Brezhnev had seemed unmoved and immovable.

During that meeting, Brezhnev was accompanied by five senior Politburo members. Kirilenko was conspicuously absent. New rumors circulated that he had been ousted from the ruling council. One source told me that Kirilenko had entered the Kremlin in his Zil limousine, a custom-made luxury vehicle that resembles the Lincoln Continental, to attend the Politburo meeting and that he was seen leaving the Kremlin in a modest Volga sedan. Confirmation came three days before the November 7 holidays. My Japanese colleague Hiroshi Imai and I drove in freezing rain to a building on Prospect Mira where the portraits of leaders are usually displayed first before festive occasions. It was past midnight and the building was not lit, but we could see that there were only twelve portraits instead of thirteen. We counted several times and than focused carefully on each of these huge canvas ikons. Kirilenko's portrait was missing. There was no doubt that he had been ousted.

Kirilenko himself was missing from the leadership lineup atop Lenin Mausoleum for the traditional November 7 military parade. A few days later, during Brezhnev's funeral, he walked in the funeral procession, an old man shuffling along with a group of Brezhnev relatives and friends, not with Politburo and Central Committee members. But by then Kirilenko was already irrelevant. A new and exciting chapter had begun.

CHAPTER FIVE

NEW DEPARTURES

WHEN BREZHNEV DIED, on the morning of November 10, 1982, the succession struggle reached its climax. It was the first death of a general secretary in office since 1953 and the second succession of its kind in Soviet history. The country had been anticipating it for some time. Even so, the end was unexpected when it came. Only three days earlier, the entire country had seen him standing valiantly atop the Lenin Mausoleum and reviewing the traditional military parade; then, after the parade, he greeted foreign visitors inside the Kremlin. Brezhnev's death marked the end of an era, but only the top members of the elite were at first aware of this moment of high drama. The strictest secrecy was imposed immediately and the country was placed on an emergency footing. In the Moscow region a military alert was ordered. By late afternoon we had an inkling that something unusual was afoot as the authorities canceled a popular annual concert honoring the uniformed police. This was followed by changes in radio and television programs, which began broadcasting classical music, and by other telltale signs that I noticed and that served me so well during the next transitions.

During the night, troops were moved into the city, so that on the morning of November 11, when Brezhnev's death was announced, Moscow had the appearance of an armed camp. The KGB and the army had set up roadblocks at all avenues leading to the Kremlin. At major checkpoints I found soldiers in brown uniforms lined up two deep across broad boulevards, and behind them police, also two deep, in blue uniforms, physically blocking all access to the seat of power. Moscow Radio announced that the city would be closed to traffic for four days. Security measures in areas up to a mile away from the Kremlin were incredibly tight. To get off the subway train in Pushkin Square, for example, people had to produce their passports and prove that they either lived or worked in the area. Closer to the Kremlin, people entering *any* building were challenged by KGB agents to show their documents and prove that they either lived or worked in those buildings.

In determining the successor, I sensed, the first twenty-four hours after Brezhnev's death were crucial. By virtue of his position and because of his links with the KGB, Andropov must have been the first senior official to be informed of the leader's death. He in turn had to direct Ustinov to order a military alert. In all other parts of the Soviet Union, the local military commander can order a military alert, but in the Moscow region, as a safeguard against a military coup, an order placing the armed forces on an alert had to be signed by the top civilian and military officials—in this case Andropov, as second secretary of the party, and Ustinov as defense minister. This meant that these two men could immediately seize the initiative and hence also the levers of power on November 10. The protocol and circumstances gave Andropov a head start but did not by any means ensure his becoming Brezhnev's successor. There remained the puzzling question of Ustinov's relationship to Brezhnev and Chernenko, as well as the fact that

Chernenko's supporters still dominated the Politburo and the Central Committee.

I was, fortunately, able to move about Moscow because of my car with special foreigner's license plates and my press card. Trying to reach people by phone was hopeless. Only those at the very top, and possibly their aides, had some information, and they were busy politicking and bargaining. By chance I had lunch on November 11 with Sayyed Moheidin, chairman of the Egyptian Progressive (Left) Party and one of the leftist officers who staged the revolt that brought Gamal Abdel Nasser to power in Cairo in the early 1950s. Moheidin's experience the previous day was interesting, since it raised questions as to the pattern in which information about Brezhnev's death had been distributed among senior officials.

Moheidin, whose cousin was prime minister of Egypt at the time, was the most distinguished Soviet ally in Egypt and leader of the main opposition party. He was in Moscow on an official visit and had been scheduled to have talks on November 10 with Boris Ponomarev, secretary of the Central Committee and an alternate member of the Politburo. The meeting was set for noon, or about three hours after Brezhnev had died. A black limousine had been sent to pick up Moheidin at his hotel and bring him to the Central Committee shortly before noon. As he was led toward Ponomarev's office, an agitated aide diverted Moheidin to the connecting office of Ponomarev's secretary. The aide, Karen Brutents, who supervised Soviet relations with the Arab countries, explained that Ponomarev had just received an important phone call and that the meeting would be delayed by only a few minutes. The Egyptian thought there was something odd about this. Previously, as leader of a party, he had always entered Ponomarev's office directly. Moreover, the Russians are sticklers when it comes to protocol. Moheidin could see Ponomarev on the phone when Brutents went into his office. A few minutes later Brutents returned, apologized profusely for the fact that the meeting had to be canceled because Ponomarev had been called to an important meeting, and offered to escort Moheidin back to his hotel. We speculate that Ponomarev either did not know about Brezhnev's death until noon or that the confusion in the Central Committee was such that Ponomarev and his aides had forgotten about his scheduled meeting with the Egyptian politician.

I was thoroughly frustrated. These were historic days, or at least so I thought, and I could not reach anyone in a position to tell me something about what was going on. I purposely headed for places where I might bump into Soviet journalists, but with little success. By late evening, I had managed a word with several contacts. By then it had been announced that Andropov would head the official twenty-five-man funeral commission, which also included Chernenko and Ustinov. In retrospect it seems clear that Andropov had already won at least half of the battle that day and was emerging as victor over prospective rivals, but there were rumors in party circles of a continued struggle between Andropov and Chernenko. A story suggesting that Andropov was part Jewish was circulating widely, and two Chernenko backers hinted to me that they felt that as a result the Central Committee might not go along with the choice of Andropov when it met the next morning. The fact that the crucial meeting was scheduled for November 12 was an important piece of intelligence. The calling of an extraordinary plenum of the Central Committee for ten o'clock the following morning could mean that the leadership decision had already been made or would be made during the night. And yet, if events followed a traditional course, we should expect a recurrence of the post-Stalin period of uncertainty and prolonged political infighting and compromises before a clear leader emerged. At the time I did not grasp the significance of the fact that Chernenko's backers were spreading ugly rumors; this was surely an act of desperation, a last-ditch attempt to mobilize Brezhnev loyalists in the Central Committee to block Andropov's candidacy after the leadership had made its decision. Later, after Andropov's brief tenure had ended, one of his associates told me that the younger members of the leadership had strongly favored Andropov over Chernenko, as did Gromyko and Politburo member Arvid Pelshe; but, he said, the crucial vote was that of Ustinov, who told his colleagues that the military chiefs "would not understand any other choice."

The next morning the city looked even more like an armed camp than before. Life came to a halt. The Central Committee, about three hundred top officials, convened in Sverdlov Hall.* The meeting broke up shortly after one o'clock and we saw black limousines barreling at great speed down Kutuzovsky Prospect. At two in the afternoon Moscow Radio announced the election of Andropov as the new general secretary. In the show of unity required on such occasions, the defeated candidate had nominated the new leader. The vote must have been close, because Chernenko felt strong enough to articulate the reservations of the bureaucratic elite and to forewarn his victorious rival against sudden changes. Chernenko credited Andropov with sharing "Brezhnev's style of leadership." Now, he said, driving in the point more directly, it was "two times, three times more important to conduct matters in the party collectively." Chernenko seemed to have expressed the fears of the entrenched *aparat* that Andropov might prove to be too strong a leader and too much of a challenge to their established way of life. They looked on him with considerable suspicion; his long tenure as KGB chairman inspired only mistrust. I had the impression that the bureaucratic establishment felt he had been imposed on the party by the other two mainstays of Soviet power, the KGB and the military, and that he would bring innovation and leadership into the Kremlin's old Senate building. Their fears were justified indeed.

---

*It was the last such meeting in Sverdlov Hall. The next year a new hall for Central Committee sessions was completed, and subsequent general secretaries were elected there.

2

A new chapter was beginning; but on that frigid November day in 1982, as Yuri Vladimirovich Andropov was facing the country for the first time as its new leader, I had no idea how short and how dramatic that chapter would turn out to be.

The northern wind blew in stinging gusts across Red Square as he performed his initiation rites, facing the coffin of his predecessor. Despite the cold, he took off his fur hat before beginning his speech and handed it to Premier Nikolai Tikhonov, saying, "Hold the hat!" His voice was clear and commanding. I recalled how fragile he had appeared to me when I saw him at the polling station the previous winter; now he seemed to have gained physical strength from the burden he was assuming.

The next funeral oration was delivered by Marshal Dmitri Ustinov, the defense minister, whose booming voice mourned a departed friend and extolled the new leader. A visibly shaken Konstantin Chernenko stood nearby but was not called upon to speak. The leaders descended the steps of the Lenin Mausoleum, whose deep rhubarb-red granite slightly tinged with ochre glistened in the sun. The waiting crowd of potentates and invited guests shivered, stamping their feet to keep out the chill. With the strain of Chopin's "Funeral March" played by a fifteen-hundred-man military band echoing through the cavernous square, the senior Politburo members carried Leonid Brezhnev's coffin to its resting place behind the mausoleum. From the start everything was done with precision, as in a choreographed and well-rehearsed spectacle. Army officers, carrying huge wreaths and Brezhnev's personal decorations on crimson cushions, preceded a gun carriage bearing the coffin, towed by an olive-green military scout vehicle. Red-and-black flags fluttered as the resplendent procession moved up the cobblestone slope past the Historical Museum and into Red Square. Moscow had not witnessed a pageant like this since the death of Stalin in 1953.

At twelve forty-five the entire country came to a halt for three minutes. With the sounds of bells, sirens, and artillery salutes ringing from Vladivostok on the Pacific Coast to Kaliningrad on the Baltic Sea, Brezhnev's body was lowered to the ground near Stalin's grave. Chernenko, Ustinov, Tikhonov, Politburo member Dinmukhamed Kunaev, and several other high officials wept openly during the final moments as Brezhnev's widow, Viktoria, and daughter, Galina, followed the ancient Russian Orthodox tradition and kissed the dead leader's forehead. So did all members of the leadership. The music stopped. One strap gave in and the coffin went down a second too early. Andropov threw the first shovel of earth into the grave, and others followed. The leaders lined up by the grave while officers shoveled in the earth. Andropov noticed that Chernenko, conspicuously dejected and fidgeting uncomfortably, was in the back of the group. With a slight nod of his head, he took Chernenko under the arm and pushed him to the fore. It seemed a magnanimous gesture of the victor toward his vanquished rival.

The leaders walked back to the mausoleum. The band struck a martial tune, and the troops staged a spirited and colorful parade, marching twenty-five abreast—infantry in brown uniforms, border units in dark green, sailors in black, airmen in blue, marines wearing green berets, and paratroopers with blue berets. As they marched past the mausoleum, snapping their heads in unison to the right, they hailed the new leader. The tsar was dead; long live the new tsar.

Andropov and the others waved to the troops. To the right and left of the mausoleum, the largest crowd of foreign dignitaries ever assembled in Moscow watched the proceedings. All the Soviet-bloc leaders were there. Also in the crowd were Vice President George Bush and Secretary of State George P. Shultz, Japanese prime minister Zenko Suzuki, Prime Minister Pierre Trudeau of Canada, Indian prime minister Indira Gandhi, West German president Karl Carstens, Pakistani president Zia ul-Haq, Prime Minister Andreas Papandreou of Greece, and scores of other ministers, princes, and potentates, from Cuba's Fidel Castro and PLO Chairman Yassir Arafat to a personal representative of the pope, Cardinal Caseroli. China was represented by its foreign minister, Huang Hua.

With the military show over, Andropov went into the Kremlin for a two o'clock reception, at which the new leader presented himself to the representatives of more than 120 nations. The presidents, prime ministers, princes, and potentates formed a long line in the corridors of the Grand Kremlin Palace. Journalists were admitted into Saint George's Hall to observe the proceedings in what must be one of the last truly imperial settings in the world.

Our attention was focused almost exclusively on the tall, gaunt, bespectacled man who emerged for the first time from the shadows of the KGB and the Central Committee into the full blaze of klieg lights. He was a man about whom I knew next to nothing; now I watched as he greeted hundreds of foreign dignitaries, calculating the time he should devote to each. I noticed a twinkle in his eye and an expression of genuine pleasure when he talked with the Hungarian leader János Kádár, an old friend. This was the only moment I saw him savoring the occasion. The rest was business—studied distance from some leaders, smiles for others. Special attention was given to Huang Hua, with whom Andropov talked longer than any other guest, holding up the line. This was a political gesture, a public indication of Andropov's interest in an improvement of Sino-Soviet relations.

I have never before been in a room filled with so many world leaders, yet they were interesting to me only to the extent that they were interesting to Andropov. Hoping to grasp what had propelled him to the top, I watched him perform, accompanied only by the premier, the foreign minister, and the first vice presi-

dent of the Supreme Soviet. Before the reception we had speculated that other Politburo members might be present to demonstrate collective leadership, but Andropov made it abundantly
clear that the general secretary of the Communist Party was the
only real boss.

The reception lasted only a bit over one hour. After the last
foreign potentates were received, the inauguration of a new Kremlin leader ended. Reporters stayed on as the dignitaries left the
hall. Andropov seemed relieved that the ceremony was over, and
he chatted and laughed with his aides, then briskly walked out of
the hall. The rest of his day was devoted to a series of private
meetings—including one with Bush and Shultz—which lasted
well into the night. American correspondents hoped for some
substantial impressions of Andropov from Bush and Shultz after
their meeting—particularly from Bush, who once served as director of the CIA and should have known more about the former KGB
chairman than almost any other American politician—but when
Bush and Shultz returned from the Kremlin to the embassy compound late that night, they looked grim and would not even talk
to reporters. A press release about their meeting with Andropov
had been prepared even before they went to see him, and now
they merely added to it a sentence saying that the exchange had
been "frank, cordial, and substantive." I caught up with Ambassador Hartman in the courtyard but his smile told me he was under
orders not to say a word. A few days later, Hartman was a bit
more forthcoming. Andropov, he told a group of us, "does not look
like a guy who has to turn around to take a vote in the Politburo."

<<< **3** >>>

WE saw a good deal of Andropov during his first few weeks
in office. The hectic days of diplomatic activity before and after

Brezhnev's funeral were followed by an equally hectic pace in domestic political life. Moscow had come alive.

The new leader held out a promise of hope. His speeches were brief, precise, and amazingly frank. He was evidently a literate man whose language was different from that of his predecessors. Contradicting all previous official pronouncements, he admitted that the Soviet economy had failed to meet its planned targets during the previous two years. The setbacks were due to "inertia" in the society and to "adherence to old ways." Some people, he said, "perhaps just do not know how to set about doing the job." The problems, in short, were massive. "The main thing" was to improve "the entire area of economic management, including administration, planning, and the economic mechanism." Then came a phrase that captured the imagination of the Russian people and led them to accept the man whose KGB associations had given him an image of firmness and strength. Speaking of the country's pressing problems, Andropov said, "I do not have a ready recipe for their solution. It is up to all of us to find answers to them." Whereas previous leaders had claimed to have solutions when they came to power, Andropov from the start conceded that he did not. Yet—with that perverse logic the Russians practice on occasion—the very admission, in the popular mind, showed that Andropov in fact knew where he was heading, that he did have a recipe.

It became apparent to me in those first weeks that Andropov had assigned, in his own words, the "highest priority" to economic and other internal issues. His call for a new beginning amounted to a repudiation of Brezhnev's domestic policy—he praised his predecessor only as a "great champion of peace." At home, however, the Soviet Union had to revitalize its economy: "We exercise our main influence on the world revolutionary process through our economic policy," he said. In trying to modernize its economy, the Kremlin must use the example of other socialist countries and draw on "world experience." In his domestic preoccupations there was a hint of isolationism. He mentioned only China and the United States in any great detail. Calling China "our great neighbor," he underscored his desire to accelerate the tentative rapprochement between the two countries. He declared that he wanted to restore détente with the United States but stressed that he would not make any "preliminary concessions" to purchase U.S. goodwill.

Exactly what Andropov planned to do about the economy was not apparent. His first moves were disciplinarian—he demanded greater social and labor discipline. But the thrust of his thinking was in line with a policy advocated by Soviet economist Yevsei Liberman a quarter of a century earlier—to promote light industry as an incentive to economic efficiency, to work toward increased production combined with increased consumption, and to push the country into the high-tech age. This was the real strategic challenge before the Kremlin, and Andropov understood that the country's ability to keep pace with the computer age rested on the involvement of the population in the process. Liberman's ideas had been briefly considered by Kosygin, but they never got very far during Brezhnev's years because they demanded radical decisions. It was clear, to me at least, that Andropov was prepared to make these decisions.* He had outlined the scope of the problem while continuing to be somewhat vague and adding protective coloration to those ideas that might provoke conservative opposition. This was part of the strategy of reassurance. Yet nothing he did could obscure a widely held perception that he was a man of power, prepared to exploit his power thoroughly to fulfill his purposes, and that his overriding purpose was to carry out national reconstruction. The sight of the new leader taking charge as

*In his first policy speech, on November 22, 1982, Andropov suggested a move toward a greater degree of economic liberalization when he said that "the independence of associations and enterprises, of collective and state farms, must be increased," and that "experiments must be carried out when necessary." In the initial stages of his rule the word "experiment" was a code word for reforms.

smoothly as if he had been groomed for it all his life naturally created a surge of optimism. The country, it seemed, was on the move again.

Andropov set the example. Every morning except Sunday I could see his limousine pass our compound at exactly twenty-five minutes before nine. He would usually return between seven and eight in the evening. By contrast, Brezhnev used to go to work at ten and was taken home around five in the afternoon. Andropov's example was infectious. Now, miraculously, I was able to phone government officials in mid-morning and actually reach them at their desks.

One of the first things the new leader did was to dismantle the large personal secretariat that Brezhnev had created. This was an equivalent of the White House staff, and under Brezhnev it had grown in size and authority to become the power center. Andropov retained only Andrei Alexandrov-Agentov, the national security adviser. He brought along several of his own aides from the KGB—serious, well-informed, and for the most part taciturn men. The chief of staff was Pavel Laptiev, a laconic former Central Committee *aparatchik* who now held the rank of KGB general. Andropov's personal secretary was Yevgeny Kerpichnikov, who supervised the flow of paper and who also held the rank of KGB general. Another key assistant was Viktor Sharapov, a gregarious former journalist. A trained Sinologist who spoke fluent Chinese, he had served as *Pravda*'s correspondent in Hanoi and Peking before he become a personal aide to Andropov in 1968.

Like their chief, these men conveyed a new thrust of action and purpose but with an overlay of secret-police determination. They were men of action who *knew* how the system worked. They were jealously devoted to Andropov and somewhat indifferent to the subtleties of Soviet politics. For instance, they saw nothing wrong in the growing number of KGB personnel switching over to political assignments.

Andropov, however, was extremely sensitive to this, primarily because of the reaction abroad. At home, the KGB was feared, of course, but it was also recognized as an elite organization. In the West, Andropov was seen as the man who ran the world's largest espionage system, who masterminded the suppression of the dissident movement in Russia, who forced Alexander Solzhenitsyn out of his homeland and sent the physicist Andrei Sakharov into exile in Gorki, who imprisoned enemies of the state in psychiatric hospitals. Abroad, the KGB chairmanship carried a stigma; at home, it endowed Andropov with an aura of authority and strength, which Russians respect. Moreover, it was immediately clear to Laptiev and Sharapov that the West would make an issue of Andropov's past KGB association. That winter KGB agents were expelled from a number of Western countries, and Italy's investigation into a Bulgarian connection with the abortive assassination attempt on Pope John Paul II gained momentum. Andropov supporters were convinced that Washington was trying to upset their chief by manipulating world opinion to underscore his KGB past.

And yet, despite Andropov's sensitivity to this problem, one of his first senior appointments was that of a former career KGB officer, Gaidar Aliyev, who was made a full Politburo member and first deputy premier. His promotion to a major job in the capital eight days after Brezhnev's funeral gave Andropov's administration, at its outset, a strong KGB tinge. So did Andropov's emphasis on law and order.

Aliyev was in his fifties at the time, an ethnic Azerbaijani who had joined the KGB at nineteen and had risen to become Azerbaijani KGB chief in 1967. Two years later he had been appointed party leader to clean up the corruption and economic crime for which the transcaucasian republic had become notorious. He proved to be an efficient and tough administrator. During one of my visits to the Transcaucasus, I had watched him at close range for several hours, and I thought of him as one of the most forceful personalities in the Soviet leadership. He was a natty dresser, well groomed, with a politician's instinct for talking with the people, kissing babies, and slapping backs. His major liability was his Moslem background, something that generated an almost atavistic resentment among Russian nationalists. Aliyev knew that, and in his first major speech as a Politburo member he made a point of paying a special tribute to the Russian people, to emphasize publicly their preeminence among the Soviet ethnic groups. But this only raised suspicions about his motives.

In retrospect, Andropov's other major appointment proved to be more significant, although it got little attention in our dispatches. A relatively obscure industrial manager and planning official named Nikolai Ryzhkov was appointed a secretary of the Central Committee. This promotion was the first step in Ryzhkov's spectacular rise, which culminated in his appointment as premier of the Soviet Union three years later. But at the time the high public profile of KGB men captured my imagination, and I focused on Aliyev's promotion as a possible signal that he was being groomed for the top governmental post once the aged Premier Tikhonov left the scene.

Ryzhkov was fifty-three, and none of my Soviet contacts knew anything about him except that he had served as director of a large factory in the Urals, where he had made a reputation as a first-rate administrator. I saw him for the first time during the second Supreme Soviet session in the winter of 1982. From his looks and manners he seemed to belong to the new breed of administrators. He was a well-groomed man who dressed like a Harvard professor and had an intelligent, slightly boyish face. Later I learned a bit more about his career. He was a graduate of the Urals Polytechnic Institute. In 1971, after a series of managerial positions in machine-tool plants in the Sverdlovsk area, he was appointed director general of the Uralmash machine-tool plant, one of the largest enterprises in the country. His successful performance there led him to Moscow, where in 1975 he was appointed a deputy minister of heavy industry and transport industries, a position he held for four years before moving into the State Planning Committee as one of a score of deputy chairmen.

Andropov's next order of business was to remove Fedorchuk, the Brezhnev loyalist, from the KGB. He did that in December, sending Fedorchuk to the Ministry of Interior (MVD) to replace General Nikolai Shcholokov, who had come under a cloud because of charges of corruption. The new KGB chairman, Viktor Chebrikov, was a longtime associate of Andropov's and a metallurgical engineer by profession. Like Andropov, Chebrikov had risen in the party under Khrushchev, but he was initially linked with the Brezhnev clique and held the job of party secretary in the Dnepropetrovsk region, Brezhnev's power base in the Ukraine, in the early 1960s. This background presumably accounts for his appointment to a senior post at the KGB the same year Andropov became its chairman. Initially, Chebrikov served as personnel chief, but in 1968 he was named by Andropov as one of his principal deputies. The two men became very close over the next fourteen years, and Chebrikov's appointment as KGB chairman was an important one as it ensured Andropov of the loyalty of his former organization.

There was another—largely symbolic—promotion. Chernenko was made chairman of a parliamentary foreign affairs committee, the job normally held by the party's second secretary. Despite this conciliatory gesture, Chernenko's political future at that point seemed extremely bleak. "We put him in Suslov's old office, and that's about the size of it," one senior official said. Andropov supporters in the press whispered privately to me that Chernenko would be out of the picture within one year. He did, in fact, disappear from public life shortly after the November session of the Supreme Soviet that elected Andropov a member of the collective presidency, or the Presidium of the Supreme Soviet. Viktor Grishin, said to be one of the main opponents of the new leader in the Politburo, nominated Andropov for the ceremonial job, which allowed him to act as head of state when the occasion required. Chernenko was spared the humiliation of making the nominating speech. From the press balcony in the Great Hall of the Kremlin Palace I watched him through binoculars. Sitting in the front bench in his favorite blue suit, he looked much older than he had only three weeks earlier; he was a troubled old man who felt he was no longer needed.

When columnist Joseph Kraft arrived in Moscow in December, Soviet image-makers were busy developing "Andropoviana." Moscow, Kraft told me, reminded him of Cambridge, Massachusetts, just after the election of John F. Kennedy. Like the men around Kennedy, many of those who played leading roles in the selling of Andropov were intellectuals, scientists, and journalists. And as in the early sixties in the United States, there was something new in the air—the energies released at periods of real political change, and hopes that the future was going to be brighter.

CHAPTER SIX

RUSSIA'S JANUS

YURI ANDROPOV seemed to me one of those Russian rulers who are formed by the events they seem to master. The fact remains that for better or for worse he changed the Kremlin's domestic political course in ways that made it possible for Mikhail Gorbachev to hit the ground running once he assumed power. But Andropov's KGB association tainted his reputation to such an extent that without historical distance and access to Kremlin files, it is difficult to assess fully his qualities as a man and a Soviet leader.

When he died on February 9, 1984, I knew very little about Andropov, despite persistent efforts to obtain information and some insight, and despite the fact that I knew several of his close relatives, friends, and associates. For the fifteen years that he was KGB chairman, a veil of mystery surrounded his persona by virtue of his job. After he became leader of the world's other superpower an even blacker and more impenetrable curtain was drawn around him; his chronic kidney ailment was a state secret shared by only a few people. Only later was I able to acquire enough firsthand information to form a somewhat balanced, if incomplete, picture of the man.

What emerged was a portrait of an enigmatic figure full of contradictions; he was a mixture of boldness and timidity, enlightenment and obscurantism and reaction, ruthlessness and gentleness, stubbornness and feebleness, a secret-police chief who hounded dissidents but wrote poems to his wife and friends.* There were disturbing allegations about KGB complicity in the assassination attempt on Pope John Paul II—allegations that could not be documented but that left a cloud of suspicion about Andropov's watch at the KGB. What was one to think of a KGB chairman who had only two adornments in his large office overlooking Dzerzhinski Square—on the wall a picture of Felix Dzerzhinski, the founder of the Soviet secret police, and on his desk a statue of Don Quixote carved in wood? Why the Cervantes hero and not Lenin? It is a Russian view, perhaps best articulated by Dostoyevski, that Don Quixote embodies the selflessness and purity of the human race, and that if humanity presented Don Quixote as its representative on the day of the Final Judgment, all its sins would be forgiven and it would not be punished by God. I wondered if this literary figure held another meaning for Andropov. Did he secretly consider himself a knight out of step with his times, dreaming at night of a world that is free while operating in the murky and brutal police world during the day? How would that explain the ruthless side of his character? His thirst for power? I did not find answers to these questions; they could not preoccupy me for long, under the pressure of more pedestrian needs—such as getting to know details about his life and collecting comments and recollections, however complimentary or one-sided, that might shed some light on his motives.

*The fact that Andropov wrote poetry came to light only after his death.

Later, trying to draw together diverse pieces of information, I began to understand a little better the complexities of mind and emotion that underlay Andropov's austere and cool exterior. Always an extremely private and reserved person, he became more so during his fifteen years at the KGB, and this excessive reserve instilled fear into the hearts of party bureaucrats; it was also the source of his fascination and his power.

Even after he moved into the general secretary's office, the outside world remained fascinated by his KGB role. What outsiders failed to realize was that Andropov gave the Russians what most of them wanted: a strong and purposeful tsar. Andropov presided over a period of transition, forcefully initiating economic and social changes and pushing forward Gorbachev and the other men who now rule the Kremlin; yet his rule was far too short to leave a personal stamp on the age or give it color. When his fifteen months in office came to an end, we wondered whether his brief tenure would turn out to be a mere footnote in Soviet history or one of its main chapters.

It was difficult to pass judgment on his administration on that frigid February morning in 1984 as his coffin rolled across Red Square shimmering in the pale sunlight. In retrospect, however, it is clear that Andropov's brief rule marked a turning point in recent Soviet history. That so brief a tenure should prove to be so crucial seemed all the more remarkable since Andropov was seriously ill for much of it. Four months into his administration his kidney problem became acute and he had to use a dialysis machine twice a week. The illness made him keenly conscious of his mortality; from that point on he was a man in a hurry. His speeches became bolder and more direct; he initiated the most far-reaching internal economic debate his country had seen and announced that a comprehensive blueprint for economic reforms would have to be completed in two years, or before the end of 1985. By advancing the public deadline, he must have sought to galvanize the lumbering bureaucracy into action.

If there is one contribution that he will be remembered for, in my opinion, it will be his bold decision to give the country a candid appraisal of its ailments, to confront both the people and the party with reality. The gap between pretense and reality had become too costly for the Soviet state; the fictions that the regime inculcated through the educational system and deliberately propagated and enforced were sapping the country's strength.

Nothing illuminated so obviously the discrepancy between utopian ideology and reality as did the Communist Party Program, the supposed bible of the party adopted at the 1961 congress, which also elected Andropov to full Central Committee membership. By the end of the seventies, the program asserted, the Soviet state and economy would be so advanced that the population would be ensured an abundance of everything. Before 1980, it specified, there would be so much food that all workers would be fed free of charge at factory canteens; schoolchildren and students would get free clothing and books; all Soviet citizens would enjoy rent-free housing; water, gas, electricity, and heating would be free of charge, as would all means of transportation; all citizens would have two months of paid vacation per year; and, needless to say, such things as medical and other social services would be free. The program, in short, promised utopia on earth. For those who did not read party documents, its promise was epitomized by Khrushchev's vow in 1961 that by 1980 the Soviet Union would "overtake America" in everything—food, wealth, comfort, industrial strength.

By the early seventies, it had become apparent that the program's pledges were in the realm of fantasy; by the eighties, the gap had become intolerable. Most people knew it, yet the rhetoric continued, as if by its own momentum. In the eighties, before the program was sharply amended by Gorbachev's congress in 1986, it had become a secret document. "They are burning it these days," one middle-level party official told me, jokingly, when I tried to obtain a copy.

What Andropov told the people was hardly a revelation—they experienced the chasm between pretense and reality in their daily lives. What was dramatically new was that the Kremlin leader spoke with a minimum of ideological sugarcoating—reaffirming his commitment to socialism but subtly yet unmistakably questioning past policies. Many of the party's stated goals, he said, had failed "the test of time"; many enshrined objectives were basically unjustified, and some contained "elements of separation from reality."

"Frankly speaking," he said, "we have not yet studied properly the society in which we live and work, and we have not yet fully discovered the laws governing its development, especially economic laws. Therefore we are at times forced to act, so to speak, empirically, in a quite irrational manner of trial and error."

For a Communist elite that was supposed to know the future and that was running the country on the "scientific principles" of Marxism-Leninism, these were staggering admissions. After sixty-five years of Soviet power, a Kremlin leader was telling the nation that the promises would not be met, that the economy and society were seriously weakened, and that this feebleness was the result in large measure of the absence of rational understanding of both and hence of a rational direction.

In making such admissions, Andropov introduced a new theme, which Gorbachev would pick up and expand later, namely, that the quest for change was inspired by economic necessity much more than by dreams of Communist triumph or Russian glory. Andropov seemed determined to create a picture of purpose and resolve. Strict disciplinary measures were combined with appeals to logic and reason, the latter suggesting that intelligence was finally being applied to national business, that the country should expect new policies and a new course. He refrained from repudiating Brezhnev directly but made it abundantly clear that the country had been at a standstill for some time and that it was ill prepared for a highly competitive future. "Now," Andropov said, "we must make up for what we have lost."

But only new people could carry out new policies.

It was clear already in the spring of 1983 that Andropov was grooming Gorbachev, the youngest member of the Politburo, for top leadership. By August, he made that formal in a televised performance that seemed choreographed for maximum impact on the party and country: Andropov collected all the surviving Bolsheviks, people who had been party members at the time of the 1917 revolution, and had Gorbachev preside over the meeting and deliver the major address, while he and other members of the leadership sat in the background. When Andropov addressed the old men and women, their breasts covered with medals and decorations, he made the case for the inevitability of change, including a generational change. The younger generations, he said, "are different; but they are not our enemies!"

In late September 1983, Andropov's condition suddenly became so grave that he had to be hospitalized. In October doctors removed one of his ailing kidneys, and from that point on, he remained restricted to an apartment inside the government hospital complex at Kuntsevo, not far from his Moscow home, so that he was always near life-sustaining equipment. And yet he continued to run the country, as if by remote control; only members of his family, Gorbachev and other close political associates, and key personal aides had access to the Kuntsevo hospital apartment.

Andropov focused almost entirely on the question of personnel. He knew that ideas and institutions are stubborn and that change has to take place through accommodation rather than destruction. But he was in a hurry. A weeding-out of old and corrupt officials intensified during that period; young people were nominated as candidates in the forthcoming Supreme Soviet elections. Andropov clearly was siding with the new generation; younger people had to be in place to carry out new policies. He had seen the dangers facing a leader seeking to make a radical change at the time when he worked as a Central Committee secretary, first for Khrushchev and later for Brezhnev. Khrushchev had been ousted in 1964 when he precipitously initiated changes that threatened bureaucratic privileges but failed to put men who shared his views in key positions. Alexei Kosygin's 1965 reforms had died a slow death in the bowels of the party bureaucracy while an ostensibly passive Brezhnev waited on the sidelines and used the failure to consolidate his preeminence in the Kremlin.

Before his kidneys gave out altogether in February 1983, Andropov told Georgi Markov, a Soviet writer, that doctors gave him only about five years to live, and "the things I want to do would require at least ten years of work." Sensing he had only a short time to live, he wanted to get things done. This urgency, rather than an excess of military ardor, was the principal reason for the remarkable visibility of senior military figures during Andropov's rule and for the high profile of the KGB. These organizations knew the meaning of obedience and responded efficiently to his orders. In his last month, he ran the country through his personal aides and with the help of the KGB. The KGB was seen by him not as an arm of arbitrary repression but as a dedicated organization, staffed by an elite untarnished by the venality and corruption of the Brezhnevite bureaucracy, certainly equipped for the struggle against that bureaucracy but more particularly for achieving political objectives. And at that stage his main political objective was to rejuvenate the party elite, to bring in fresh blood. So Andropov advanced young and energetic people who were building their careers, hoping his vision would be carried out by his disciples; apart from Gorbachev, all the top men who today run the Soviet Union came to the fore during Andropov's fifteen months in office: Nikolai Ryzhkov, Yegor Ligachev, Vitali Vorotnikov, and Viktor Chebrikov.

I felt that the end was near in December when I read a speech, which he was too ill to deliver before the Central Committee, whose last portion seemed to me his political testament, almost an appeal to the Central Committee. The course had been set, he said; "we have raised people's expectations." It was the duty of all Central Committee members to stay the course.

A poem he wrote a month before his death (and which I read much later) confirmed that impression. It was a curiously lyrical description of his realization that mortality is "the most terrifying truth" and that after his death, "white summers will mow down the memory of me." But he ended it optimistically:

> *Yet the essence born in dusk*
> *is indestructible on its way to dawn.*
> *Other generations on the earth*
> *will take the torch of life even farther.*

⋘ 2 ⋙

ANDROPOV was essentially a self-made man, even in the Soviet context; a combination of both talent and luck shaped his destiny. But this could not be seen in his official biography; at the time of his death even the most basic things about Andropov were not known.

His official biography, published on his accession to power, began with an inaccuracy and an omission. The inaccurate statement—that he was born on June 15, 1914, when in fact he was born a year later—was a source of jokes in the Andropov family on those special birthday celebrations—the fiftieth, the sixtieth, the sixty-fifth—when Andropov, like all senior officials, was given high awards. Andropov had made himself a year older to qualify for admittance to a technical school, as many young people did in the twenties and thirties.

The omission is slightly more interesting for it was a deviation from the standard format for official biographies, such as Brezhnev's, Chernenko's, or Gorbachev's, in which the birthdates were followed by the word "Russian." Andropov's biography did not give his nationality. Although he was a Russian and regarded himself as such, one of his grandparents (his father's mother) was Jewish; and in a country known for its anti-Semitism, the fact that he had even a drop of Jewish blood was not the sort of information an ambitious young man or an aspiring politician would volunteer.

But ethnic roots were not an important determinant during the first decades of the Soviet state. What defined Andropov's life in a deeper way was World War I and the enormous privations the Russians suffered in its aftermath. He was born into what was at the time a middle-class family; his father was the stationmaster at the Negutskaya Station in the Stavropol region, a white-collar government employee; his mother was a piano teacher. Both came from families of higher social status than Gorbachev's, Chernenko's, Brezhnev's, Khrushchev's, and Stalin's, but not than Lenin's. Andropov insisted that he came from the family of a railway worker. Vladimir Andropov's house, which still stands at Negutskaya, is a handsome bungalowlike one-story single-family home with a large attic and a fenced-in yard. Family albums show a Steinway piano in a well-furnished middle-class living room adorned by paintings and the oval-framed photographs popular at the time.

Initially, Stavropol was far away from the front, a rich agricultural area from which food was shipped to the capital and also to the troops at the front. Negutskaya was a station on the main Moscow–Baku line; and Baku was the center of the Russian oil industry. That was why Vladimir Andropov was not drafted; he was needed at his railroad job. But during the Bolshevik revolution and the ensuing civil war, the famine and disorders reached the Stavropol region. The young Andropov was four when he lost his father; Vladimir died of typhus while traveling to neighboring Georgia to buy food. Amid famine and internal turmoil, the demand for music lessons in that remote part of the country evaporated. Evgenia Andropov took a job in the local elementary school. In later years Andropov almost never talked to his own children about his mother, except that when he heard Rachmaninoff or Chopin piano pieces on the radio he would sometimes say, "My mother played that." Nor did he ever talk about his stepfather; when he was six Evgenia married again, and the family moved to the town of Mazdok, in the northern Caucasus, where his half sister, Valentina, was born the next year. In 1929, when Andropov was fourteen, his mother died.

What he did for the next few years cannot be established with precision. He did leave his stepfather's home and, according to a family story, was making it on his own, like Jack London, one of his heroes at the time. He was tall, bigger and stronger than other boys, and always claimed to be older than his age. He was a bookworm even then, and his interior life was shaped not only by Russian classics—the works of Maksim Gorki in particular—but also by such American writers as London, Mark Twain, and James Fenimore Cooper. (Years later, while running clandestine operations against the Finnish army in Karelia, Andropov chose as his code name "The Mohican.")

His natural curiosity and lifelong passion for learning led him first to a job, as an assistant to the projectionist in a movie house at Mazdok; the newsreels of the time opened a new world to an impressionable young mind. They showed distant European capitals, other peoples. But they also revealed to him the vastness of Russia; soon he left the Caucasus and roamed around southern Russia, supporting himself by doing odd jobs. When he made his way to the Volga River he became fascinated by ships. The Volga may have conjured up the picture of the Mississippi of Huckleberry Finn; for, as people who knew him testified, Andropov had a strong romantic streak, even in later years. He worked as a porter at the Volga River port of Ribinsk, then as an ordinary sailor on a tugboat, and eventually decided that he wanted to become a captain.

His enrollment at the Ribinsk Water Transport Technical College in 1932 seems to reflect a conscious decision on the part of the seventeen-year-old Andropov that he wanted to get ahead in the world, not roam around as a romantic vagabond. It was then that he gave an incorrect birthdate, making himself one year older to qualify. Russia at that point was going through Stalin's chaotic industrialization, and young people were encouraged to *do* things; the dictator knew that to capture the imagination of the nation he had to capture that of its youth, and he succeeded in doing so in the thirties. The Komsomol, the young Communist youth organization, became the pool of new cadres, young men and women who were quickly promoted to the jobs vacated in Stalin's murderous purges, when tens of thousands of party members and ordinary citizens were executed and countless others were exiled to Siberia. Extremely rapid mobility was the order of the day. Young men were placed in charge of big projects; they were rebuilding the country.

Andropov not only joined the Komsomol but became its leader at the school.

After Andropov's death, a young Soviet filmmaker, Oleg Uralov, who was making a documentary about the late Soviet leader, interviewed several people who knew Andropov at the river navigation school. His chemistry teacher, Nadezda Miloradovna, remembered the young Yuri as calm, hardworking, and serious, which set him apart from his more extrovert colleagues. He was, she recalled, a natural leader of men. The boys sometimes behaved in class in a way that embarrassed the young teacher, who was only a few years older than they, but young Yuri knew how to calm things down. A classmate, Ivan Polyarkov, said he wondered at the time why a man who grew up in the steppes of

Stavropol and the Caucasus range would want to become a Volga boatman. Andropov's answer was "always the same," Polyarkov recalled. "He loved the wide spaces along the Volga and he wanted to become a ship's captain."

He never became a captain, however. Immediately after his graduation, in 1936, he was appointed head of the Komsomol organization at the largest industrial enterprise in Ribinsk, the Volodarsk shipyard. In accepting the appointment, he opted for a political career. One photograph from that period shows him dressed in a black tunic buttoned up to his neck, a Komsomol badge pinned near his heart, with bushy black hair and full sensuous lips but the stern expression of a Komsomol leader; another shows him laughing with a group of shipyard activists; in yet another he is wearing a Russian national tunic, looking shy and uncomfortable.

In 1937, as Stalin's purges depleted the ranks of the party, Andropov was sent to the city of Yaroslav to become third secretary of the regional Komsomol committee. Two years later he became its first secretary. For a young man twenty-four years old, this was a major promotion. He was given an apartment in the center of the city, in one of the massive buildings where party and government officials lived. In 1939 he joined the Communist Party—his card number is 2,605.010. He met and married Tatyana Filipovna, an attractive, petite brunette who was a Komsomol activist, and they remained very close throughout their lives. Andropov was one of the few top Soviet officials who never had a mistress; on Tatyana Filipovna's fiftieth birthday he wrote her a lyrical sonnet in which he alluded to this by saying:

> Let them laugh at the poet
> and let them envy us doubly
> because I write sonnets to my own wife
> and not to another man's.

He had written her a sonnet a quarter of a century earlier, and now, when his hair was almost white, he was recalling that they had gone through moments of great "misery" and also "happiness" to remain eternally faithful friends.

⫷ 3 ⫸

In 1940, Andropov was transferred to Petrozavodsk in Karelia to take over the job of first secretary of the Komsomol.

Over the next ten years, Karelia gave him a peculiar slant on Soviet society; for all the ravishing beauty of its forests, streams, and lakes, the atmosphere of the region was tense. Its Finnish and Russian population lived in separate worlds, which could be bridged only by outsiders who had no stake in either. Andropov entered this environment at an explosive moment; the historic animosities between these national groups were aggravated by the Russo-Finnish war of 1939–1940, known as the Winter War. At high cost in casualties, Stalin took a large slice of Finnish territory and merged it with Soviet Karelia. Stalinist terror reached monstrous proportions in the province, and it became one of the most sensitive border areas of the time. When Nazi Germany attacked Russia in the summer of 1941, Finnish troops crossed the frontier into the Karelo-Finnish Republic and imposed an almost equally brutal and harsh rule on the Russians. German troops surrounded Leningrad in the rear. Andropov became one of the organizers of partisan resistance, working behind Finnish lines, living the precarious existence of an underground operative, the "Mohican" who signed radio messages to partisan units.

His headquarters were in Belomorsk, on the southern coast of the White Sea. As Komsomol leader, his main task initially was to mobilize the population to build a railway line east from Belomorsk to Obozerskiy, deep inside Russia. With the southern part of the Belomorsk–Leningrad railway link already in enemy hands, the Northern Railway connecting the heartland with the port of Murmansk, in the far north, had become unusable. The Belomorsk–Obozerskiy line was completed by October 1941 and helped to maintain a link that proved crucial for Western military assistance to Moscow under the Lend Lease program, which was channeled mainly through Murmansk. For the rest of the war, as Komsomol leader, Andropov was responsible for Soviet partisan activity. In his first known article, published in the journal *Smena* in 1942, Andropov extolled the heroism and skill with which young men and women fought against the Finnish army. But he noted that courage and heroism were not enough; the partisans, he wrote, must "skillfully combine courage, caution, and precise calculation to achieve positive results."

The war's end in Karelia was messy. Before evacuating the area, the Finns burned down or destroyed all public buildings, industrial enterprises, and power stations. When Andropov entered Petrozavodsk, the provincial capital, on June 27, 1944, with the troops of the Red Army's 368th Division, he found more than 660 of its public buildings and industrial enterprises destroyed. After the war, he was one of the officials who sovietized the province and its sullen Finnish population; it was a job only a thoroughly dedicated and ruthless man could do. After Andropov rose to prominence in the sixties, some people in Helsinki hinted that he also had dipped his hands in the blood, and it is true that Stalin made everyone who survived in the party seem a participant in his crimes. But the Finns were by then reluctant to provide evidence or say anything publicly against the man who was on the move in Moscow.

Andropov got to like Karelia and learned to speak Finnish; in an ethnically explosive situation this helped him cement friendships and lightened the burdens of everyday life, and it also be-

131

came an important political asset. As administrator, he made an intellectual investment in understanding the Finns and the nature of multiethnic relations. Years later, Jakkoo Kalela, foreign policy adviser to Finnish president Mauno Koivisto, told me that during a meeting with Andropov in 1983, Finnish officials were stunned by his grasp of Finnish affairs and Soviet-Finnish relations. "In a single sentence," Kalela said, "Andropov was able to summarize the nature of our relations and to tell us exactly how he wanted to see them develop in the future. He showed an amazing insight."

Andropov's ties to Karelia were both personal and political. Both his children were born there, Igor in 1942, and Irina in 1946. In 1944 he became secretary of the Petrozavodsk City Party Committee and in 1947 he was second secretary of the republic's Central Committee. In Karelia he established a personal and political relationship with Otto Kuusinen, a colorful Finnish Communist who served as head of a puppet Communist government in Finland during the Russo-Finnish war of 1939–1940, became leader of the Soviet Karelo-Finnish Republic, and eventually became a full member of the Soviet Politburo. This relationship, as we shall see, eventually helped propel Andropov toward the peak of Kremlin power. According to people who knew both men, Kuusinen had a very high opinion of Andropov, admired the cool efficiency of his operation and the flexibility and subtlety of his mind, and regarded him with paternal fondness. (Andropov later enjoyed a close personal relationship with another Baltic Communist who became a full member of the Soviet Politburo—Arvid Pelshe of Latvia.)

Others, too, held Andropov's work in high esteem, and at the end of 1943 Moscow proposed that he become the first secretary of the Komsomol in the Ukraine, the second most important Soviet republic after Russia; but the Karelian leaders opposed the transfer, which would have been a major promotion for Andropov. They wanted him to stay in Karelia.*

*Gennady Kuprianov, *Ot Barentsovo Morya do Ladogi,* Leninzdat, Leningrad, 1972.

Over the years, Kuusinen was a civilizing influence on the young man from Stavropol. He was a highly cultured Finnish poet and historian and an old-fashioned Marxist with broad experience. In the first two decades of the century, he had served as a member of the Finnish Parliament while working as a leftist journalist and editor. He then helped to organize the abortive Communist revolution in 1918 in Finland and was member of the Revolutionary Government before fleeing to Russia. He was also one of the founders of the Finnish Communist Party. In the twenties and thirties he served on the Comintern executive committee, until Stalin sent him in 1939 to organize and head the Popular Government of the Democratic Republic of Finland, which was established at Terioki, now Zelenogorsk, in Karelia. The Winter War, however, disabused the Russians of their hopes to establish a Communist government in Finland, and Kuusinen's subsequent career was confined to Soviet politics. Kuusinen became a member of the Soviet Central Committee in 1941 and was elected to the Politburo before Stalin's death. Under Khrushchev, he was again elected to the Politburo and also became a secretary of the Central Committee. He moved to Moscow in 1944 and remained there until the end of his life, although he was chairman of the Karelian Supreme Soviet. Kuusinen's presence in Moscow meant that Andropov had a friend in court.

Despite these lofty positions, Kuusinen was not a mover and shaker in the Kremlin; in fact, the number of historical books he managed to write during that period and his activities in the Academy of Sciences, of which he was a member, suggest that his presence in the top echelon of Kremlin authority may have been due to his revolutionary past and to his ethnic background, an important consideration at a time when the Russians still maintained the pretenses of being an international revolutionary movement. The fact that he could serve in both Stalin's and Khrushchev's Politburo reveals a strong streak of opportunism, as do his later writings. In the thirties, for instance, Kuusinen advanced some elaborate schemes for subverting Western democracies, but he modified this position in his later works, after Khrushchev began to pursue détente with the West.

Yet Kuusinen was in a position to advance careers of junior officials, and to protect Andropov when he got into serious trouble in 1950.

Up to that point Andropov's ascent had been smooth; everything had broken right for him since he became Komsomol leader at Ribinsk. In January 1950, however, a team of inspectors from Moscow arrived in Petrozavodsk to investigate allegations of mismanagement and inefficiency in the republic. Back in Moscow they presented a report that formed the basis for a sharp Central Committee denunciation of the Karelian leadership, of which Andropov was the second in command. The indictment, published in the newspaper *Leninskoe Znamya* of Petrozavodsk on February 17, included Andropov's name. His chief, the republic's party leader, Gennady Kuprianov, was arrested, as were some local officials in the food and dairy industries, who were involved in embezzlement schemes. Andropov later told friends that he went to bed every night expecting a knock at his door by agents of the NKVD (the predecessor of the KGB). It was probably then that he became fully aware of the mindless arbitrariness of Stalin's regime; and it was at that time, the time of Stalin's anti-Semitic paranoia, that he realized his partly Jewish ancestry was a potential liability. So he became more of a loner. Later, when he rose in the party hierarchy, he surrounded himself with people who were internationalists and temperamentally anti-Stalinist, men and women who questioned not the system but rather the despotic character of Stalin's rule. In the high party circles he became known as a man who opposed police arbitrariness and insisted on regular procedures; this was one of the reasons he was eventually given the job of running the KGB.

How Andropov escaped arrest at that point can be explained

only by Kuusinen's intervention in Moscow. Andropov publicly conceded mistakes, or as the record of the Karelian Central Committee put it, "he acknowledged that he was to be blamed since he had had the responsibility for these areas." And he endured scathing public criticism; one speaker rose to reject sarcastically the "self-criticism" by Andropov and two of his associates who said they did not notice mismanagement in the food industry. "What do you want?" a speaker identified as Comrade Klishko said. "A health certificate from the party saying you temporarily lost your political vision? No, It's not that they didn't see. They didn't want to see."

It was clear that the blemish the affair left on Andropov's record would sidetrack him in his political career, but obviously not for long. In 1951, he moved from Karelia to Moscow and joined the bureaucracy of the Central Committee, first as an inspector and later as a minor official in the subsection dealing with European Communist parties. It was a temporary haven after his public reprimand in Karelia. There was little doubt that he owed his transfer to Kuusinen. He was the only man to whom Andropov ever became seriously politically indebted throughout his career.

In the latter part of 1952, a number of junior regional officials were moved to the Foreign Ministry to prepare for ambassadorial assignments. It is not quite clear why this was done; some senior Soviet officials told me that the party had decided that foreign diplomatic assignments should not all be held by professional diplomats and that reliable junior cadres should be given important diplomatic posts. A more convincing explanation is based on the increasing paranoia of a xenophobic Stalin, who in his last years became murderously suspicious of the professional Soviet diplomats in general. It is known that Stalin began to suspect even his foreign minister, Vyacheslav Molotov. Among junior officials from the provinces who joined the Foreign Ministry at the time were a number of persons who would later rise to prominent party positions, including Mikhail Zimyanin and Sergei Lapin. The High

Diplomatic Academy was set up for officials who were preparing for assignment in the capitalist part of the world; it provided crash courses in diplomacy and languages.

Andropov joined the Foreign Ministry in 1953, after Stalin's death. According to a story told by dissident historian Roy Medvedev (which I could not verify), this was arranged by Kuusinen to rescue his protégé's career. While still in the Central Committee bureaucracy, Andropov was said to have unwittingly found himself in the midst of a power struggle between Khrushchev and Georgi Malenkov, who succeeded Stalin as premier. Malenkov wanted to dislodge the party secretary of Soviet Lithuania, and Andropov was sent to investigate alleged irregularities in the Lithuanian party. Andropov, however, gave the man a clean bill of health and thus incurred Malenkov's hostility.

Kuusinen at that point was a member of the Politburo and therefore in a position to advance Andropov's candidacy for a diplomatic assignment. As an official who had helped sovietize the heavily Finnish Karelia and who spoke Finnish, Andropov seemed ideally suited for rebellious Hungary, whose language shared roots with the Finnish. He did not, however, attend the High Diplomatic Academy—it was believed that those to be assigned to socialist countries did not need the tools of the diplomatic trade, something very much in the spirit of that period when Stalin regarded East European countries as an extension of the Soviet empire.

<<< **4** >>>

HUNGARY made a deep impression on Andropov; his experience there shaped his outlook more than any other, according to persons close to him. Hungary was to place him at the center of a major international crisis and allow him to distinguish himself for his incisive mind, limitless capacity for work, and cool judgment under pressure.

The job of Soviet ambassador to Hungary had been an insignificant one. Stalin treated Hungary as a colony. The real power was in the hands of the Soviet military commander in Hungary, and substantive business between Moscow and Budapest was conducted through the party bureaucracies, with the Russians, in effect, issuing guidelines for the Hungarians to follow. The Kremlin did not pretend otherwise; the ambassador was no more than a messenger, lacking political clout to act independently. The regime of Hungarian Communist boss Mátyás Rákosi was as subservient to Moscow as it was deadly oppressive at home.

Andropov arrived in Budapest in the fall of 1953. The entire Hungarian leadership had been summoned to Moscow the previous June and ordered to reform itself. It was decided that Imre Nagy would become prime minister and initiate a series of reforms. Rákosi, however, remained the party's general secretary. But after a hopeful and reasonably tranquil period of eighteen months, Nagy was suddenly removed from power and replaced by a Rákosi clone, Erno Gero. From that point on, the Hungarian Communist leadership would be sharply divided over the future of the economy, budgetary allocations, and the scope of the de-Stalinization and liberalization that would progressively weaken the ruling party and produce political instability in a country sliding toward a popular revolt against Communist rule.

Initially, the diplomatic life offered an opportunity for Andropov to read and reflect, write poetry, and study Hungary's history and language. Despite his skimpy formal education, he had an insatiable appetite for learning, and his reading and reflection during that time broadened his perspective and gave a historical grain to his intelligence, something that he admired in his mentor, Kuusinen.

He and his wife also enjoyed leisurely weekends in Vienna, in neighboring Austria, which was then under four-power occupation, and they toured the sights he had once seen on the screen as a projectionist's assistant. He attended few diplomatic dinner parties, mainly those given by his Communist colleagues. He began taking English lessons. But he also attended to his job, trying to learn about Hungary and to get to know the people who were running the place. The job became increasingly complex and demanding as various factions in the leadership fought each other and sought supporters in Moscow. Day by day he witnessed a weakening of the system.

More than a quarter of a century later, when he became convinced that Russia had to reform its system, he would cite to friends the lesson of his diplomatic years. The once-imperial city of Vienna, now the capital of a small country, was for him the symbol of the Hapsburg empire's failure to adjust to new economic, social, and political conditions. Unless checked and reversed, economic and social stagnation could eventually push the Soviet state onto a familiar historical path—a dangerous path, which had led other great nations, trapped by bureaucracies and habits too rigid to accommodate new problems, to lose their empires. Moscow had to deal with its own problems, and at the same time control events elsewhere in the Communist world. Andropov's experience in Hungary made him aware not only of the need for reform but also of the impact an uncertain period in the Kremlin leadership could have on the unrest in Hungary, Poland, and the rest of Eastern Europe.

In the first year of Andropov's ambassadorship, Khrushchev emerged as the main force in Moscow, amid confusing signs of change in Soviet domestic and foreign policies. The next year Moscow moved to ease its relations with the West; but more significant, from Andropov's vantage point, was Khrushchev's rapprochement with Tito's Yugoslavia, which had been expelled by Stalin from the Soviet bloc in 1948. In 1955, the year the four occupying powers signed the Austrian peace treaty and withdrew their troops, Khrushchev traveled to Belgrade in an act of contrition demanded by Tito. It seemed that a new Soviet attitude toward Eastern Europe was emerging. This posed a political problem for the East European Communist regimes, which were thoroughly identified with the Stalinist policy.

Each passing month of 1956 placed Andropov closer to the center of decision-making in the Kremlin. Early on he foresaw the potential for social upheaval inherent in the unresponsive and obtuse Rákosi leadership in Hungary. But Khrushchev was engaged in a complicated struggle against his political opponents in the Politburo, a struggle that would not be resolved until 1957. At the beginning of 1956 he delivered the "secret speech" at the Twentieth Party Congress, exposing Stalin's crimes. In the spring he removed Molotov from the Foreign Ministry; but Molotov and other Stalinists remained in the Politburo. There was also unrest in Poland that summer, which would culminate in the removal of Marshal Konstantin Rokossovski from Warsaw. Rokossovski, although a native of Poland, was a Soviet citizen and marshal who for the past seven years had served as Polish defense minister. I do not know of any other country where a citizen and officer of a foreign country could serve as defense minister, but this was typical of Stalin's attitude toward Poland.

But by early summer the issue of Hungary began to dominate Kremlin discussions. First Mikhail Suslov and then Anastas Mikoyan, both Politburo members, traveled to Budapest to shore up the Rákosi regime. The first street demonstrations in July were full of foreboding. Nikolai Inozemtsev, who was on Khrushchev's staff at the time (and whom I got to know well much later when he served as director of a Moscow institute), told me that Andropov's dispatches came to the attention of the Soviet leader that summer as the gravity of the crisis became apparent. Their tone was clinical; they foresaw the weakening of the Rákosi-Gero position. Imre Nagy was the only alternative, although he was not a player at that point. Yet Andropov distrusted Nagy as a nationalist and a weak figure. Another source told me that Andropov's assessments of Hungarian leaders produced disagreements in Moscow.

As the crisis deepened, the previously obscure ambassador to Budapest became well known in the Kremlin; his dispatches, and there were sometimes up to ten cables in a day, were read by the entire ruling elite. With events progressing into a revolutionary stage, it was Andropov, and not the Soviet military commander in Hungary, who provided the political analysis that implicitly questioned the Kremlin's somnambulism. He also advanced the candidacy of János Kádár, who until 1954 had been languishing in prison on charges of espionage, treason, and nationalism—charges fabricated by Rákosi and Gero.

Andropov must have brought up Kádár's name with Suslov and Mikoyan in early 1956, for Kádár was exonerated. As the crisis deepened, Andropov saw Kádár as the only potential leader. He argued that Kádár was an old Communist who spent the war years in the underground and in prison, not in Moscow, like Rákosi, Gero, and Nagy. That, plus the fact that he was victimized in the Stalinist purges, would give Kádár greater stature in his own country. On the minus side, people like Kádár were less subservient to Moscow than Rákosi and his followers. But at that point Moscow had nothing vaguely resembling a policy; the sole objective was to halt the slide toward chaos and restore Communist rule.

But what if Kádár faltered? Andropov was the only Soviet official who had had contact with him since he was released from prison. Moreover, Andropov's recommendation, according to one source who had access to the archives of the period, "was not fully supported in Moscow." The stakes were high as the inevitable showdown approached, and Andropov's career was at risk. But he trusted his analysis and his instincts; he also got to like the Hungarian, a sentiment that he would retain for the rest of his life. Of all the Communist leaders he met and dealt with, Kádár was the only one whose photograph was displayed in Andropov's apartment. I suspect that he told Kádár in those days that he himself was nearly a victim of Stalinist terror, that by a miracle he escaped the fate that befell others; that may have been the initial bond between them. I saw a long televised interview with Kádár after Andropov's death, and what struck me most was the degree of intimacy that existed between the two men.

What persuasion, political maneuvering, and diplomacy could not enforce in Hungary, the Soviet military would have to undertake at gunpoint. Andropov's role again became subsidiary, for Khrushchev and his top advisers made the decisions. Up to the point when Soviet tanks moved into Budapest to crush the open rebellion, Andropov was a diplomat, carrying out instructions and —in dealing with the Hungarians—displaying a high degree of firm and decisive treachery by offering counsels of moderation and hopeful but unfounded assessments of Soviet intentions. Diplomacy, needless to say, rests on the art of dissimulation. After Andropov became a major figure in Moscow, Hungarian émigré sources attached a particularly sinister meaning to his deceptive techniques, as if to suggest that the ambassador of a country about to invade another one should be decent and gentlemanly enough to tell his hosts about it in advance. I could not, of course, check out these things, nor could I check out Soviet tales of Andropov's fearless behavior and personal courage in the face of armed anti-Communist street gangs in Budapest. Both seemed somewhat self-serving. However, there is no doubt that the Soviet intervention caused Andropov great personal anguish, but his performance as a diplomat in October and November of 1956 was assessed as superb by his chiefs in Moscow.

5

HIS role in Budapest raised Andropov's status in Moscow, particularly as Kádár quickly consolidated his position. Yet, according to a friend of his, Andropov was worried about his future when he returned to Moscow in April 1957. Such worries were not entirely misplaced. In the previous year he had met and dealt directly with Khrushchev, Suslov, Mikoyan, and other members of the leadership. They were all impressed favorably by the cool, self-contained man whose personality lacked pretense and whose judgments were well argued and sound. But Khrushchev's own position was shaky, and that may have been the source of Andropov's anxiety.

In June Khrushchev survived an attempt by his political enemies in the Politburo to depose him; in turn, Molotov, Lazar Kaganovich, and other Stalinists were purged from the leadership. Moreover, Andropov's mentor, Kuusinen, had sided with Khrushchev and was returned to the top leadership as a full member of the Politburo and a secretary of the Central Committee. Andropov was awarded the Order of Lenin, the nation's highest civilian decoration, for his ambassadorial performance.

Kuusinen advanced Andropov's candidacy to head a new department in the Central Committee created to deal exclusively with the socialist countries. Until then, such matters had been handled by the International Department, headed by Boris Ponomarev and under Suslov's control. The Hungarian revolt and the unrest in Poland and other Communist-bloc countries and the looming difficulties with China made the establishment of the new division both rational and necessary: Ponomarev was going to handle relations with Communist parties in the rest of the world; Andropov became responsible for the Soviet-bloc area.

Since Khrushchev wanted to adjust and modernize relations between Moscow and other Communist-bloc capitals, he was easily persuaded by Kuusinen that Andropov was ideally suited for the job. He had just lived through the high political drama created by the first major popular revolt against Communist rule in a Soviet-bloc country; and he had firsthand understanding of the problems in smaller Communist-bloc countries and presumably of ways for dealing with them.

Andropov's Hungarian experience was important to him in a more fundamental way. A man without formal knowledge of foreign affairs—who had largely taught himself through reading and observation—Andropov had been thrown into a major international crisis that had forced him to analyze and act, to pass judgments without the benefit of consultations or instructions, to be an independent agent. He matured in the process. In the bureaucratized world of Soviet politics, players normally take a long time to acquire such skills and then only on the regional level. It must have occurred to Andropov at the time that high office was not outside his reach; people he saw running countries and determining their fate must not have seemed conspicuously better qualified than he. A man who worked for him at the Central Committee told me that he detected traces of this attitude after Andropov became a secretary of the Central Committee in 1962.

Yet Hungary was also a traumatic experience, emotionally wrenching, involving treachery and deception. Several of his associates told me how deeply Andropov felt the impact of the Hungarian revolution and its suppression, yet no one could be specific about the source of his anxieties. He had tricked General Pal Maleter, commander of the "rebel" forces, to visit him under safe-conduct at the Soviet embassy to discuss the situation; inside the embassy, Maleter was seized by Soviet troops and was eventually executed. I doubt, however, that this particular incident disturbed Andropov's sleep; Communists feel loyalty to other Communists, not to those whom they regard as class enemies, and

Maleter was a nationalist soldier. The main source of his anguish must have been the arrest by the Soviet military of Imre Nagy and his cabinet after Kádár had guaranteed their safe-conduct in a written note to the Yugoslav government. Could Kádár have issued such a guarantee without consulting the Soviet ambassador? Highly unlikely. Nagy and his cabinet had taken refuge in the Yugoslav embassy in Budapest after Soviet forces occupied the city. They were holed up in the basement of the small building for three weeks, until the new Hungarian government, in a note endorsed by Kádár, guaranteed their safe-conduct and pledged that no charges would be lodged against them for activities connected with the revolt. Nagy and his colleagues, having read the note, decided to leave the embassy and return to their homes. Seconds after they left the building, Soviet soldiers swooped down on them, seized them, and took them to a military camp. Subsequently, Nagy and his top associates were executed.

Did Andropov know that would happen? I do not know. Unlikely, most of his associates said; if he had known, he would not have been convincing enough to persuade Kádár to sign the safe-conduct guarantee. I have discussed this point with several high-ranking Western career diplomats; all believed that Moscow would not tell its ambassador anything beyond his basic instructions; no government would do more. But even if he was not told by his superiors in Moscow that Nagy and his associates would be executed, Andropov must have intuitively known it. Clearly he had no choice; yet this placed Kádár in an awful situation vis-à-vis his people. Moreover, it was a monstrous betrayal of men they both knew and had worked with in the past. Andropov's subsequent actions suggest a deep sense of guilt; in his new job in Moscow, he used his position to help Kádár when he began the slow process of social and economic reforms that turned the regime they both helped install into the most accepted and popular government in the Soviet bloc.

After Budapest, Andropov developed high blood pressure. Like many a superstitious Russian, he wore a silver bracelet around his right wrist. Such bracelets, imported from Japan, were expensive; according to popular belief at the time, they had medicinal properties. Later, however, when he became seriously ill, he did not give in to the irrational streak in the Russian makeup and refused the services of various folk healers.

⫸ 6 ⫷

UPON returning from Hungary, Andropov took up a job at the Central Committee in Moscow and moved his family into a two-room apartment in a huge, rambling building at Kutuzovsky Prospect No. 30. They lived there until 1967, the year he was appointed chairman of the KGB, when the family moved into a more distinguished building at Kutuzovsky Prospect No. 26.

He cut a strange figure in his Central Committee days. His black topcoat, an oddity in Russia, made him look like a tall, gangling Protestant minister. He always wore a tie, except when he went to work on Sundays. Although a workaholic, he spent a large chunk of his time reading books or brainstorming with associates. Alexander Bovin, who worked for him at the time, told me that he once went to visit Andropov and found him reading Plato's *Dialogues.* "Why are you reading Plato?" Bovin asked. "If I want to argue with you I've got to know philosophy," Andropov responded. Bovin, a Falstaffian figure who is now a senior commentator for *Izvestia,* was fifteen years younger than Andropov but had two university degrees, one in law and another in philosophy. Andropov had no university education and he was busily educating himself.

Other associates noted on his desk volumes by Hegel, Kant, and Oscar Wilde, as well as various Russian classics. In Andropov's home, the tradition was to present books as gifts for birthdays or other occasions. Books lined the hall of his apartment up to the ceiling. He collected, in particular, editions of Cervantes, including English editions. After he returned from Budapest he resumed his English lessons, with a teacher who came to his office twice a week. Georgi Arbatov used to bring American detective novels to Andropov so that he could practice his English. Andropov wanted to read Oscar Wilde in English and was frustrated, telling his children he would never be able to catch the nuances. Why Oscar Wilde? Was there something of Dorian Grey in Andropov? Several poems of his that I have read reveal Andropov to be a man aware of the world's limitations, not a revolutionary trying to change it. Perhaps we should be reminded that Dorian, Salome, and Lady Windermere were not Wilde's only creations, that he also wrote *The Soul of Man Under Socialism,* in which he predicted a utopian future when the abolition of private property will make possible the full development of the individual, when there will be no want and no insecurity, no ugliness and no waste of the human spirit in senseless rivalries, a world in which there will be no crime since there will be no economic reason for crime.

Was Andropov's reading taste a function of his inquisitiveness, something that met the needs of his interior life as well as his thirst for power? His son, Igor, described him as someone with a "tremendous thirst" for getting to know people. Each time he met an interesting person, Igor said, Andropov would come home and talk about him or her. "It was an event for him; I can say without qualification that he knew how to understand others."

This quality translated into a gift for attracting and using bright young men and earning their loyalty. During his ten years in the Central Committee, he gathered a team of "consultants" that included some of the most intelligent and able people in the country. Andropov insisted that his advisers not only be well educated—virtually all had doctorates—but that they also possess imagination and initiative. (He would make the same demands on personnel when he took over the KGB in 1967.) There was another common denominator among his counselors: In addition to being intellectuals, all felt disgust for Stalin and his murderous rule, or as one of them put it privately, "We were all children of the Twentieth Party Congress." This, in the Soviet context, meant they had a less dogmatic and somewhat reformist cast of mind. His team became a Kremlin stable of speech writers, analysts, and idea men. Among them were Lev Tolkhunov, who later became editor in chief of *Izvestia* and moved up to head one of the chambers of the Supreme Soviet; Georgi Shahnazarov, a well-known writer who became a senior official of the Central Committee; Fyodor Burlatsky, a leading political scientist and journalist; Oleg Bogomolov, now director of the Institute of the Economics of the World Socialist System; sinologist Lev Delyusin, former Beijing correspondent for *Pravda* and now of the Institute of Oriental Studies; and Georgi Arbatov, head of the Institute of the U.S.A. and Canada.

There were stirrings of reform in the early sixties, instigated by Khrushchev, in fact, before he was ousted in the palace coup of 1964. Kosygin, who initially shared power with Brezhnev, also talked about reforms but his plans came to naught. The country was still deeply divided on the question of Stalin, as was the party. Despite Khrushchev's de-Stalinization campaign, Stalin remained in the hearts of many Russians. It was not a time for profound changes; had they been initiated at the time, Andropov's men would have risen much higher in the Soviet hierarchy than they did eventually. But already at that time, according to émigré Soviet writer and biologist Zhores Medvedev, liberal Soviet intellectuals looked upon Andropov as a hopeful and positive figure in the leadership. Medvedev was involved in a struggle over the officially approved genetics theories of Trofim Lysenko, a charlatan who has since been completely discredited. He reported that Andropov was against Lysenko although the latter still enjoyed Khrushchev's support.

When Kuusinen returned to the Politburo and Secretariat in

1957, he assembled a personal staff of advisers, who reported only to him; Andropov, elected a full member of the Central Committee in 1961, originally managed Kuusinen's brain trust and then took it over from his ailing mentor in 1962, when he himself became a secretary of the Central Committee, a major promotion that set him on the road to supreme power. Kuusinen died two years later.

Andropov's main preoccupation in his Central Committee days, as was noted earlier, was foreign policy, particularly relations with socialist countries. His first major assignment came in 1957, when he and Ponomarev traveled to Belgrade to persuade Tito to take part in the November world conference of Communist parties. They failed.

In his new position he was learning the limits of power. He was no longer a lowly ambassador but the man in the Kremlin who helped shape policy toward the other socialist countries. He put a lot of energy and effort into a speech in which he sought to chart a new course in relations between socialist countries. Every word, every idea in it was debated and thrashed out a number of times in an effort to gain a consensus for innovation without alarming dogmatic Communists. The man who helped Andropov write the speech recalled numerous rewrites and the adjustment of material to satisfy Andropov's fastidiousness. And when he delivered the speech in East Berlin at a major Communist gathering, nothing happened. It was just a speech; subsequent events were shaped by other, more basic, factors, such as national interests.

By far the most significant issue was China, and this gave Andropov's assignment a strategic scope that placed him at the center of ideological disputes. China's Mao Zedong, appalled by Khrushchev's denunciation of Stalin the previous year, had already begun to distance himself from Moscow. Signs of more profound irritation in Beijing became apparent on the issue of Moscow's reluctance to give China nuclear technology. Tito had cracked the unity of international communism in 1948, but Mao was to split it wide open in the early sixties.

Brezhnev family portrait. From left, front row: Brezhnev's wife, Viktoria; Brezhnev's only great-granddaughter, Galya, eight; and Brezhnev. Standing, from left: Brezhnev's son, Yuri; a woman believed to be Viktoria, Brezhnev's only granddaughter, and her husband; Brezhnev's daughter, Galina, and her husband, Yuri Churbanov; an unidentified woman; Brezhnev's daughter-in-law, Ludmilla, wife of Yuri Brezhnev; and Yuri Brezhnev's son, Andrei, twenty.

RIGHT: Brezhnev with "Misha," the official symbol of the 1980 Summer Olympics, relaxing in Budapest, 1979.

BELOW: Soviet Communist Party leader Leonid I. Brezhnev and his wife, Viktoria, keep watch over their granddaughter, Viktoria, in Moscow.

Brezhnev walking away from a Kremlin reception on November 7, 1982, three days before his death.

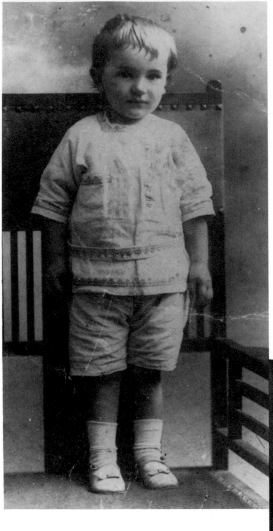

Yuri V. Andropov, age three, 1918.

Andropov and his half sister, Valentina, with
their grandmother, 1929.

ABOVE: Andropov *(right)* with two classmates at
the Ribinsk Water Transport School, 1933.

RIGHT: Andropov as Komsomol activist,
between 1934 and 1936.

BELOW: Andropov with his daughter, Irina,
sometime after their return from Hungary
in 1957.

RIGHT: Andropov, while still KGB chairman, visiting János Kádár in Kádár's office in Budapest.

Да, все мы смертны, хоть не под утру
Мне за теты, страшней, котрой нету;
Но в час положенный и, как все умру
И память обо мне сотрут седая лета

Мы бренны в этом мире, под луной;"
Жизнь-только миг; небытие - навеки.
Кружится во вселенной шар земной
Живут и исчезают человеки.

Но сущее, рожденное во мгле.
Неистребимо на пути к рассвету,
Иные поколения на Земле
Несут все дальше жизни эстафету.

LEFT: Andropov's last poem, in his own handwriting, written in January 1984.

*Yes, we are mortal, even though I do not accept
this truth, the most frightening of all.
At the appointed hour I will die, as everyone must,
and the memory of me will be erased by the kingdom
    of the dead.
We are transients in this world under the moon.
Life is but a blink; nonexistence is eternal.
The earth is spinning in the universe
as people live and people die.
Yet the essence born in dusk
is indestructible on its way to dawn.
Other generations on the earth
will take the torch of life even farther.*

The author interviewing Chernenko, October 1984. Clockwise from left: General Secretary Konstantin
U. Chernenko; Leonid Zamyatin, former head of the Central Committee Information Department;
Andrei Alexandrov-Agentov, former national security adviser; Alexander Sazonov, counselor in the
Soviet Ministry of Foreign Affairs; Dusko Doder.

Andropov and his protégé, Mikhail Gorbachev, on a leisurely walk through the woods.

A month before assuming power, Gorbachev votes in parliamentary elections, accompanied by his wife, Raisa, and granddaughter Ksanochka, 1985.

Gorbachev and his wife, Raisa, at the Geneva summit, November 1985.

The major events that led to a grave rift between the two giant Communist nations came during Andropov's watch. In 1958, Mao announced his Great Leap Forward policy, which seemed a repudiation of Khrushchev's internal policy; the next year, after Khrushchev's tour of the United States and his subsequent visit to Beijing, the Chinese dismissed Khrushchev's rationale for détente with the United States—the effort to avoid nuclear war—by publicly stating that the United States was "a paper tiger." In 1960, Khrushchev impulsively withdrew all Soviet technicians and aid personnel from China.

The feud came into the open in a curious fashion. At various international meetings of Communist parties, the tiny and Stalinist Albania, which sided with China, became a whipping boy for Moscow. Attacking Albania was a way of castigating China, and many speakers did so at the Twenty-second Soviet Party Congress in 1961. (Suslov and Andropov delivered speeches on Sino-Soviet relations, but their content is unknown because they were not published.) It was the most anti-Stalinist congress of all. A few weeks later Andropov wrote an article in *Pravda* condemning the Albanian leadership for its Stalinist views and singling out Molotov, one of Stalin's closest associates, who was then in diplomatic exile, for sharp criticism. But its real target was Mao. During the 1962 Chinese-Indian war, Moscow remained neutral, to Beijing's irritation. The Cuban missile crisis the same year, and Khrushchev's retreat, further annoyed Mao, although it gave added force to his argument that Khrushchev was a bumbling and incompetent leader. Andropov accompanied Suslov and Ponomarev to Beijing in 1963 for talks with the Chinese, who were led by Deng Xiaoping, but no common ground was reached.

A senior Soviet foreign affairs official told me that Andropov had been "among the first to notice" in 1958 that China was becoming an enemy of the Soviet Union, that this involved "personal hostility of Mao toward us, that Mao saw himself, after Stalin's death, as the leader of international communism." Later, in 1964, Andropov had no illusions about Khrushchev's being the source of the problem. "But Andropov," the official continued, "was also the first to see changes in China's policy and to press for positive gestures on our part to start the process of rapprochement."

If that was indeed so, Andropov seems to have carried out contradictory instructions with great diligence. In 1959, he wrote an article in *Pravda* praising Mao's Great Leap Forward in glowing terms. In 1964, in his first major speech as a member of the Soviet leadership, he held out hopes for a reconciliation with China. This was the first time he had been selected to deliver the keynote address at the Kremlin celebration of Lenin's birthday on April 22; the selection was a clear sign of his growing importance among the twenty or so men who ran the Soviet Union. His speech was targeted at China, which he described as a "socialist country"; the differences between Moscow and Beijing, he said, were temporary and would be overcome. The Russians, it seemed, were still hoping that the dispute would be patched up.

The ouster of Khrushchev in October of 1964 coincided with the first explosion of a Chinese nuclear bomb. When Zhou Enlai arrived in Moscow the next month, ostensibly to attend the celebrations commemorating the 1917 Bolshevik revolution but in fact to sound out the new Soviet leadership, he came as a leader of a new nuclear power. The downfall of Mao's enemy seemed to provide an opportunity for rapprochement; but the gap between Mao and Khrushchev's successors was too wide by then.

The last effort to patch up relations involved a Soviet attempt to create a united front in defense of North Vietnam. Andropov accompanied Kosygin to Hanoi and Beijing in 1965; but the Beijing talks failed and the downslide in Sino-Soviet relations, which included armed border clashes in 1969, was not arrested until 1982, when Andropov succeeded in his bid for power. The 1965 Hanoi visit was significant, for it colored Andropov's view of the United States. While he and Kosygin were there, the United States began bombing the North Vietnamese capital—an action that destroyed Moscow's diplomatic leverage for pushing Hanoi toward a negotiated settlement.

In the early summer of 1965, Andropov suffered a heart attack. He had been working too hard; long days at the office were followed by long evening debates and discussions. Doctors told him he had to slow down. In the hospital he read extensively and used his long convalescence to write and think. Two of his consultants, Arbatov and Bovin, jointly wrote a poem for the boss. They tried to make it funny; they wanted to lift his spirits. Andropov responded in kind with a long poem chiding his aides for presenting him with "a collective madrigal." He laughed at his illness in a bawdy way and used an imaginative play on words. Yet despite his cheerful tone, the prospect of death affected him profoundly. His verses include the thought that you can be "Socrates one hundred times over" *(stokrat Sokrat)* and yet one day you will die.

⟪⟨⟨ 7 ⟩⟩⟫

IN May 1967 Andropov was appointed chairman of the Committee on State Security, the KGB. It was a major surprise, most of all to Andropov. Moreover, Brezhnev promised to make him an alternate member of the Politburo, which he did later in the year.

The image of the secret police as an omnipotent and omniscient instrument of oppression is deeply embedded in the Russian psyche. A remark Andropov made at the time to a friend proved particularly illuminating. They were passing by the notorious Lubyanka building, the KGB headquarters, the friend recalled to me, when Andropov said: "All my life I have been walking past this building with a feeling of unease and awkwardness. Imagine, now I'm going to become its boss."

His first day in office was a happening at the Lubyanka. He

discovered that there were no normal doors leading into his office on the high second floor overlooking Dzerzhinski Square; instead he had to go through what was known as the *shkaf,* a contraption in the secretary's room that resembled an antique wardrobe closet. He entered, then stood in total darkness inside the closet, until an aide found the special button that opened the entrance into his room. Nobody could tell him who had built the contraption and why. The *shkaf,* he was told, had *always* been there!

When a person close to Andropov told me the story, I felt disappointed; after so many James Bond movies and *Mission Impossible* evenings, I had become convinced that such contraptions were simply a figment of the burning imagination of a screenwriter who had never been close to a real intelligence operative, let alone the office of a Communist spy chief. But anything is possible. Andropov's predecessors in the KGB office included a gallery of villainous rogues and criminally inclined characters ranging from the murderous N. I. Yezhov and Lavrenti Beria to Viktor Abakumov, General Ivan Serov, and more recently Alexander Shelepin and Vladimir Semichastny.

His first order—and the only decision of Andropov as KGB chief that I can report with absolute certainty—was to have the *shkaf* demolished and replaced by regular doors. The decision was intended to send a signal throughout the huge security establishment that a new style of authority had begun.

It was clearly not a simple task to take charge immediately of such an organization, in anything more than a superficial sense. The KGB had grown into a small empire. Half the member nations of the United Nations maintained armies smaller than the KGB's uniformed border guards; together with the network of espionage agents and operatives abroad and the vast force of plainclothes agents and paid informers at home, they probably accounted for a total of about one half million persons. The KGB also operated big complexes of communications, transport, maintenance, and procurement, as well as special services dealing with nuclear arms and gold and diamond production, among other things. The organization's budget must have been huge, but, like everything else about the KGB, it was a secret.

The demolition of the *shkaf* may have demonstrated Andropov's determination to impose his own style of authority on the KGB, but it was far harder to gain a genuine hold on the vast structure, which over the years had come to exert a disproportionate influence on Soviet life through a mixture of intrigues and pressures, and within his own lifetime, through brutal terror.

I could never determine to my satisfaction how in the end Andropov managed to impose his personal authority. Was he merely coopted by the security establishment to become its spokesman and champion in the high council, or did he indeed assert himself sufficiently to change the character and composition of the organization? Or was it a combination of both? Andropov kept himself in the background. I know of only one authentic account that sheds some light on his work in the KGB, by quoting a dissident and a Crimean Tatar representative who had actually met him.* Yet it is generally agreed that the Soviet political police changed substantially during his tenure, that it grew in size (particularly in the area of industrial and technological espionage), and that the quality of personnel in general was upgraded.

One thing worked in Andropov's favor. He took over during a time of political and administrative crisis in the security establishment, which had been discredited since the death of Stalin. Moreover, the KGB had been in the hands of people loyal to Brezhnev's serious rival, Shelepin. An ambitious and aggressive former Komsomol leader, Shelepin had been appointed KGB chairman in 1958 but in 1961 moved into the Secretariat, where he was responsible for the KGB and other security agencies; his job at the KGB was given to Semichastny, another young and crude Komsomol leader

*Eric Abraham and Jonathan Steele, *Andropov in Power,* New York: Doubleday, 1984.

and a friend and protégé of Shelepin's. As a Politburo member and secretary of the Central Committee, Shelepin was in a position to challenge Brezhnev, who had not yet fully consolidated his authority and shared power with Kosygin. In the spring of 1967, Brezhnev moved to neutralize Shelepin; while Shelepin was hospitalized for abdominal surgery, the Politburo replaced Semichastny with Andropov and the next month ousted Shelepin from the Secretariat.

Apart from Kremlin power intrigues, however, there were other reasons for appointing an experienced and intelligent politician as KGB chairman. For the first time there were stirrings of organized political dissent in Moscow. Khrushchev's liberalization, symbolized by the publication of Solzhenitsyn's *One Day in the Life of Ivan Denisovich,* had been stopped; this in turn had generated popular pressures on the more rigid Brezhnev regime.

Even more significant may have been the escalating Soviet-American arms competition. Technology and science were creating problems ranging from the selection and design of weapons systems to the determination of strategy. Soviet intelligence needed engineers and scientists who could analyze American technological advances and men and women who could obtain scientific and technological information in the West. The old KGB of criminally inclined toughs was ill suited for such purposes. The struggle had reached a new phase, one in which the pace of American innovation threatened to leave the Russians further behind technologically. The situation called for a security outfit versatile enough to meet the full spectrum of Soviet needs. Western specialists I talked to believe that this was the main thrust of Andropov's activity for most of his fifteen years at the KGB.

Andropov seemed well suited for the job. He was an intelligent politician who, during his days in Karelia, had dealt with the difficult issues of internal control in a subtle way; his Hungarian experience had taught him the perils of dissent in a socialist society; he had acquired considerable experience in foreign affairs during his ten years in the Central Committee; and he knew the strategic issues at stake.

Those who had worked with him previously described his style of operation. He was demanding and fair; but his assault on a problem began with a battery of specific questions, directed at specific individuals, demanding precise answers at a designated time. One could argue with him and disagree, provided one's arguments were logical and based solidly on facts. Whether he followed this approach at the security establishment is not known. Eventually, or so I was told by various Soviet sources, his decisiveness, intelligence, and directness won him the lasting loyalty of the KGB; but no man could have reasonably been expected to exercise complete authority right away.

At that time Andropov changed his living quarters from Kutuzovsky 30 to Kutuzovsky 26, a move that befitted his new standing in the leadership as an alternate Politburo member and KGB chairman. The No. 26 structure had been built for high officials and had special security arrangements. Unlike the vast majority of high officials, Andropov did not enjoy alcohol and only on occasion would he drink dry white wine. This made him an odd man in the company of the hard-liquor aficionados who gathered at Brezhnev's apartment. Brezhnev occupied almost an entire floor in the building; his crony, General Nikolai Shcholokov, the interior minister, had an apartment only slightly less palatial than the leader's. Andropov's ascetic nature and innate modesty were reflected in the apartment he and his wife chose. They lived for the rest of his life in a one-bedroom apartment on the sixth floor of the massive building, retaining it even after he became general secretary.

The apartment consisted of a kitchen, a small dining room, where they could seat a maximum of eight persons around their oval dinner table, a small bedroom, and a large living room—a total space of about 900 square feet. The living room faced the inner courtyard, while the windows of the bedroom and dining room overlooked the boulevard. That worked fine in the sixties, since there was hardly any traffic in Moscow. But after the Russians began mass-producing a small Zhiguli passenger car in 1970, the traffic volume and noise on Kutuzovsky Prospect increased sharply, so the Andropovs shifted their bed into what was previously the living room, which overlooked trees in the quiet inner courtyard, and Andropov turned the former bedroom into a small study, selecting a light green wallpaper with a flower pattern in yellow and white. There he kept a large statue of Don Quixote, carved in oak, and another small black iron statue of his hero, which stood on his desk. On the wall in his study hung a large framed watercolor of a typical Russian landscape, apparently representing the view he had from the balcony of his two-story dacha at Usovo. Apart from his family and work, that dacha was his great love; he rushed down the Uspenskoe Highway to Usovo whenever he could and lived there for the greater part of the year.

By all accounts, Andropov was a genuine political animal who enjoyed the pleasures of power—not the special phones, the secret files, and the black limousines, but the *real* power of shaping events and manipulating people. He was always interested in larger issues, and these preoccupied much of his time at the KGB.

His policy toward internal dissent became the most controversial aspect of Andropov's image in the West. Andropov's public speeches emphasized "persuasion" where infractions were manageable and legitimate, and "different measures" where they were not. Peter Reddaway, one of the leading specialists on Soviet dissent, writes that the leaders of an authoritarian system "have an even stronger incentive than those of a pluralistic one to see grievances settled" by persuasion at the local level; in this way, he argues convincingly, the formation of groups of aggrieved individuals can be averted. Reddaway also says that under Andropov the KGB had standing orders to avoid making political arrests if at all possible.

It is in the area of "different measures" that the KGB, under

Andropov, began to resort to unorthodox pressure techniques, including a wide use of psychiatric prisons and of forced emigration. To these were added the use of the draft against young dissident activists, and various forms of blacklisting, such as preventing admissions to universities or forcing young graduates to work in distant parts of the country.

There is evidence that the expulsion of Solzhenitsyn in early 1974 disturbed even Andropov's most loyal friends and supporters. A few of them wrote him private letters expressing their concern. Some, resorting to literary forms, gently questioned his integrity. I did not see these letters, but from Andropov's answer it was clear that people were wondering whether power had changed him, whether it had spoiled him. He defended himself through poetry. In a poem addressed to a friend and dated June 1974, he said that the old adage about power corrupting men is often repeated, but those who quote it simply ignore the fact that "it is people who spoil power."

If there was any clear pattern to his efforts to demolish the dissident movement, which emerged at the time he took the KGB job, the strategy was to exile or incarcerate its militant leaders and leave it without a sense of direction. The emigration of Soviet Jews in the seventies provided a vehicle for getting rid of many such leaders. By the time Andropov left the KGB, most important dissident intellectuals had left the Soviet Union; others were in exile, and the movement had ceased to exist in an organized form, at least for the time being.

There remains a bad odor about Andropov's KGB, especially because of its use of psychiatric prisons, where sane people would be "treated" with drugs that damaged their mental health. But it would be an oversimplification to focus all the blame on Andropov and his KGB. Contrary to the prevailing view in the West, the KGB is not a penal empire, as it was in the *gulag* days of Stalin; it no longer runs the country's prisons, camps, and psychiatric wards—these are under the control of the Ministry of Internal

Affairs (MVD). Andropov's direct influence on the MVD was not great—he had a very poor personal relationship with its minister, General Nikolai Shcholokov, a personal friend of Brezhnev's who became the first major figure to be fired once Andropov took power. Brezhnev's son-in-law was Shcholokov's first deputy. This is not to minimize the KGB's role in suppressing dissent, but to make clear that the blame has to be apportioned with greater accuracy. After all, the political leadership has ultimate control of the security establishment and its actions.

The imprint that the KGB years left on Andropov became apparent once he achieved supreme power. The job had given him the best available information about foreign and domestic issues. He knew the *real* state of the country's economy, the aspirations of its people, the potential for maintaining adequate levels of military capability, and perhaps most important, the morale within the ruling party and the country. He was by far the best-informed man in the leadership. His KGB experience had also made him more pragmatic than many others, in the sense that he was freer from dogma and sought to make sensible use of existing conditions, rather than relying on ideological formulas. When he took charge, he dismissed Brezhnev's notion that the Soviet Union was in the stage of "developed socialism"—rather, he said, the country was treading the first steps on a long road to developed socialism. He appealed directly to the workers to put their backs to his program for economic efficiency, and he did so without mincing words. "There are no miracles," he told the Ordzhonikidze engineering factory hands. If they wanted higher wages and better conditions, this could come only from hard work, increased productivity, and a crackdown on "shirkers, bad work and idlers."

His KGB experience may also have sharpened the resoluteness of his decision-making but added a tendency to act from behind the scenes, covertly. The circumspection of his political instinct was the other side of the coin. People who loved him conceded later that he had become more secretive during the fifteen KGB years, more suspicious, and more withdrawn. "He should have left the KGB much sooner," one of these persons told me long after Andropov's death.

During that stage of his life, he had few hobbies. He was interested in studying people, and the KGB files provided him with a wealth of material about the major figures on the international scene. He was fascinated by Henry Kissinger; I was told that he studied profiles of all the leading American politicians, including Nixon, Carter, and Reagan, and also of some leading American businessmen, particularly self-made men such as Donald Kendall of Pepsi-Cola and Donald Regan of Merrill Lynch. He enjoyed visiting the Caucasus resorts, where he first met Gorbachev. And he cherished his dacha at Usovo, a rambling two-story wooden building with gables, set high above the steep bank of the Moskva River, surrounded by tall birches and spruces. He spent most of his free time there, often sitting in an aluminum easy chair on the second-floor balcony. The river makes a bend near that secluded spot, and over the birch and pine trees one can see a typical Russian landscape, a seemingly endless valley. He no longer played his guitar, as he had in his youth and middle age, but instead listened to classical music or, more frequently, Gypsy music and old Russian romances on a tape deck.

One day, not long before he became supreme leader, his daughter, Irina, and her husband, actor Mikhail Filipov, arrived at the dacha for the weekend with their son, Dima, who was eight at the time. Andropov was sitting on the balcony, reading a book, while the sounds of Gypsy music, going at full blast, spread all over the forest. He played it so loud that he did not hear their car engine as they parked, almost directly under the balcony. But when he heard Dima's shout, he turned down the tape deck, drew himself into a theatrical pose, and shouted back from the balcony in a self-deprecating voice, "Here you see Fedya Protasov—in the stage of developed socialism." (Protasov is a character in a drama by Leo Tolstoy—a wealthy merchant who, disappointed by life, abandons his family and business, loses himself in drinking and reveling, hires a Gypsy band to play for him all the time, and eventually commits suicide.)

Later, when he became general secretary, he had to give up his dacha and use a far more elaborate country home in Barvikha, not far from Usovo, which was equipped with the communications system and support facilities the leader required. I was told that he yearned for Usovo and would drive out to that spot where the river makes a bend and where, from the high northern bank, he could look at the familiar Russian landscape that he loved so much.

<<< **8** >>>

THE enduring measure of a man as a political leader should take account not only of his human failings or even his grave mistakes, but also of his concept of his country's direction and its place in the world. Andropov's record during his fifteen months as general secretary remains the main basis for taking his measure. Yet his long association with the KGB cannot be ignored. His supporters maintain that in establishing political control over the secret-police establishment he imposed a degree of legality on its procedures and in general softened its oppressive nature. His critics, while conceding that such changes occurred, contend that as a result, the KGB became an even more diabolical tool in the hands of the Kremlin leadership. Hence, our evaluations must be tentative.

In the context of Soviet history, Andropov may be judged more charitably by his countrymen than Westerners might expect. I recall the assessment of a friend who had suffered at the hands of Stalin's secret police, whose literary career was ruined by the system, who spent years in exile, and who died in near obscurity in Moscow in 1970 at a moment when his reputation was being revived in the West. That was Nikolai Erdman, whom Maksim Gorki hailed in the twenties as "our new Gogol" and the first truly Soviet playwright.

I knew Erdman and his wife, Ina, during the last three years of his life. He lived in a massive apartment building across from the U.S. Embassy, where I met a number of Moscow's prominent cultural figures. His first play, *The Mandate*, was staged in the late twenties and was an instant success. His second play was *The Suicide*, a Kafkaesque description of Stalin's Russia that can be understood only as a scathing criticism of totalitarianism. In Stalin's Moscow, one of Erdman's characters says, "Only the dead can say what the living are thinking." Although the legendary director Meyerhold rehearsed the play in 1931, it was never performed in Russia during Erdman's lifetime. In 1932 Erdman was arrested and exiled to Central Asia for having written a short satirical story that was deemed insulting to the Kremlin. He came back to Moscow after World War II. In one of those ironies that sometimes occur in Russia, the long-forgotten author was visited in 1967 by a Czech scholar who was interested in the twenties, the only period of Soviet cultural exuberance; Erdman was the only surviving playwright from that era. The scholar asked him for a copy of his manuscript of *The Suicide*, which he took with him to Prague, and eventually the script wound up in Sweden, where the play had its world premiere in Malmö in 1969. (It had successful runs some years later in London, New York, and Washington, where I first saw it.)

I heard from a Swedish colleague that an anti-Stalinist play was to be performed in Malmö; everyone thought its author long deceased. I remember telling Erdman about it, then arranging a dinner at my house to celebrate the premiere and read the reviews, which I obtained courtesy of the Swedish Telegraph Agency. I had to drive Erdman and his wife, Ina, into our compound; at sixty-seven, he was beaming with pleasure but unsure as to the reception the play would receive in a foreign country. A Norwegian colleague, Per Egil Hegge, and his wife joined us for dinner, and Hegge translated the reviews. One headline, I recall, suggested that Erdman was one of the greatest satirists of the century. The old man was clearly trying to hide his pleasure and said with a deadpan expression, "After that, you don't have to read any more." Ina was beaming like a youngster. Later, after Hegge translated all the reviews, which were extremely complimentary, spirits were high in our apartment. But Erdman turned philosophical. In his own country he was, he said, completely forgotten; his life as a playwright had ended long ago. "This," he said, pointing at the reviews strewn around our dining table, "this will probably not change my life at all, but my fate [as playwright] apparently has already changed." Both Erdman and Ina were long dead when *The Suicide,* in a somewhat sanitized version, was given its Moscow premiere and had a short run in the summer of 1982, courtesy of Andropov, who at the time was the party's second secretary and ideological watchdog.

Erdman was a wise old man and a friend who was generous in sharing his views and assessments. One day in 1969, I went to visit him, just at the time of a political trial involving Pavel Litvinov and a group of dissidents who had protested the Soviet invasion of Czechoslovakia. I was indignant that we had to witness the procedure from outside the courthouse because KGB agents were there to keep us out and, presumably, to intimidate us as well. But when I vented my indignation, Erdman smiled at me with an impish expression in his deep-set eyes. "You, you are right, from your point of view," he said, "but you have to look at it from our point of view as well. You know, when I was arrested there were no trials, no lawyers, no journalists standing outside a courthouse. An NKVD man knocked on the door; he had a piece of paper, which I did not read—I didn't even ask to read it! You are shipped into exile—period. You wait, you write appeals. And now they have to follow procedures, they have to prepare the case, they have to go before a panel of judges. And perhaps you are right, everything is predetermined and the end result is the same. Yet all these steps serve as a small deterrent to the absolute arbitrariness of the KGB. They cannot do things they used to be able to do! And that is progress in our country."

But not everyone holds such a charitable opinion of Andropov. Years later, while discussing the role of the KGB under his leadership, I recounted Erdman's view to a young Soviet intellectual who was disappointed by the continued disciplinarian approach Andropov used once he became the country's leader. Of course Erdman's point was valid, my interlocutor said. "Of course, of course." But that was not the issue, in his view. The real problem was that progress was far too slow, and that it slowed down in the years after Khrushchev's ouster. Erdman was of a generation that had experienced the Stalinist past; the new generations have not, and they measure things by a different yardstick.

CHAPTER SEVEN

MORE TRANSITION TRAVAIL

WITH THE ACCESSION of Andropov the Soviet Union seemed to have entered a new phase in its history; it appeared that a real power transfer had been accomplished smoothly and painlessly and that the country would be spared the long power struggles that had marked each preceding change in the Kremlin. After Lenin's death it took Stalin years to consolidate his authority. When Stalin died, Khrushchev had to battle Malenkov and others for almost four years before reaching preeminence in the Politburo. The removal of Khrushchev was followed by a similar uncertain period, during which Brezhnev shared power with Kosygin and Podgorny before becoming the undisputed master of the Kremlin.

What we did not anticipate—and what almost seemed an act of God—was that Andropov would be so quickly undercut by weak health that he could do no more than set the stage for real change by advancing Gorbachev, the exponent of the new generation and its only representative in the Politburo. Nor did we expect that the Kremlin gerontocracy would make its final stand by choosing Konstantin Chernenko as general secretary at the time of Andropov's death in February 1984. In hindsight, the events that followed the short tenures of Andropov and Chernenko reinforced the pattern that each succession is followed by power struggles that last a few years before the real successor emerges.

At the beginning of the year, the mood was different from that of the Brezhnev years. Beneath the drab surface of life there was a ferment of anticipated change. Moscow's political life bustled as never before in my experience. A major house-cleaning was under way; hundreds of officials were being retired or demoted—most of them with the face-saving expression of Kremlin gratitude— like dinosaurs being driven from their caves. The conservatives did their best to thwart Andropov, but there was little they could openly do, for this gaunt disciplinarian knew just how serious corruption was, and how many party figures were tainted by it; and the anticorruption drive continued with almost weekly arrests of officials, including those with powerful connections. The Brezhnevite machinery was in disarray; the contest between the old guard and the new generation was under way. Quite evidently the mood of the ruling class was changing. New decrees were being issued from the Central Committee almost once a week; new laws were being prepared and debated. Tass began issuing a weekly communiqué on the business transacted by the Politburo. A wide-ranging debate on economic reforms was initiated when Andropov visited a Moscow factory in January to talk to the workers about economic and social conditions; in the spring, the country's economists, economic managers, and government experts began deliberation at conferences in Moscow over the future course.

There was, however, a disturbing aspect to Andropov's internal tightening: It extended beyond the country's social and labor problems to the realm of creativity. Erdman's play *The Suicide* was quietly dropped from the repertoire of the Satire Theater. The censors banned a production of *Boris Godunov,* which director Yuri Lyubimov was preparing to stage at his Taganka Theater; it seemed that Pushkin's play about Russia's time of troubles in the seventeenth century carried too many unpleasant associations in the post-Brezhnev period. Historian Roy Medvedev was threatened with prosecution if he continued to write about contemporary Soviet politics; novelist Georgi Vladimov, who represented Amnesty International, was harassed to such a degree that he decided to leave the country and applied for an exit visa. I greatly admired Vladimov's *Faithful Ruslan,* an allegorical novel about the dismantling of the Stalinist penal system as seen through the eyes of a police dog, Ruslan, whose services were suddenly no longer needed. This deeply moving story of a dog is also a subtle and scathing indictment of Stalinism. The problem with his novel, from the official point of view, was that it went beyond criticism of symptoms to criticism of causes. Soviet writers and dramatists can and do write about the scandals arising from corrupt or idle officials and bureaucrats, but they cannot suggest that the system be held responsible for the behavior of such individuals. I went to commiserate with the Vladimovs before they left for West Germany, joining thousands of people whose departures from Russia—like those of their predecessors under the tsars—impoverished the local cultural scene while enriching the societies to which they migrated.

Another disturbing development that coincided with Andropov's accession was the end of Jewish emigration, which quickly dwindled down to a trickle. The exodus had reached its peak in 1979, when 51,320 Soviet Jews were allowed to emigrate; the figure for 1980 was 21,471, and in 1981 it was down to 9,447. In the fall of 1982, rumors had it that the Jewish emigration would finally be terminated, and the figure for that year was 2,688. Almost immediately after Andropov took charge, heavy pressure was put on Jews who had applications for exit visas pending; they were told to withdraw their applications and resume their lives as if nothing had happened. There would be no more exit visas. Indeed, the figure for 1983 was down to 1,314, and for the next year it was 896. In addition, the Kremlin decided to take the offensive and established a Jewish Anti-Zionist Committee headed by General David Dragunsky. Its purpose appeared to be to assure the world that all Soviet Jews who wanted to leave the country had already done so; several hundred Jewish families who wanted to return to the Soviet Union were permitted to do so and their "plight" in the West was trumpeted by the media as evidence that Jews were better off in the Soviet Union.

The tough antiemigration stance produced a profound gloom among Jews who still wanted to leave. It was something many Westerners in Moscow felt as well, for our Jewish friends were in a state of despair. My friends were already in a spiritual exile, merely vegetating in Moscow, but that was endurable as long as there was hope that sooner or later they would receive their exit visas. One of my friends, in particular, was distraught. I saw him regularly because, to help him a bit, I asked him to give math lessons to my son. The problem for Jewish couples who made the commitment to go to Israel while their children were still young was that as months of waiting stretched into years, the children grew up in an inimical atmosphere. My friend had now waited almost seven years, and his children were seniors in high school, ostracized by their peers.

I asked a well-known Soviet television commentator, who himself was partly Jewish, to explain the sharp switch in policy. Was Andropov behind it? The commentator assured me that Jewish emigration had been one of the more contentious issues in internal debates for at least five or six years and that already in the second half of the seventies there had been forceful arguments against permitting the exodus because of its adverse social consequences. "I can tell you that this was the issue on which we made our major mistake in dealing with the United States," he said. "We should have never allowed this emigration."

Andropov partisans, when questioned about internal tightening, argued that it was temporary and necessary because of the scope of political struggles over the country's most important single issue—restructuring its economy. No leader, they said, could take on the old guard and the bureaucracy as directly as Andropov did and at the same time loosen up restraints against liberal intellectuals, who constantly criticize the system, and Jewish refuseniks, who reject it altogether. The explanation seemed, at least to me, to be largely self-serving.

Yet the scope of political activity was indeed broad, and those were exciting days for Moscow correspondents. Each night, as I made my way home, I was eagerly anticipating the next day's stories; I did not feel mentally worn out from the daily grind. The Soviet press had become more lively and outspoken; it seemed that Andropov was trying to generate pressures from below in his struggle against the bureaucracy. The Kremlin had become sensitive to domestic public opinion, and Soviet citizens were even encouraged to write conspicuously forthcoming letters to the editor. Some of these letters leaped out from the pages of *Pravda* and *Izvestia; Pravda,* for instance, published a letter written by a worker in Chita complaining about "dishonesty" among officials and "lies" about production goals. "Everything is allegedly going fine," the letter said, "but that is a pure lie. We have to live with the truth no matter how bitter it may be. The lies are a corrosive which undermine the human spirit and destroy the people." A flurry of similar letters seemed to echo the new policy line.

I also found officials more candid when it came to discussions of the internal situation; all that was required to evoke their responses was a measure of skeptical silence coupled with tactful but serious questions. It was possible to engage my interlocutors in meaningful conversations by accepting the premises of their internal debates, in which the word "reform" did not imply a restoration of capitalism in Russia but rather a structural adjustment of the existing system. In fact, the word "reform" was shunned in the course of Andropov's tenure because it implied a qualitative change, an earlier error in judgment, a mistake—and the party was incapable of saying that it had made mistakes.*

In April, a major economic debate involving hundreds of top economists and managers began in Moscow. The tone and substance of this debate was echoed in my conversations with people at the fringes of the elite—journalists, experts in various institutes, middle-level government officials. The trend was against systematic mystification, against the Kremlin's traditional preoccupation with appearances at the expense of reality; under Andropov, it seemed that intelligence was finally being applied to the nation's business.

Perhaps the best example of the contradictions and confusions of Soviet thinking about the economy and society was to be found in the serious analyses of Soviet society prepared for the leadership. I obtained one such confidential document in April from an official who was on the staff of one of the leading personalities in the country and was closely identified with Chernenko. The document, printed in seventy numbered copies, dealt with the issue of economic change and questioned the entire system created by Stalin. I was told that a number of similar papers were being discussed at a high level, which suggested not only the urgency and seriousness of the internal debates but also the difficulties encountered in seeking solutions.† Also in April a new journal, *Problemi teorii i praktiki upravlenia (Problems of the Theory and Practice of Management),* appeared in Moscow; the title was

---

*The word "reform" pertaining to contemplated economic changes appeared in *Pravda* for the first time on December 26, 1983. Up to that point, the authoritative newspaper talked about economic "experimentation."

†The document, about which I wrote a story in August, became known as the "Novosibirsk Report" because it was prepared at an economic institute of the Soviet Academy of Sciences in Novosibirsk.

revealing, as one of Andropov's stated objectives was to change the system of economic management.

Both the character and the timing of this debate reflected the difficult position into which the Soviet Union had been allowed to drift in all domestic matters during Brezhnev's eighteen years. The line of least resistance had been to delay difficult decisions, to temporize. Stalin had had an immense and backward country to run and to bring forward so that it could compete with the West, and his method of doing this was to use brute force and mass terror. The economic benefits of his rule were apparent; he telescoped into decades developmental processes that took centuries in the West. But the political price and the cost in human suffering were horrendous. His rule was far more despotic than that of the worst Romanov monarchs. The system he built now had all the top players in its grip and had become the main impediment to progress. This was the conclusion of the "Novosibirsk Report." And the debate was, broadly, the familiar argument between the reformers and the conservatives.

Andropov also set a new trend in another political arena. Immediately upon his accession, he struck several blows at the Soviet tendency to rewrite the past. The significance of this move was far greater than I perceived at the time. It challenged, in a modest way at least, the autocratic tradition of relegating to instant oblivion dead or disgraced politicians. In November, Andropov publicly thanked Andrei Kirilenko for his long years of service to the Soviet state; he carefully avoided criticizing Brezhnev directly and made sure that his predecessor was assigned a place in Soviet history; in January, the name of Nikita Khrushchev appeared in print for the first time in two decades—and even in a positive context for his role in the battle of Stalingrad.

Busy covering the rush of daily events, I had not fully noted in my dispatches that what was taking place in the Kremlin during Andropov's rule was a major battle between two generations and their complex interests: between the orthodox, dogmatic section of the party, with its vast satrapy of bureaucrats and provincial bosses and their followers, and the party's reformist elements; between the Brezhnev establishment, which had strong regional bases of power, and Andropov's men, who were younger and had no similar regional bases but were given strong positions in Moscow, and were backed up by the KGB and the military high command. By moving these younger men from the provinces into the centers of power in the Kremlin, Andropov not only gave his administration an infusion of energy but also formed the kernel of the future leadership, Mikhail Gorbachev and his new team. Andropov cast his lot with the new generation and used the KGB to identify loyal and energetic young men and women throughout the country who could be prepared for management positions.

The situation at the top was more difficult. Except for Gorbachev and Gaidar Aliyev, who was moved from Azerbaijan to become first deputy premier and Politburo member, the figures Andropov placed in key strategic positions were largely unknown —Chebrikov as head of the KGB; Ryzhkov, in the Secretariat to guide economic policy; Ligachev, also in the Secretariat, to supervise personnel matters; and Vorotnikov, in the Politburo and the top position in the Russian Federation, the largest republic, which accounts for roughly four fifths of Soviet territory. Only Gorbachev and Aliyev were in the Politburo; other Andropov allies in the ruling council were Arvid Pelshe, the octogenarian Latvian Communist who was personally close to Andropov, and Andrei Gromyko, whom Andropov named first deputy premier, a clear promotion, since he retained the foreign ministry portfolio. (It seemed to me at the time that Andropov wanted to broaden Gromyko's responsibilities and raise his status to compensate for the fact that the veteran foreign minister was in reality being pushed aside by Andropov himself, who was his own foreign minister.)

All outward signs at that stage pointed to Gorbachev's leading position in this group, especially after Andropov selected the youngest Politburo member for the signal honor of delivering the keynote speech at the Kremlin celebrations of Lenin's birthday on April 22, 1983.*

In May, Gorbachev was sent to Canada for a long trip that was his first real official exposure to the West, and he performed splendidly. People around Andropov said the chief was profoundly pleased with the way Gorbachev handled himself in Canada, although his trip there was barely noticed elsewhere in the West. Canadians were also impressed. Geoffrey Pearson, the Canadian ambassador to the Soviet Union, who was a shrewd observer of the Soviet scene, was the first person I heard say—with a degree of assurance that surprised me at the time—that Gorbachev would become the Soviet leader. He described as superb Gorbachev's performance in a meeting with Canadian parliamentarians and offered to provide a transcript of it. "I don't understand your paper, not to mention the rest of the American press," Pearson said. "No U.S. paper paid attention to the visit; and here was a chance to see the man who will soon run the Soviet Union, to assess him and to talk to him."

By the summer, Gorbachev seemed to be carrying the thrust of Andropov's policies, and next to the leader himself, he was the most visible political figure on the scene. He appeared to be in overall charge of the economy, and he was noticeably more active in foreign affairs, beginning to take part in talks with foreign visitors. I only dimly suspected that all this had something to do with Andropov's kidney ailment; because of the secrecy sur-

---

*The speech revealed the thinking of both Gorbachev and his mentor about the thrust of economic policy. Referring to Lenin's New Economic Policy, which reintroduced a degree of private enterprise in the early 1920s, Gorbachev said: "Our reliable support, here as always, is Lenin's legacy, his teaching of democratic centralism. . . . Lenin persistently defended centralism as the point of departure in the organization of the economy of socialism, which represents a uniform entity. At the same time he called for giving free rein to creativity and initiative at the base. Our main task [Lenin said] is to provide an impetus everywhere in the country, to mobilize a maximum of initiative and to display a maximum of independence."

rounding his health, we had no reason to doubt that Andropov would be around for a long time.

On the other hand, the Brezhnevite opposition seemed impressive, including five of the eleven Politburo seats, although initially it was completely mute. With Chernenko as its leader, it included Premier Nikolai Tikhonov, Moscow party boss Viktor Grishin, Ukrainian leader Vladimir Shcherbitsky, and Kazakh leader Dinmukhamed Kunaev. The faction's strength was even greater in the next tiers of party bureaucrats and managers.

One member of the Politburo was viewed as a loner, though inclined to side with Chernenko's team. Grigori Romanov, the diminutive but tough party boss of Leningrad, with steely blue eyes and a boyish complexion, was known for his corruption. He was one of the more unpleasant figures on the political landscape and behaved like a Mafia chieftain. His roots were in Novgorod, the ancient citadel of Russian nationalism, and there was an air of arrogance about him. We were puzzled as to why Andropov brought him into the Secretariat, a move that seemingly enhanced Romanov's power and prestige. Some held that removing Romanov from his power base in Leningrad would weaken him and make him dependent on Andropov; others said the new leader needed a tough and ruthless executive in Moscow to impose discipline on the party bureaucracy. What went almost unnoticed at the time was the fact that Andropov replaced Romanov with a man who later was elevated to the peak of Kremlin power—Lev Zaikov, the mayor of Leningrad. From that relatively minor position, Zaikov was appointed party chief in the country's second-most-important industrial region.

In the middle stood Marshal Dmitri Ustinov, the defense minister. Despite his old links to the Brezhnev group, he represented the armed forces, whose leadership was behind Andropov. Their voice, as articulated by Ustinov, was crucial in his election; and Ustinov consistently supported Andropov to the end.

The balance of forces did not seem to justify the conclusion I had drawn, almost immediately after Andropov's accession, that he was in uncontested charge of the Kremlin. But the numbers did not take into account the political dynamics and the "fear factor." In addition to his discipline campaign, Andropov also intensified the anticorruption drive, which sent terror into the hearts of the party establishment. Almost all those at higher levels were afraid their KGB files contained damaging information. Moreover, the Chernenko group had no program of its own and was united mainly by the negative impulse of holding the line, resisting change.

It seemed to me that Andropov had the backing of two of the three main pillars of power, the military and the KGB, but not of the third, the party itself, which had been largely controlled by Chernenko. However, the party had been weakened by the bureaucratic blight and corruption of Brezhnev's years. Enjoying lifetime job security, some regional barons had been allowed to run their big or small fiefdoms almost independently, provided they met production quotas for the central government and flattered Brezhnev with the splendid gifts they repeatedly laid at his feet. This meant almost automatic job security for countless officials in the middle and lower levels of the bureaucracy. The power ran by way of the great barons, such as Romanov in Leningrad, Shcherbitsky in the Ukraine, Kunaev in Kazakhstan; or powerful Central Committee members controlling smaller fiefdoms, such as Sergei Medunov in Krasnodar, Nikolai Banikov in Irkutsk, Leonid Kulichenko in Volgograd, or Yuri Khristoradnov in Gorki. The party bureaucracy of these regions had come to resemble a secular priesthood and most of its members associated their interests with valid policy; most did not want any reforms. Andropov's modernization drive, however innocuous he tried to make it, was a threat to their entrenched positions.

I had the opportunity to meet with one such regional chieftain, Nikolai Kirichenko, the first secretary of the Odessa region, a few months before his enforced retirement. He seemed to be a man of basically inaccessible mind and authoritarian manners; he recited so many statistics and clichés that I had the impression that, while extending the hospitality of his office, he was filibustering to forestall any questions during the brief time allotted to me. Odessa, as the largest Black Sea port, was known for its political and economic corruption, prostitution, and many other vices criticized publicly in the press, yet I never got a chance to raise these issues with Kirichenko. The only distinct thing I remember from that encounter was his emphatic statement, "No, our system does not need any reforms." When I quoted ideas from an Andropov speech, he backtracked, but only a bit. "Of course, we have to improve some things. But we have been doing that since nineteen seventeen."

It would be a gross oversimplication to assume that only the corrupt elements were resisting the new course. In the higher echelons, many orthodox Communists feared systemic changes on the ground that, once initiated, reforms could acquire an uncontrollable life of their own. The question was whether the party could hold the society together and make changes smoothly, particularly while confronted by President Reagan's rearmament program and Moscow's extended commitments to Communist allies and various other clients throughout the world. So the old guard was lying in wait, publicly acquiescing in the new policies but covertly speculating, after Andropov's illness in February, about how long he would last.

This was part of a deeper polarization of the political world that was taking shape. The coalition for change included powerful groups in society—including technocrats, younger people in general, senior military men who had become increasingly concerned about the feebleness of the economy, the KGB, and much of the population, who favored discipline, order, and the anticorruption drive, and above all expected changes that would improve their lives. In strictly numerical terms, this coalition constituted a huge majority.

At first glance, this seemed to make the political job a simple, straightforward one in an authoritarian environment. But when one speaks of changes in the Soviet economy, one is talking about reshaping the entire society, for all citizens work for the state and are subsidized by it in one form or another. The changes had to involve not only new legislative steps, but also changes in the psychology and attitudes of the population. Even the introduction of a more rational pricing system would be a revolutionary step —a step that would be opposed by the population because it would mean higher prices as government subsidies on basic commodities were cut or terminated. The trouble in Poland, after all, had begun with price increases. I talked to many persons from all walks of life about economic reforms. The more we talked of these things, the harder it was for me to pin down and formulate their opinions—for they depended on values and attitudes inherent in a whole way of life based on the Stalinist system. What most people truly wanted they also feared. Soviet life offered security and the satisfaction of basic needs but few material advantages —most citizens were above the poverty level yet far from comfortable. Seven decades of socialism had turned Russia into the world's largest welfare state. At bottom this is what makes Russia's problems intractable. Were the people prepared for high taxes or higher rents? Could the food prices be brought closer to a market level, which meant a sharp increase? Questions of this kind were debated at the very top, for however compelling the need for change, political considerations came first. This in turn meant that reforms would have to proceed slowly, cautiously, and that the population would have to be properly prepared for them.

This point was brought home to me by a young, well-educated friend who was wholly behind Andropov's program. She fully supported the changes that were being debated, including the pricing mechanism. But when I told her in the course of a long conversation that a change in the pricing system would eliminate, at least in part, massive government subsidies for such things as rent, food, and energy, she looked absolutely amazed and almost offended. "Oh, no," she said firmly. "The rents cannot be raised." It was a Catch-22 situation: The monthly rent for her one-bedroom apartment, including heating and gas, cost the equivalent of about ten dollars, or less than one bottle of Stolichnaya vodka, which sold for the equivalent of eleven dollars.

Later, a political associate of Andropov's told me that this was the crux of the problem. "We can take care of the bureaucracy," he said. "The problem is that when you come down to the real changes, most people would be against them." He told me that surveys the government had conducted showed that roughly three out of four persons were not prepared to make personal sacrifices, although they fully subscribed to the idea of economic reforms. This was an enduring feature of Soviet life that haunted Andropov, and also Gorbachev and his men.

Although Andropov's disciplinarian approach quickly lifted the economy from its slump, this was a temporary phenomenon in what was clearly a protracted economic slowdown. The annual rate of expansion of the Soviet GNP, which was under 6 percent in the early Brezhnev years, had dipped to 2 percent in the early eighties. The rate of economic consumption, the goods and services the Soviet household gets from the economy, had also declined. For the period from 1976 to 1980 growth in per capita consumption dipped to 2.2 percent, as opposed to a 5.1 percent growth for the years 1970 to 1975. It was projected to rise only 1 percent for 1980 to 1985, and that was an optimistic estimate. Net agricultural output, which advanced 3.7 percent in the decade of 1961 to 1970 and grew by only a puny 0.9 percent from 1971 to 1980, dipped below production targets to such an extent that no official statistics were provided after 1980. Moreover, Soviet economic growth lagged significantly in relation to that of other industrial economies; after outstripping the average growth rate of the sixteen Organization for Economic Cooperation and Development (OECD) countries by 0.4 percent during Brezhnev's first five years in power, it fell 1 percent behind during his last years. A key indicator known as total factor productivity—the increase in output per added unit of capital and labor input—after rising in the sixties and seventies, began to decrease by about 1 percent annually in the early eighties.*

It was apparent to me that the economic debate would continue for months to come. Most of my daily dispatches at the time reflected a preoccupation with Andropov himself, who seemed to be beyond conventional Kremlin politics, because he used the instruments of power, and particularly his former organization, the KGB, to subdue the party bureaucracy. Moscow buzzed with talk about corruption, and there were juicy stories about high police officials in trouble with the authorities.

The personnel changes began in a big way with the firing of the interior minister, General Nikolai Shcholokov, a Brezhnev crony and neighbor, in December; this was followed by a purge of the ministry. Because of his military rank and his seat on the Central Committee, Shcholokov himself could not be interrogated, but members of his immediate family, including one son who was a senior official in the Komsomol, could. Rumors of the general's staggering corruption began to circulate. Some were outlandish, but what could be established with reasonable accuracy was that the general had managed—illegally, no doubt—to supply members of his family with sixteen Mercedes and Volvo sedans. He also had a habit of sending an assistant to appropriate things the minister needed from the Moscow Customs Office's storeroom of confiscated goods.

In January and February, the Lefortovo prison, operated by the KGB for interrogation of pretrial detainees, became filled with

*Statistics from *USSR: Measures of Economic Growth and Development, 1950–1980.* Washington, D.C.: U.S. Government Printing Office, 1982.

police officers, including those of senior rank. The wife of a detained political dissident, who visited her husband at Lefortovo,
reported that he and other prisoners were being moved to another
prison to make room for MVD officials. Common criminals had
been separated from the detainees earlier, after two police officers
were murdered at the prison. In March, Shcholokov's wife died,
and rumor had it that she had committed suicide.

The house-cleaning of the higher echelons involved mainly the
Cabinet and the Central Committee bureaucracy in Moscow.
Among those in the first wave of ousters were a deputy prime
minister, Valentin Makaveyev, as well as the minister of railways,
the minister of trade, the deputy minister of the aviation industry,
the deputy minister of light industry, and the chairman of the state
committee for construction. All were members of the Central
Committee. Andropov also replaced in quick succession nine
of the nineteen powerful department chiefs of the Central Committee.

There was another facet of news that had to be covered. Relations between the United States and the Soviet Union had continued to deteriorate, with a great deal of huffing and puffing on
both sides. The atmosphere was not only acrimonious but confused, and became more so as the date approached for the deployment of new American medium-range nuclear missiles in Western
Europe. President Reagan's "zero option" proposal—namely, that
the Russians would have to dismantle all of their medium-range
nuclear missiles capable of reaching European targets in exchange for nondeployment of U.S. Pershing Two and cruise missiles in five West European countries—was clearly a nonstarter.
I did not find one person willing to discuss it seriously. They saw
it as an easily understood formula tailored for the Western man
in the street and an ingenious device to put the Russians on the
propaganda defensive. The Russians were convinced that the
Americans were determined to deploy these missiles and had no
interest in the ongoing talks in Geneva; but they hoped that the

pressure of European public opinion might at least limit the scheduled U.S. deployments. It was a major propaganda battle, and it gave full sanction to the fears and tensions of the time—Reagan invoking the image of "evil empire" and the Russians describing the president as a power-thirsty lunatic about to blow up the world and likening him to Hitler. Such charges traded by the world's two superpowers make the front pages. Sitting in Moscow at a time like that, I thought the propaganda war fascinating, bizarre, and irrational. It seemed to me that the two countries had made their basic decisions and that the noise was merely polluting the atmosphere and preventing a clear view on their respective policies.* Yet, American correspondents were supposed to write intelligible stories about Moscow's reaction to this or that pronouncement by Washington. I was slightly resentful at having to spend so much time on these "reaction" stories when the changes in the country seemed so much more interesting.

⟪ 2 ⟫

THE summer of 1983 was warmer than the two previous ones, promising a good harvest after four consecutive disasters. Economic indicators for the first half of the year showed a sharp turnaround in industrial output and labor productivity, obviously a result of strict disciplinary measures. "God is smiling at An-

---

*In their loud protestations that Pershing Twos were to be positioned close enough to "decapitate" the Kremlin's command-and-control center, the Russians conveniently ignored the fact that their nuclear submarines were positioned far closer to Washington. I was in Moscow when President Carter's Presidential Directive 59 was made public; the directive envisaged such a "decapitating" move as a possibility. The next day I talked with Vikenty Matveyev, senior *Izvestia* commentator. "Don't you realize that our submarines are off the coast of Washington, D.C.?" he said, bristling. One expert whom I saw at the time, Oleg Bykov, thought Carter's directive "highly irresponsible." Don't you have similar scenarios? I asked. "Of course we do," Bykov replied, "but we have not raised them to the level of national policy."

dropov," superstitious Russians said. For his supporters, that summer was the crest.

In June, Andropov convened an ideological plenum of the Central Committee. He also was formally elected head of state, or
chairman of the Presidium of the Supreme Soviet. As such he was
the country's tenth president; it had taken his predecessor thirteen
years to gain that post after he became general secretary. But
unlike Brezhnev, Andropov did not want the largely ceremonial
position. Authoritative sources later told me that he was persuaded to take it only because not doing so would have sent a
wrong signal to the outside world. I wondered at the time whether
his opponents in the Politburo were covertly rejoicing at the prospect of an ailing leader acquiring the additional burden of countless ceremonial duties. I watched him in the Grand Kremlin Palace
on that June morning as he thanked the Supreme Soviet deputies
for their trust. He was pale and distinctly thinner—his shirt collar
looked at least three sizes too big; he chose to speak from his seat
rather than walk down the steps to the speaker's podium. And
when all the delegates jumped to their feet to give him a standing
ovation he stood there looking dejected—a lonely, gaunt man
surrounded by Politburo members and secretaries of the Central
Committee yet displaying a detachment so pronounced that I suspected even then that, as he watched those proceedings, he felt
that he had only a short time to live.

Ideological plenums are rare events and perhaps as complicated as Vatican ecumenical councils. Only one such plenum had
been held since World War II. It was called in 1963 by Nikita
Khrushchev and had the Sino-Soviet dispute as its main theme.
Khrushchev had earlier called an ideological plenum in 1956, three
years after Stalin's death. But literally on the eve of the plenum,
he was outvoted by his colleagues in the Politburo on the question
of his rapprochement with Tito, whom Khrushchev had invited to
attend. A furious Khrushchev canceled the scheduled plenum and

proceeded to maneuver against his enemies, whom he ousted from the Politburo in 1957.

That Andropov was capable of calling an ideological plenum after barely seven months in power testified to his preeminent position; he had entrenched himself more deeply in the Kremlin than any of his predecessors had in a comparable period. Endorsing his rapid ascendancy to nearly unchallenged authority, the ruling elite voted unanimously to take his speech at the plenum as the basic document guiding the party's actions.

It was a major speech, proposing a new program to replace the 1961 document drafted by Khrushchev. In it Andropov said unrealistic plans and exaggerated expectations had to be jettisoned. The main objective was to raise labor productivity and improve the organization of production. He proposed that "civilized" conditions be created in the countryside to deal with the apathy of the rural population and the flight of the young to the cities. Changes were mandatory, he said; the existing system of planning penalized innovative managers while rewarding those who stuck to traditional methods; the whole economic mechanism was blocking technological progress; industry was producing goods "nobody wants to buy"; there were shortages of food and other products.

The program of economic "experiments" was being prepared. But he injected two new ideas that sounded heretical to orthodox ears. One dismissed the notion of equality, or equal pay for work rendered by persons whose productivity and efficiency differed—the famous *uravnilovka.* Those who work better should have higher wages, he said, adding: "As to full equality in the sense of equal use of the material boons, this will be possible only under communism"—in short, in the very distant future. The other new idea was that the economy should work "rhythmically," not on the basis of Stakhanovite principles, a Stalinist method of shock work to meet constantly increasing production quotas. His immediate aim, Andropov said, was "to bring to order what we have, to ensure the most rational utilization of the country's productive resources . . . and the smooth and uninterrupted work" of the entire economy.

⟨⟨⟨ 3 ⟩⟩⟩

BUT Andropov's health became an issue that summer. I noticed that his limousine was no longer passing our compound at eight thirty-five in the morning.

At the beginning of June, Averell Harriman, the veteran American diplomat and former ambassador to Moscow, found Andropov "vigorous" and his presentation "clear and intelligent." The ninety-one-year-old Harriman was impressed by the new Soviet leader and his grasp of the issues. Pamela Harriman, who accompanied her husband, told me later that summer that Andropov struck her as a man of power and charm—looking like a "suave Western businessman."

A few weeks later the new Finnish president, Mauno Koivisto, professed to be equally impressed; he found Andropov open and charming during their private conversations. But the Kremlin changed its protocol in June: Andropov greeted Koivisto in the Kremlin instead of riding out to the airport to meet him. Finns who attended the state dinner reported that Andropov seemed "weak and unsteady" and that he read his formal speech sitting down.

By the end of June, when leaders of the Warsaw Pact nations held a summit in Moscow, stories about the Kremlin leader's deteriorating condition circulated in East European quarters in Moscow. The Hungarians were silent; much later János Kádár described in a television interview his private meeting with Andropov—their last—recalling that the Soviet leader spoke about his illness "matter-of-factly, without self-pity" and talked about his plans and policies when, in Kádár's words, "another man would have sent everything to hell and busied himself with his illness."

In July, West German chancellor Helmut Kohl arrived for an official visit, but his first-day meeting with Andropov was canceled at the last moment. This touched off speculation that Andropov either was ill or wanted to administer a gentle snub to his visitor. Andropov turned out to have been ill; he met with Kohl the next day. An official West German photographer who traveled with Kohl and who photographed the two men came out of Andropov's office saying to a senior Bonn diplomat, "This is a man with the mark of death on his face."

I was involved at that point in trying to arrange an interview with Andropov for Katharine Graham, chairman of the Washington Post Company, and several *Post* editors. Graham had requested the interview through the Soviet ambassador in Washington, Anatoly Dobrynin, earlier in the year; I was trying to do what I could at my end, an enterprise that brought me into contact with persons close to the leader. The interview was set for early October, since Andropov, I was told, would be vacationing in September. But the timing, I figured, was also tied to the last major Soviet effort to stop the deployment of new American missiles in Europe the next December. Moscow was preparing yet another "last offer" to cut its missile forces in the European theater and sought the maximum media exposure to announce it. Intimations of a shift in the Soviet position came during talks in July between Marshal Sergei Akhromeyev, then deputy chief of staff, and a group of U.S. congressmen led by Representative Thomas J. Downey of New York; the marshal suggested that Moscow was now prepared to negotiate on the basis of the so-called walk-in-the-woods formula, under which the United States would deploy cruise missiles but not Pershing Two missiles, while the Russians would sharply reduce their SS-20 force.

That summer for the first time I heard rumors in official circles that Andropov also suffered from diabetes. But August was a busy month for him, and I could not allow my preoccupation with his health to interfere with the more congenial task of analyzing his performance. The frenzy of August seemed all the more remarkable because it was usually the dead month on Moscow's political calendar, when the entire ruling elite was on the Black Sea or in the Caucasus. Andropov's schedule was hectic. He met various foreign visitors, including Americans—the president of the Machinist Union, William Winpisinger, and a group of ten senators led by Claiborne Pell of Rhode Island. He told Winpisinger that he was prepared to meet Reagan halfway "on many points." At the meeting with the senators on August 18—Andropov's last public appearance—he offered to negotiate a ban on the use of antisatellite weapons, telling the senators that he had decided to impose a unilateral moratorium on the deployment of such Soviet weapons. It was, he said, a gesture of "goodwill."

But the most exciting things were happening in domestic policy. By August, it was clear that Gorbachev was no longer simply the man in charge of agriculture, but that as Andropov's heir apparent he was shaping a national economic reconstruction program. He was presented as such to the surviving old Bolsheviks in the new conference hall of the Central Committee on August 15, and it was that appearance that brought him for the first time to the center of the national consciousness. Gorbachev presided over the gathering, outlining the problems to an audience of old men and women whose black suits and dresses set off their white hair and shining gold medals and decorations. Andropov was, in effect, asking the oldest party members, who represented whatever was left of the old Bolshevik flame and who were known for their conservatism, to give their trust to a young man who could be the son or even grandson of most of those present.

When Andropov addressed the old men and women, he delivered the boldest speech of his career. The country, he said, had entered a new stage, in which "increased social requirements dictate the need" for reforms. This "demanded, among other things, changes in planning, management, and the economic mechanism itself"—in short, the entire economy. In the past, he said, meaning the Brezhnev period, the leadership was "not vigorous enough . . . and resorted to half-measures which . . . could not overcome the accumulated inertia." A cautious step would be made, he said. On January 1, 1984, partial reforms would be undertaken in some sectors of the economy "to examine quietly and calmly what effect the suggested innovations will have." He was being cautious, he asserted, following the old adage "Do your measurements seven times, for you can only make one cut." He also returned to his "law and order" theme and complained about "conspicuous" lack of discipline, parasitism, and passivity among the young—themes close to the conservatives' hearts. But, he said, the future is with the young, who are "not alien to our generation, just different." And he set the date for the formulation of a new program for the economy—it would have to be done before the end of 1985 so that the country could "enter the new five-year period, so to say, fully armed."

⟨⟨⟨ 4 ⟩⟩⟩

THAT summer I had my first serious encounter with the KGB. In the beginning of August, I finally wrote a story about the confidential economic study prepared at Novosibirsk. I do not recall a similar document ever reaching the hands of Moscow correspondents. (I did obtain two other "for official use only" documents printed in editions of several hundred copies.) Its intrinsic value was that it revealed the tone and substance of the internal debates on economic reforms. It was a powerful indictment that focused on the causes, not merely the symptoms, of the country's economic slowdown. What I found significant was that sections of the elite had stopped pretending that everything was for the best in the best of all possible worlds and that only some fine-tuning was required to reverse the downward trend. The paper said that the economic system created by Stalin fifty years ago had been "incredibly compromised and outdated," that it had not changed "to reflect the fundamental change" that had taken place in the society and economy, and that it was no longer suitable for the Soviet Union. Moreover, the study said, the Stalinist system itself was the main reason for declining Soviet economic performance. It was unusually frank in describing problems ranging from demography to bureaucracy and in questioning the stultifying system of central planning.

The paper was written by a member of the Soviet Academy of Sciences, Tatyana Zaslavskaya, an associate of the well-known reformist economist Abel Aganbegian, also of Novosibirsk. It was one of a series of papers discussed during a major closed-door economic debate involving the entire economic establishment of the country. Such papers were distributed to the offices of top officials; the source who gave me the copy of Zaslavskaya's paper also provided brief oral summaries of some of the other documents. The story created a minor stir in the West, although I had tried to be low-keyed and to avoid sensationalism. The purpose of my story was to give the flavor and specifics of internal debates without compromising my source or the author of the document.

Almost immediately I had the feeling that the police were closing in on me. I sensed it everywhere, inside our compound and driving around Moscow. My telephones began to act up. The police guard inside our compound rushed to his booth when I came out of my office. I didn't think this was a paranoid reaction, but I wanted to check whether I was imagining that a white Zhiguli sedan with three persons inside was constantly behind my car; I took a wrong turn, turning to the right just outside the Tass headquarters, and the white Zhiguli, which was in the left lane, had to proceed straight ahead. But from the corner of my eye I saw the car stop after the intersection and two persons jump out of it. This was not conclusive proof but that evening, when I set out to keep an appointment with a person who lived on the outskirts of Moscow and who, fortunately, did not have a telephone at home, I again noticed a car at a discreet distance following me out the Domodyedovo airport road. I turned off the highway and drove up to a traffic light; the white Zhiguli halted at a distance. I decided to violate traffic rules by turning into a one-way street going in the opposite direction; the white car followed, no longer trying to maintain a discreet distance. So I decided to return home at a leisurely pace, knowing that once the KGB had focused on me, there was little chance that I could elude it. In situations like this, the best thing was to lie low and avoid contacts, because any person I got in touch with would subsequently be interrogated by police agents.

I had anticipated all this and had kept the document hidden for four months because I knew that would make it very difficult for the police to discover my source. For the same reason I had not mentioned in my story the author of the document or the Novosibirsk institute, where it was prepared, but rather had described it as one of a series of documents being considered at the high levels of government.

Here was a curious situation: Government officials were intrigued that I had managed to get a classified document and seemed genuinely interested in debating its content with me. I sensed no animosity nor any unusual suspicion toward me among officials of the Foreign Ministry, the Central Committee, or Arbatov's think tank on American affairs. Yet the KGB pressure was palpable; a friend at Tass hinted to me over drinks at the Press Club that I was suspected of having espionage connections—to which I gave the standard reply, a series of four-letter words.

But I had acted in an imprudent manner, which probably raised a KGB control officer's suspicions. Back in April, when I showed the document to a few trusted colleagues to get their views, I had also given a copy to a friend at the U.S. Embassy. I had not thought through the consequences of such a move; looking back, I believe I must have felt that it was important that somebody in the U.S. government be aware of the contents of the document in order to assess the changes contemplated by the new leadership. It never occurred to me at that point that I was doing something improper and potentially self-incriminating; all too frequently in Moscow we tended to view the world in simple terms—*we* and *they*—and the instinct to go with our pack was occasionally so strong that it overruled judgment and experience. On August 3, 1983, with the story causing something of a one-day sensation, the only people who failed to phone me and seek additional details were the American diplomats.

In the claustrophobic world of Moscow, where we were under fairly close scrutiny most of the time, the conspicuous lack of American interest inadvertently made it plain to the police that the embassy already had this particular document, which meant either that I had given it to the embassy or that the embassy had leaked it to me in order to embarrass the Soviet Union. In either case, my role seemed dubious. I decided that day never again to give any confidential information to U.S. officials in Moscow.

The Novosibirsk paper did, however, give me an insight into the internal struggle over economic reforms. Why did my source give me this document? I was not sure, but I knew him to be a firm advocate of change, and I suspect that he probably figured that a report about Zaslavskaya's document in the *Post* would get extensive readership in Moscow. He must also have been confident that I would not do or say anything that could lead the police to my source. Whether he acted on his own or with the knowledge of his powerful boss I do not know. But when I talked that August with another powerful man, Deputy Premier Nikolai Baibakov, chairman of the State Planning Committee, who had earlier denied the existence of Zaslavskaya's paper, and offered to send him a Xerox copy of the document, he said, "That's not the point. What you people make out of it is all wrong. Nobody is talking about re-forms."

Meanwhile, as the full text of Zaslavskaya's study was printed in major European and Japanese newspapers, and pundits in the United States speculated that the KGB was circulating this document, I was deeply disturbed by a feeling that I had inadvertently betrayed my source's trust. I heard indirectly that a KGB investigative team had been sent to Novosibirsk and that my acquaintances in the scientific world were suspected—wrongly, of course. There was no way for me to approach the source or any possible intermediaries for another year.

But there was one possible lead that could help the KGB figure out the leak. Back in April I had made two Xerox copies and secreted one away. To eliminate any traces that could identify the source, I had covered with whitener the markings and comments that were written on the margin of the original document, and I had eliminated, of course, the number of the document. It was this cleaned-up version that I gave my friends and colleagues. But I did not destroy the copy with the markings and handwriting in the margins; I hid it—in such a good place that at first I was not able to find it. Only after frantically searching for several days did I find it and burn it in my kitchen sink.

In addition to my concerns about the KGB shadow, I also grieved and worried in this period about the fate of one of my closest Soviet friends, who had been picked up by the police and placed in a psychiatric hospital for examination. I knew that the publication of the Novosibirsk paper had nothing to do with it, because he had confided to me in July that he was hiding from the police (not the KGB). He told me that as I drove him from our compound after a dinner at my house for a visiting Colorado congressman, Timothy Wirth, and his charming wife, Wren. Also at the dinner were James Billington, director of the Wilson Center in Washington, poet Andrei Voznesensky, and his wife, Zoya. They had no idea, and neither had I until late that night, that a fugitive from justice was seated at our table. My friend had read Billington's suberb book about Russian cultural history* and had wanted to meet the author. The next day he had acted as a guide to the Wirths. He was seized by police a week or so later and taken to the notorious Kashchenko hospital for examination— ostensibly because he did not hold a steady job. Never before had I felt so angry and so frustrated in Moscow as I did at that time. I tried to keep my personal indignation and resentment to myself, which meant that I was exceptionally ill-tempered toward everyone around me.

Late at night, after work, I drove by the Kashchenko, a massive building that looked to me like a prison, wondering whether he was being forced to take some horrible drug that would make him ill. All the gory stories about the abuse of psychiatry suddenly became a personal reality that haunted my mind. And there was nothing I could do. I was tempted to write an article about it, a scathing article, for I was a witness to tremendous injustice; I would draw a comparison with the arbitrariness of Nicholas I, who also sent people to insane asylums. But what would that accomplish, beyond making me feel better about myself and reducing my feeling of impotence? Driving late one night to the home of a mutual friend, I recalled our evenings of mellow intellectual arguments, and my resentment and bitterness swelled into fury. But several friends cautioned me to do nothing, for the involvement of a foreigner would merely complicate things, would make his incarceration a state case. A group of his friends became active in the affair, including several Soviet journalists, a prominent physics professor, and two film directors, who involved a vice president of the Academy of Sciences, Yevgeny Velikhov. Fortunately, their advice turned out to be right, and our friend was released before the end of August.

My own situation did not get any better, however. I had con-

---

*James H. Billington, *The Icon and the Axe,* New York: Knopf, 1966.

stant company in my nocturnal shuttlings around Moscow. The surveillance had become blatant—a sign that it was meant as harassment. I finally decided to confront the issue head-on by bringing it up with my acquaintances in the Foreign Ministry and with some high-ranking political figures I could reach, including a man who was close to Andropov. My telephones no longer worked, I said; my telex was being switched off and on in an unpredictable manner. I was forced to use the communication facilities of my Japanese neighbors. I had no problem with the KGB trying to find out the source of the Novosibirsk paper, I added, but I did object, and object vigorously, to the disgraceful harassment, which interfered with the performance of my duties. These were Gestapo methods, I said pointedly. I would describe them as such in an open letter to Andropov, which would be published on the op-ed page of the *Post.* The men I contacted seemed genuinely surprised. A well-connected friend told me, "But all this is not directed against you. You must understand they are doing their job; they have got to find out who leaked the document. They do the same things in Washington."

A few days later the pressure suddenly evaporated; or at least I did not feel it any longer.

It was at that point that a Russian I had known for a long time told me about the unpublished memoirs written by Stalin's deputy, Vyacheslav Molotov. Was I interested? There was a way, he said, to obtain a copy of the manuscript, which is held at the Institute of Marxism-Leninism. He outlined the plan in detail: It seemed that almost effortlessly I could get hold of interesting historical materials through Molotov's daughter, Svetlana, whose husband I knew. Needless to say, I was interested in obtaining a copy. And yet I declined. I felt, perhaps unjustifiably, that I was being set up.

The last days of August were warm and pleasant. We celebrated with champagne the release of my friend from the Kashchenko psychiatric hospital; there was hope, after all. I felt low and drained yet relieved after those nightmarish weeks of grueling psychological pressures; moreover, Mrs. Graham's interview with Andropov was firmed up and I was looking forward to accompanying her into the Kremlin. We were also looking forward to our home leave in September and were thinking with considerable anxiety about being for the first time without our son, Peter, who was entering a boarding school in Connecticut.

At the end of August, Andropov left Moscow for a vacation. My family and I boarded an Aeroflot plane on the morning of September 1, flying directly to Montreal. My colleague Michael Dobbs in Paris had a Soviet visa in hand in case he was needed to cover events in Moscow, but everything seemed quiet there. I did not know that during the previous night a Soviet air force plane had shot down a Korean Air Lines passenger jet and that more than fifty Americans were among the 269 persons who lost their lives. From that point on, the confrontational mode between the superpowers was firmly established until Andropov's death.

It was a luminous September afternoon when we arrived in Montreal and checked into the Dorval Hilton, anticipating a pleasant dinner in a French restaurant. We had heard from a Haitian taxi driver something about a plane being shot down by the Russians. When we turned on the TV set in our room, the shooting-down of KAL 007 was on every channel, but for some inexplicable reason I did not grasp what had happened; there were too many words and too few facts.

I phoned the *Post*'s foreign desk. The question was raised as to whether I should fly back to Moscow. It was the last thing I wanted to do. Rick Weintraub read to me the Tass statement on KAL 007, which ended with a vague phrase saying the plane was seen heading "in the direction of the Sea of Japan."

I said, "That means they have shot it down. The phrase should be taken literally—it went into the Sea of Japan." My editors mercifully did not order me back; Dobbs was ready to go to Moscow, and we proceeded the next day to New Hampshire on our vacation.

So the shooting-down of the KAL jetliner became the one major story that I did not cover during my tour. The Russians were soundly condemned for the incident, which seemed to most of the world a brutal and repellent action. However reprehensible it may have been, the downing of the plane did not surprise me. If past experience is any guide, it can be assumed that the Soviet pilot tried to force the plane to land on Soviet soil, but when he failed and saw it leaving Soviet airspace, he shot it down. But such an explanation would have had a heretical sound in the atmosphere that I found in the United States.

I also sensed that our interview with Andropov was no longer possible. When I arrived in Washington after a brief vacation, I accompanied Mrs. Graham, Editorial Page Editor Meg Greenfield, and Jim Hoagland to various meetings with administration figures and Soviet specialists. But we were going through the motions, carrying out a previously scheduled program of preparations for a meeting with Andropov. Mrs. Graham knew that an interview now was not likely to take place, yet she persisted with vigor. Andropov would have certainly found her a formidable interlocutor.

⟪⟪ 5 ⟫⟫

Moscow seemed in a different mood when I returned in the beginning of October. By now it had become clear that the Russians had suffered a devastating propaganda defeat and that it would inevitably lead to an equally devastating political defeat when U.S. missiles were deployed in Europe. Whatever Andropov's strategy to stop the deployment had been, it now lay in ruins. In late September he dramatized this perception with a statement so confrontational in tone and substance that I wondered whether the two superpowers would be able to talk with one another in the near future. Andropov challenged the basic premise of Brezhnev's détente policy. While desirable, Andropov said, accords with the United States did not seem possible. "Even if someone had illusions as to the possible evolution for the better in the policy of the present U.S. administration," he said, "the latest developments have finally dispelled them." The KAL incident, it was claimed in Moscow, was deliberately engineered by the U.S. administration to poison the atmosphere and to ensure the December deployment of new U.S. nuclear missiles in Western Europe. No evidence for this was ever produced, however.

Those were strange, moody days; people were anxiously talking of war. Beginning in September and continuing throughout the year, the public temper was gradually rising, octave by octave, and the shrillness made it obvious that the need to counteract would soon force active decisions upon the Soviet government. Tensions increased under the stimulus of Reagan's "evil empire" rhetoric and the poisonous insinuations of Tass. Under these stresses, Marshal Nikolai Ogarkov, the chief of staff, renewed warnings in late September that Moscow would respond to the new U.S. medium-range missiles in Europe with measures that would pose an equal military threat to the United States and Western Europe. Marshal Viktor Kulikov, the Warsaw Pact commander, warned that Reagan's plan to gain strategic superiority "could play the role of a detonator in the current explosive situation." Top officials talked more and more about adopting a "launch on warning" posture—no longer in whispers to foreign visitors but in strong public statements. In practice that would mean that the Kremlin would rely on its computers to determine whether the country was facing a mortal threat and to retaliate automatically against the United States. It was a war of nerves on the grand scale, since senior U.S. spokesmen continued to insist that superpower relations were not particularly dangerous, that

the Soviet leadership was pragmatic, and that serious negotiations would start only after Pershing Twos were deployed. Perhaps the situation was not too serious, though it seriously affected
judgment on the spot.*

The Soviet propaganda machine had conspicuously moved into
high gear. As the thoughtful Norwegian ambassador, Dagfinn
Stenseth, put it, "One has the impression of the Soviet leadership
taking to a submarine, going down, and looking through its peri-
scope at the rest of the world." Stenseth had one of the best
analytical minds among foreign ambassadors; he and the Turkish
envoy, Vahit Halefoglu, were the envoys I frequently sought out
for conversation about Soviet developments. Both men had noticed, early on, that senior military officers had emerged as Kremlin spokesmen. That fall their prominence became apparent to me,
and I began keeping a list of their names—names I had never
before encountered in public life. The main Kremlin spokesmen,
in addition to Gromyko, were Ustinov and Ogarkov. But my list
of other marshals and ranking generals who publicly talked about
military policy grew long that fall. This departure from the standard practice, under which the top brass had always been visible
but silent, could partly, but only partly, be explained by the fact
that the "Euromissiles crisis" was to a large extent a military
matter. But one had the impression that the armed forces chiefs
were no longer an inert tool of the leadership but rather its equal
partner; what made this ominous was their clearly stated position
that they would throw all their weapons at the United States once
the first American missile was detected heading in the direction
of Soviet territory. Halefoglu's explanation—and I did not fully
appreciate its savvy—was interesting in view of his experience

---

*However, a group of eight U.S. senators who visited Moscow in August and met
with Andropov for two hours concluded that the situation was dangerous, in their
report to the Senate, *Dangerous Stalemate: Superpower Relations in Autumn of 1983*,
U.S. Government Printing Office, October 3, 1983. The senators, all Democrats, were
Claiborne Pell, Russell B. Long, Dale Bumpers, Patrick J. Leahy, Howard M. Metzen-
baum, Donald W. Riegle, Jr., Paul S. Sarbanes, and James R. Sasser.

with the role of the Turkish military in Turkey's political life: "The generals," he said, "become visible when the political life of a country is seriously weakened."

The Kremlin also started a broad effort to mobilize the population; friends told me that at closed party meetings throughout the country a Central Committee letter was read asserting that there was no chance for an agreement at the Geneva talks over the intermediate term—the Russian word used was *v perspetive*—and hence there was no chance for an improvement in relations with the United States. In mid-October, Kulikov forecast that Moscow would introduce nuclear weapons in Eastern Europe. By the end of the month, the Defense Ministry announced that preparations for deployment of new nuclear missiles in Czechoslovakia and East Germany had begun. Meanwhile Tass had started to escalate its vitriolic accusations, charging that Reagan was spouting "lies," and describing his White House as "a center of international terrorism." This was level five or six on the Richter scale of Soviet abuse. The American invasion of Grenada brought the invective to the year's all-time high. The president was held personally responsible for what was described as a "criminal act" of "international banditry."

What I did not learn until much later was that Andropov was gravely ill in October and that one of his ailing kidneys had been removed. The impact of the KAL incident on Andropov's health and his state of mind remains a mystery. I was told that he had not been consulted about the incident until after the plane was brought down; given the nature of the system, that seems to me entirely plausible. He had returned to Moscow from Kislovodsk to deal with the crisis but he remained in the background.

His health took a sharp turn for the worse in the last days of September, although that was not known even in high party circles. At the beginning of October, Sergei Losev, director general of Tass, disclosed privately at a reception for an East European delegation that Andropov would go to Bulgaria on a state visit in the second part of October. This was confirmed by Bulgarian diplomats. As is customary on such occasions, Soviet television began a series of special Bulgarian programs. Suddenly we were told that the visit had been canceled because of the tense international climate.

In the latter part of October, a friend of mine, Harvard cardiologist Bernard Lown, arrived in Moscow to present a message to Andropov from International Physicians for the Prevention of Nuclear War. But he and his Soviet counterpart in the group, Yevgeny Chazov, were received not by Andropov but by Vasily Kuznetsov, the first vice president, and I began to suspect that something serious had happened to the Soviet leader. Since Chazov was the head of the department responsible for medical treatment of the leadership, he knew the exact details of Andropov's condition. "What does Chazov say about it?" I asked Lown during a long chat one evening in his hotel room. But Lown, who has a strong sense of social responsibility and is one of the finest men I ever met, professed not to know anything. I knew that it was unfair for me to press Lown on this issue, but I suspected that Chazov had consulted him privately. Eight days later Lown, already back in the United States, received a cable from Andropov, apologizing for his failure to receive the doctors and saying he had a "cold."

I interpreted the telegram as a damage-control enterprise, intended to soften the rumors that inevitably spread after Andropov failed to appear in Kremlin celebrations on November 7 commemorating the 1917 Bolshevik Revolution. This was significant—in Russia a ruler has to be able to assert himself in physical terms if he is to have control over the Kremlin. Even if he were to recover from his ailments, Andropov's spell over the country was gravely damaged, and the impression of physical vulnerability so graphically conveyed by his absence from the most important public ceremony on the Soviet calendar placed the question of succession on the agenda. One year after the death of the perpetually ailing Brezhnev, the same problem that had plagued Kremlin councils during his declining years came to haunt the ruling elite again.

Not that it was possible to dislodge Andropov, given the backing of the KGB and the armed forces. But in the shadow of Andropov's illness there were stirrings in the party elite. His opponents were regrouping. I saw signs of it in the press as well as in rumors emanating from Chernenko supporters. On November 5, in his keynote address in the Kremlin Palace of Congresses on the eve of the three-day anniversary celebrations, Romanov failed to include a single complimentary phrase about the hospitalized leader. That was highly unusual, and I thought—and reported—that Andropov's enemies in the Politburo were plotting against him. Rumors in official quarters had it that Andropov would be asked to retire from his job, but these were promptly quashed on November 11, when the armed forces issued a ringing endorsement of Andropov's policy and sent greetings to him and the Central Committee—notably omitting the Politburo. Tass, in its Russian service, quoted Ustinov as saying that this message was the outcome of his meeting with all senior officers of the Defense Ministry, the Moscow military district, and the antiaircraft forces; but the English Tass merely reported Ustinov's meeting with the military leaders without mentioning their message of "ardent support" to Andropov. Soviet television and radio, controlled by Chernenko's ally Sergei Lapin, failed to report the high command's endorsement. But the armed forces daily, *Krasnaya Zvezda,* carried the Tass dispatch in full and prominently, a clear signal that stopped rumors of Andropov's retirement.

An air of Byzantine intrigue hung over the city that winter. The absent leader's power was beginning to be severely circumscribed in the Politburo, where Gorbachev lacked the personal authority to impose decisions on the senior and more experienced men of the old guard, who still held a majority of seats. But Andropov could control the operations of the Secretariat, where Gorbachev and his men ran the show on behalf of the leader. In practice, this stalemated the old guard leadership.

One development in late November reminded Andropov's opponents of his power. A court in Moscow sentenced to death Yuri K. Sokolov, a personal friend of a number of prominent Brezhnevites, including Moscow leader Grishin and Brezhnev's daughter, Galina. Sokolov was director of Gastronome Number One, better known as the Yeliseyevski Magazine, its name during tsarist days, which supplied Moscow's elite with food delicacies and other scarce goods. An equivalent of four million dollars in various foreign currencies, gems, and rubles had been found in a cache hidden under the parquet floor in Sokolov's apartment following his arrest a year earlier. That a senior Politburo member such as Grishin could not save his friend—he was eventually executed—illustrates the atmosphere of the times.

There was one other important consideration: A major diplomatic setback over the deployment of new American nuclear weapons in Western Europe was now at hand. The battle for West European public opinion had been lost, and it was evident that domestic and foreign considerations gave Andropov an almost desperate feeling that he had to do something. If he had not carried out his public threat to break off the Geneva talks once the Americans began deploying new missiles, he would have risked a humiliation that would have weakened him at home and made the Reagan administration doubt the firmness of the Kremlin. The latter point weighed heavily on his opponents in the Politburo, who did not want any signs of disunity to further weaken the country's international position.

Very few persons at that point knew the exact state of Andropov's health. Western diplomats and journalists spent a lot of time staking out positions along Kutuzovsky Prospect following reported sightings of Andropov's limousine. His supporters talked about his recovering and attending the December plenum of the Central Committee; the illusion of his presence in the Kremlin was maintained by a series of public pronouncements on arms control and East-West relations. Gorbachev went so far as to receive a visiting Iowa banker, John Crystal, through whom he conveyed Andropov's "oral message" to the readers of the Des Moines *Register*.

But Andropov failed to appear at the December plenum. Yet his grip on power was shown by a series of important changes at the top: Vitali Vorotnikov, fifty-seven, a protégé of Andropov's, became a full Politburo member, as did Mikhail Solomentsev, seventy, whose career had been blocked by Brezhnev. Viktor Chebrikov, fifty-nine, Andropov's top assistant during his KGB years and now KGB chairman, was appointed alternate member of the Politburo, and Yegor Ligachev, sixty-three, was named secretary of the Central Committee. These changes, which broke the old guard's hold on the Politburo, constituted Andropov's crucial legacy to Gorbachev. In less than two years, Ligachev would become the party's second secretary, assuming the post once held by Suslov.* It was with the men Andropov elevated that Gorbachev eventually came to power.

One thing became increasingly obvious at the end of 1983: the vigorous propaganda effort to portray Andropov as more active than ever. When he failed to appear at a Supreme Soviet opening session on December 28, the main television news show devoted its first twenty minutes to statements by various figures extolling Andropov's wisdom and leadership, and to clips of his old speeches. The Supreme Soviet session, which was attended by all

---

*Ligachev, a graduate of the Moscow Aviation Institute, became a party official while working in an aircraft factory in Novosibirsk in 1945. He had been a Komsomol leader and later an official of the Novosibirsk regional party committee. He became a top official in the region, where the Siberian center of the Soviet Academy of Sciences was being built in the late 1950s. The establishment of Akademgorodok was his responsibility. In 1961, he was brought to the *aparat* of the Central Committee in Moscow and was moved in 1965 to Tomsk as first secretary of the regional committee, the post he held until 1983, when Andropov brought him to Moscow. According to various reports, he enjoyed a fine reputation in Tomsk as an undogmatic person and an efficient and uncorruptible manager.

top figures in the country, was barely mentioned at the end of the broadcast. I conducted a totally unscientific sampling of opinion on this issue and I was stunned to find that only about one out of ten persons was aware that Andropov had failed to attend the Supreme Soviet session and the Central Committee plenum, although the first sentence of his speech, published in all the newspapers and magazines, expressed his regrets that he was unable to be there. When I mentioned this fact to the historian Roy Medvedev, he smiled. His own twenty-three-year-old son, Medvedev said, was convinced that Andropov was at work and that he had attended the plenum. This instance of successful public relations enhanced my respect for the power of propaganda.

Despite Andropov's high profile during those last weeks, some of his central domestic policy themes virtually disappeared from the press; others appeared only sporadically. We wondered about the absence of information on the economic experiments, which were to start on January 1. But I was caught up in the Soviet propaganda war over the deployment of Pershing Two and cruise missiles and the walkout from the Geneva talks. It was Ogarkov, a firm Andropov loyalist, who held a press conference on December 5 to explain the walkout, lashing out at the United States for having sabotaged arms control. The sound and fury over this issue obscured the fact that the government was paralyzed.

Much later, a senior Soviet official recounted to me Andropov's final days. Everything had been done to fix his hospital apartment at Kuntsevo in such a way as to make him forget that he was inside a hospital compound. He was constantly on the phone. When he called senior officials in for talks, he would greet them in his living room, wearing a soft blue robe and seated in a comfortable armchair. A battery of phones was nearby. He had good days and bad days. On a bad day, the official recalled, Andropov's "voice was weak."

He described a meeting with Andropov in late December 1983. "When we finished discussing the business at hand and I was about to leave, he got up from his armchair and embraced me. He did so as if he knew that we were seeing each other for the last time, and I was tremendously shaken and saddened. But then I talked to him by phone two weeks later and his voice was firm and cheerful and I thought, well, he was going to recover, that I was being a sentimental fool to mourn him prematurely."

By January of 1984, it was virtually impossible to divine what was going on in the Kremlin, although the signs and portents of the day were disquieting. Another Andropov friend, Lev Tolkhunov, who was then editor in chief of the government daily *Izvestia,* published on January 21 an article that seemed to suggest public parting with the bedridden leader. Under the headline "Parting," the paper talked about the last days of the semiparalyzed Lenin, who continued to plan and think about the future, preparing a speech for the forthcoming congress although he was "not destined to accomplish this." Knowing the links between Andropov and Tolkhunov, I was led to believe that the leader's days were numbered. Yet the parallel was too Russian, too arcane, to be taken as a piece of evidence.

It was a stroke of luck that my *Post* colleague Don Oberdorfer arrived in Moscow that month to sound out the Kremlin's attitudes following the breakdown of the Geneva process. Don was a great boon to the bureau; in Moscow he enjoyed a good reputation for his work and hence was in a position to meet people who were near the centers of power. I accompanied him to a series of meetings, of which those with Vadim Zagladin, deputy chief of the Central Committee International Department, and General Viktor Starodubov, an arms control expert for the General Staff, were the most interesting.

Zagladin was the prototype of a modern top-level Soviet bureaucrat. He was courteous and friendly, a man of formidable intellectual breadth, wearing what seemed to me an expensive Western suit and tie; he was a Marlboro man, preferring American cigarettes to Soviet ones, an odd thing for a senior Central

Committee member. Close to the end of our lengthy conversation Don asked him, as he had asked everyone else, about Andropov's health. It was January 28, and in retrospect we know that Andropov's condition had seriously deteriorated a day or two earlier. Zagladin told us that he was in constant touch with the leader, receiving written or oral instructions daily. He pointed to a battery of phones near his desk. When Don persisted in asking whether he actually held daily phone conversations with Andropov, Zagladin replied indirectly, with studied conviction, "What is a telephone for?" Don and I talked about it afterward; the topic of Andropov, as Don put it, was the hole in the doughnut of every conversation.

Another conversation, with Valentin Falin, former Soviet ambassador to Bonn and now an *Izvestia* commentator, reinforced our impression that Andropov was a more transitional figure than anybody had guessed a month earlier. Falin revealed to us as "information" that he had heard that an *Izvestia* colleague had recently spoken to Andropov. The comment bordered on the ludicrous. The leader of the world's second superpower was invisible even to those in the high circles. Were it not for the loyalty of the KGB, Andropov probably could not have retained personal authority at that stage and the leadership situation would have been much more volatile.

Since Falin did not tell us the name of the colleague, I suspected that it must have been Tolkhunov, the editor. But Alexander Bovin, the *Izvestia* commentator who once worked for Andropov, told us over a lunch at the Foreign Ministry Press Club that he had talked to Andropov by phone for twenty minutes.

In late January, the word filtered out that Andropov's days were numbered. His opponents were waiting. They were no longer frightened of the dying former KGB chairman. A remark at the time by Ignaty Novikov, a senior Central Committee member, illustrated the point. Six months earlier Novikov had been dismissed from his job as chairman of the State Committee on Construction Affairs. "What's all this about Andropov?" he said with evident contempt to a group of young people at a wedding party in the Hotel Moskva. "He is just an old, sick man." Novikov was a charter member of the Brezhnevite group; he came from Brezhnev's hometown in the Ukraine and was chairman of the organizing committee for the 1980 Moscow Summer Olympics.

Also in January, a new edition of the official *History of the Soviet Communist Party* appeared in bookstores; its final chapter dealt with the Andropov period. I read it twice, then compared it with similar chapters in other party history books. In what was a striking departure for such volumes and a signal of things to come, it mentioned Chernenko alongside Andropov as architects of the party's strategic course.

During that last month of his life, Andropov suffered physically and was no longer able to move, as his muscles became weaker. In the fourth week of January, his condition deteriorated sharply. Early in February he lapsed into a coma, never to regain consciousness. The phone calls stopped; the government came to a standstill. Pavel Laptiev and two other close personal aides moved into the Kuntsevo apartment; the medical team was there around the clock. He died on February 10, as his son Igor was flying to Moscow from Stockholm.

CHAPTER EIGHT

THE CHERNENKO INTERLUDE

KONSTANTIN USTINOVICH CHERNENKO was a man of no special virtues and qualities and never appeared as someone destined to rule Russia. He came to power not because he was the most intelligent, the most eloquent, or the most forceful politician around but because the older generation was not quite ready to turn the reins over to younger leaders. His was a caretaker regime, the last stand of the old guard resisting change.

Once again, on a frigid winter day, we witnessed the accession of a new tsar. As a physically exhausted Chernenko, the fifth successor to Lenin, stood atop the Lenin Mausoleum presiding over the funeral rites for his predecessor on February 14, 1984, the scene on Red Square had an almost dreamlike quality of unreality and impermanence.

First impressions often jell into lasting images, and in Chernenko's case these were devastatingly negative. As the Kremlin's Spassky Tower chimes signaled twelve noon and the new leader, about to present his speech, seemed unsure how to proceed, the voice of Andrei Gromyko was clearly heard over the loudspeakers. "Don't take off the hat," he said, turning toward Chernenko. The new leader looked to his left, got an approving nod from Politburo member Victor Grishin, and began to read his speech. One could see his breath in the freezing cold of the vast square. It was the shallow breath of a man with a lung problem. He slurred his words, and I often could not make out where his sentences began and where they ended.

The next speakers were Gromyko, the veteran foreign minister, whose eulogy was a masterpiece of eloquence, and Marshal Ustinov, the defense minister and another grand old man of the party. Both seemed to deeply mourn Andropov. These two powerful figures, speaking forcefully and appearing physically far more vigorous than Chernenko—who was about four years younger than they—made the new leader appear a feeble and indecisive old man surrounded by powerful party barons.

Precisely why the men in whom political power was vested decided to turn to Chernenko instead of Mikhail Gorbachev, Andropov's real heir, was never fully explained. When the choice was announced, it came as a shock. I had never witnessed such widespread and strong discontent with a Kremlin decision before. During those days I sampled opinion as best I could, but failed to come across a single person who could say anything positive about the new leader. People within the government bureaucracy were mum; those I knew better indicated privately that they found the choice disheartening. At seventy-two, he was the oldest man to hold the job and was clearly in poor health. Persons whose business it was to sell the Soviet image abroad had difficulty in coming up with the most routine laudatory clichés. Even thoroughly apolitical people, if they held any opinions at all on such lofty issues beyond their control, would have liked to see a younger man take charge. The age factor in itself made Gorbachev the overwhelming favorite of the population. But the old guard apparently wanted a grace period to sort things out before the inevitable; they and their loyalists in the ranks feared for their positions and privileges and argued that Gorbachev was untested for the very top.

I was told, however, that a section of the population was rejoicing—but more over the death of Andropov, the stern disciplinarian, than over the choice of his successor. It was a curious company: Moscow's underground world of black marketeers and speculators joined the orthodox bureaucratic *aparat* in champagne parties on the night Andropov's death was announced.

The sense of gloom and even despair that was initially so pervasive was summed up at the time by a prominent Russian novelist. "I can tell you that as a Russian writer I honestly feel hurt in my national dignity," he said privately. "I love my country, I'm proud of it, I am not a dissident, but I do not want such a man to be at the head of our country."

Yet these initial impressions were not entirely justified. It would be difficult to imagine a truly indecisive and feeble man rising to membership in the Politburo, let alone aspiring to become the country's leader. For nearly three decades Chernenko had served as the most intimate aide to Brezhnev. He knew all the secrets and he saw all the papers before they came to Brezhnev's desk. During Brezhnev's last, ailing years, it was Chernenko who in effect ran the country in his mentor's name.

Once in power, Chernenko turned out to be conservative on domestic issues. But he shared Brezhnev's inclination toward détente with the West, and he left his mark in foreign affairs by almost single-handedly forcing a shift in policy toward the United States, which opened the way for the resumption of dialogue between the superpowers.

People who knew Chernenko well described him as a man of above-average intelligence who possessed a talent for organization and a mastery of technical details. My own impression after talking with him was of a man at home with the arms-control issues and fully conscious of just how far he could go in talking about American domestic politics and the arms issue without saying something that could damage the interests of his country. His eyes were steely and entirely without warmth, even when he laughed. They widened only when he tried to make a point, slightly tilting his head down and focusing his gaze on you to make sure the point was understood. His intellect had been shaped in the party, and by the time he moved into the general secretary's office he was completely set in his ways. He believed with a kind of holy passion in the need for regular procedures and rigorous bureaucratic protocol. Only through discipline and order could material prosperity and cultural development be achieved. He drew strength from this belief. He had worked his way up through the party bureaucracy from the lowest level before he latched on to Brezhnev and was propelled by him into high orbit. He had always been an administrator, and even his detractors conceded that he was an efficient one, easier to deal with than any other member of Brezhnev's entourage. Yet his mind, for all its clarity, was conventional and in the traditional mold of a successful party bureaucrat. He was a grand master in the bureaucratic game, knowing how to make himself indispensable, making the right friends, lying low and waiting. He never lost track of his support within the system; he drew on his long-term service in the party and on the loyalty of his generation.

A harsher portrait of Chernenko is drawn by former Soviet diplomat Arkady Shevchenko, who became an American agent and eventually defected, in 1978. In his book *Breaking with Moscow* * he describes Chernenko as a "pragmatic, businesslike man" who knew what he wanted, "a master of wheeling and dealing on the Central Committee" who used his friendship with Brezhnev to the utmost, arousing his colleagues' resentment. He was, Shevchenko says, "demanding, rude, authoritarian, arrogant."

*New York: Knopf, 1985.

I heard a similar view from a senior Soviet politician and Andropov loyalist who, after Chernenko's death, described him privately as "a tremendously average man" who had risen too high. Another Central Committee member described Chernenko as "an ideal number-two man"—shrewd, sensible, but unimaginative. What propelled him forward also held him back once he assumed supreme power. He was a prisoner of his background, tied to Brezhnev's ideas, style, and approach.

But the defeat he had suffered in his first bid for the top job had a profound psychological effect on him. During the first months of 1983 he practically withdrew from public life and his health suddenly deteriorated. Chernenko felt that the government had fallen into the hands of amateurs, people who wanted to experiment, to play with the processes of Kremlin power, in short, into the hands of intellectuals, even if the KGB was behind them. Andropov's belief in the importance of people and their attitudes and his contention that one changed policies by changing people was distasteful to Chernenko, smarting from hurts he suffered during the power struggle. When he reappeared in public on May 1, 1983, I noticed for the first time that he was breathing with difficulty. Atop the Lenin Mausoleum that May Day, a once bouncy and energetic Chernenko looked like an old man. Achieving the final rung of the Kremlin hierarchy eight months later must have been a singular personal triumph for him—in Soviet politics losers are generally relegated to oblivion. His accession, however, had more to do with the fact that Andropov, during his brief tenure, had shaken up the country to such an extent that the ruling elite questioned whether they really wanted another strong and forceful figure to continue so disturbing a challenge to their accustomed way of life. The challenge, for many of them, seemed too exacting; they preferred the familiar, safe Chernenko. But most Russians saw his elevation in the context of the generational struggle: The old guard did not want to relinquish power to a new and younger leadership.

So Chernenko emerged partly by default, partly as a result of his own adroit maneuvering. He was chosen to hold the line, slow down the dynamics of change, protect the interests of the entrenched officials whom he, as Brezhnev's confidential aide, had placed in their jobs during the previous two decades.

This was the low point in the protracted Kremlin transition.

Everything seemed stacked against Chernenko. Any Soviet leader would have been at a disadvantage, at least initially, as Andropov's successor. Given Chernenko's public image, the disadvantage was colossal. Even his physical appearance was a negative—women were not merely indifferent to him; they disliked him. The sheer contrast in personality and style worked against Chernenko. There had been an element of intellectual passion in Andropov's speeches, an attempt to deploy rhetoric as a tool of change. Andropov clearly believed what he said and cared about the way he presented his ideas. Chernenko's speeches contained no ideas and were made not because he wanted to say something—he was an exceptionally bad orator—but because that was his duty. Moreover, Andropov after his death immediately became a Soviet folk hero. Like John F. Kennedy, to whom he otherwise bore no resemblance, he died before one could determine whether he would have been able to implement his vision for his country, but in the popular mind he was seen as the leader who would have done what he pledged to do had his health allowed it. Partly, the myth may have been created by the KGB, which had a vested interest in seeing *their* man, their former chairman, in the pantheon of the country's heroes. But many of my colleagues who traveled across the country and talked to a variety of Soviet citizens on trains and planes, in remote small towns and cities, came back with stories of popular sentiment toward Andropov that left no doubt that the myth was indigenous.

Chernenko must have sensed the potency of the Andropov myth. He insisted, at least rhetorically, that he was continuing

Andropov's course; he had no program of his own. Andropov had charted the main direction of policy and had brought a number of his men into key positions to establish a degree of control over his legacy. Gorbachev was the party's second secretary under Chernenko and thus also in a position of influence.

So Chernenko's thirteen months in power were to a large extent a period of truce, a stalemate between the Andropov forces and those associated with the new leader and his old mentor, Brezhnev. Chernenko took no direct action to dismantle Andropov's program of economic experimentation. He did not try to stop the anticorruption campaign. It was during his watch that one of his —and Brezhnev's—close friends, the former interior minister Shcholokov, committed suicide to avoid standing trial on corruption charges. Shcholokov's suicide was true to the tsarist military tradition: He put on his general's uniform, pinned on all his medals and decorations, placed the muzzle of a rifle in his mouth, and pulled the trigger. Chernenko could not reverse proceedings already under way against other high-ranking officials, but he could slow things down and move against some Andropov loyalists just to show who was the boss.

It is difficult to overestimate the importance of the style and instincts that a general secretary of the Communist Party brings with him to the office. The office itself not only is the vital hub of action in the ruling bureaucracy; in a strictly hierarchical system, it also sets the tone and pace. What Chernenko did during his tenure was to calm down sectors of the country shaken by Andropov and to reassure the bureaucracy after fifteen turbulent months. Andropov's programs continued, but without energy and without enthusiastic support from Chernenko. He reversed one of Andropov's last decisions, which called for a cut of nearly 20 percent in the bureaucracy—an effort to eliminate a number of jobs that officials had dreamed up to take care of their protégés and friends, who, in turn, had come to regard the positions as sacred and unalterable. The decision against the cut was convenient; it postponed the reality of change and perpetuated the comfortable illusion of order and control within the bureaucracy. The pace of political life set by the new leader seemed to recall the Brezhnev years and served as a brake on the modernization drive. Andropov's appeals for hard work and sacrifices were gradually short-circuited by Chernenko's promises of benefits. The stalemate was a setback for the reformists. "Chernenko," one Soviet politician told me much later, "could not slam on the brakes. But he simply took his foot off the accelerator and everything slowed down."

The Soviet Union, a thoughtful journalist friend of mine said a few months after Chernenko's accession, "is now on automatic pilot."

2

DURING the first months, Chernenko presided seemingly benignly over a divided elite and a placid country, although he did not hold all the threads of power in his own hands. It was one thing to make a foreign policy shift, to move from the confrontational path to the old Brezhnev furrow. But it was quite another thing to make adjustments in domestic policy, an area where Andropov's men were far better positioned and where resolutions of problems were far more complex. Andropov's first direct meeting with citizens had involved a surprise visit to a machine tool factory, where he discussed the pressing need for economic changes. Chernenko chose a dramatically different setting for his first major public appearance. He met with the Central Committee *aparat* to reassure them that the changes would be gradual, that the frenzied pace of his predecessor was winding down. "In the renewal of the economic structure, we would do well to observe that wise old saying 'Look before you leap,' " he said. He himself

213

was a creation of the *aparat*, the ultimate *aparatchik* who became tsar, and the *aparat* could trust him.

However, from the start, the new leader sought to assert his personal authority.

His victory had been made possible by Ustinov, who threw the support of the armed forces behind Chernenko; but according to Kremlin insiders, the old guard had to accept Gorbachev as second secretary—which meant that he was the next in line—as part of a compromise engineered by Gromyko, who had acted as a bridge between the two generations. But Gorbachev's standing was not immediately made clear. As the second man, he made the concluding remarks at the Central Committee session that elected Chernenko; but this was not mentioned in press accounts of the proceedings, a deliberate slight administered by the new leader. Only a week or so later, following a series of rumors about Gorbachev's role at the plenum, a pamphlet was published revealing his standing and providing the text of his speech.

Chernenko took the offensive. He wanted to say that the new generation did not yet deserve full trust, that Gorbachev had not yet earned his spurs. This was how the Russians interpreted Chernenko's conspicuous disclosure in his first major speech of yet another agricultural setback. Agricultural production figures had become a state secret over the years, and I generally relied on the estimates of the U.S. Department of Agriculture, which proved remarkably accurate. But Chernenko wanted to make a point that would be clearly understood. The 1983 grain harvest was something in excess of 190 million tons, he said, better than in the two preceeding years but clearly not as high as Andropov's men had been vaguely suggesting. And Gorbachev had been the man responsible for agriculture.

Chernenko also moved against several Andropov loyalists who were highly visible in the media but who had weak political bases. Perhaps the most visible victim was Alexander Bovin, one of the country's finest journalists and a member of the party's Auditing

Commission. Like Andropov and Gorbachev, Bovin came from Stavropol, where he had served as a judge while Gorbachev was a junior party official. After a time he had moved to Moscow to study philosophy and, upon graduation, he joined Andropov's staff at the Central Committee. When Andropov moved to the KGB in 1967, Bovin went to work for Brezhnev as a speech writer. He had always been an outspoken and gregarious person, a gifted and well-educated writer who enjoyed the company of artists, journalists, and actresses far more than that of Central Committee bureaucrats. He also was freer and more imaginative in his way of saying things than an *aparat* man was supposed to be, which annoyed many people, despite the fact that in substance Bovin did not deviate from the party line. Chernenko was one he irritated, and as Brezhnev's chief of staff, he fired Bovin in 1971. Bovin then moved to the job at *Izvestia* that he has held ever since. But he had many powerful friends and admirers and was repeatedly elected deputy to the Supreme Soviet, until Chernenko's accession, when his name was taken off the list of candidates in the March 1984 elections. Bovin also was immediately removed from television, where he had had a weekly program dealing with foreign affairs. Why? I asked a Central Committee official close to Chernenko whom I met in the Foreign Ministry. "Why?" he said. "He's got a tongue a mile long."

We could feel the internal tightening that spring, especially on the cultural front. Moscow was shaken by the defection of Yuri Lyubimov, the well-known creator and director of the Taganyka Theater. It was a blow far greater than the defections of ballet dancers, such as Nureyev or Baryshnikov, or the cellist Mstislav Rostropovich. Lyubimov was an institution in Russia, a firm fixture on Moscow's cultural scene, whose theater was patronized by the elite as well as anyone else who could get tickets. He was irreplaceable; with him gone, the Taganyka began a swift downward slide.

I again felt pressure from the KGB, as did other American correspondents. The monthly magazine *Journalist* carried a scathingly sarcastic article attacking Serge Schmemann and John Burns of the New York *Times*, Bob Gillette of the Los Angeles *Times*, Howard Tyner of the Chicago *Tribune*, and me. We were charged with an assortment of abuses of our "power," of hanging around with the dregs of Soviet society, and of deliberately misrepresenting Soviet realities. It was a silly article, yet it reflected the new mood in the capital.

The authorities also moved against Jewish dissidents and arrested several Hebrew teachers. Police guards were placed outside the doors of dissident historian Roy Medvedev's apartment to prevent foreigners from contacting him. They installed a special telephone in the stairwell and brought a table and chairs to ease the round-the-clock duty.

I maintained regular contacts with Roy, as did most of my colleagues, and, whenever the opportunity arose, I sought to let the authorities know that he is respected as an author in the United States. On one occasion, I had taken Medvedev to lunch with Robert Borsage of Washington's Institute for Policy Studies. We were at the Praga Restaurant, a place frequented by important establishment figures, and Borsage noticed Harvard economist John Kenneth Galbraith at a distant table, lunching with several Soviet officials. Roy does not speak English, but Borsage and I quickly cooked up a scheme to invite Galbraith to meet him. I saw it as a small but important demonstration, something that could not go unnoticed at the Praga. Yet I was unsure whether Galbraith, whom I had never met before, would go along. Over the years I had come across people who professed to hold strong feelings about civil liberties but who would not do anything to offend their official hosts. Another category of "distinguished Americans," on the other hand, did not care about their hosts' feelings at all and would do anything to get publicity back home. There was a fine line between asserting one's values and taking actions that offended one's Soviet hosts; I always felt I had to do the first without doing the second. And that was just what Galbraith did. When Borsage went to his table and invited him over, the former ambassador to India excused himself with a bow, rose to his full height—which is considerable—and walked over to our table to meet Medvedev and chat with him, using me as interpreter. I felt profoundly pleased by Galbraith's gesture, although I noticed the Soviet officials staring at me with obvious displeasure. Such stares tell a great deal in a society in which communications are frequently conducted through a gamut of gestures and looks that, to an outsider, could seem like a special code. These stares conveyed extreme hostility.

Another incident that spring made me feel proud of a colleague, Charles Labroschini, correspondent of the Paris daily *Le Figaro*. During a press conference conducted by Leonid Zamyatin, the Kremlin spokesman, a question came up on the condition of Dr. Andrei Sakharov, the dissident physicist living in exile in the city of Gorki. We were not able to have any contacts with him since Gorki was a city closed to foreigners and Sakharov was under constant surveillance, but we had heard reports that his health had deteriorated after a hunger strike. Zamyatin assured us that the physicist was fine and healthy. At which point Charles stood up. "You told us that Mr. Andropov had a cold and we now know that that wasn't so. And you told us that the KAL plane was going in the direction of the Sea of Japan, and now we know different [it had already been shot down]. Why should we believe you now?" I have never heard such a bold question at a Moscow news conference. Zamyatin himself seemed shocked and flustered; his face turned red, and he obviously had to make an effort to control his behavior. "The next question," he quipped, looking around the hall; then, focusing back on Charles, he added, "Your question was tactless."

<<< **3** >>>

BY the time Chernenko became general secretary, the Kremlin's relations with the United States had moved in an almost complete circle—from Cold War hostility to détente and back again to enmity. As Brezhnev's closest aide, Chernenko had seen from the inside the growth of the empire, as one after another Third World country embraced socialism—Angola, Mozambique, Ethiopia, Laos, Cambodia, Afghanistan, Nicaragua. Under Brezhnev, the Soviet Union achieved strategic parity with the United States and détente with the West; simultaneously it enlarged its imperial holdings by acquiring new toeholds in distant parts of the world. Chernenko was formally promoted to the top leadership in 1976—he was made secretary of the Central Committee—when his mentor's conservative regime reached the high-water mark of optimism and when Brezhnev himself could say, with evident self-satisfaction as he celebrated his seventieth birthday, that "never before over the length of its entire history has our country enjoyed such authority and influence in the world." In 1984 the shape of the empire on the map, ominous and vast when looked at from the outside, had a very different appearance when viewed from the Kremlin. Its maintenance costs had gone up sharply. Poland was a heavy burden. So was Afghanistan, more politically than economically, however. The downward slide in the price of oil, gold, diamonds, and other metals since the seventies had depleted Moscow's hard-currency earnings. Then there was the iron logic of figures indicating a decline in the rate of economic growth, which had been between 5 and 6 percent annually at the beginning of Brezhnev's rule, to roughly 2 percent in the last year of Brezhnev's life. To top it all, the Americans, as seen from Moscow, were on the march, using the same techniques against the Kremlin's socialist allies that the Russians deployed decades earlier against America's allies—financing and supporting guerrillas fighting the established governments. Reagan's Strategic Defense Initiative, a quintessentially American venture, threatened to impose even greater restraints on the Soviet treasury. The détente of the seventies, in retrospect, seemed the golden age of Soviet power, a policy that permitted military buildup sufficient to secure strategic parity but at the same time resulted in higher living standards for the Soviet people.

So Chernenko, throughout 1984, seemed principally concerned with foreign affairs. He had come to power two months after the Kremlin's crushing diplomatic defeat on the issue of Euromissiles. After a political and propaganda battle that lasted more than three years, the Russians had failed to persuade the West Europeans not to accept the new Pershing Two and cruise missiles. When the first Pershings arrived in West Germany in December of the previous year, Andropov ordered his negotiators to leave the Geneva talks. Meanwhile, the American president had advanced his Star Wars program for an antimissile defense shield around the United States. As seen from Moscow, the Americans were breaking all the rules of the nuclear game; they had embarked on the path of permanent modernization of nuclear weapons in an effort to exhaust the Soviet economy. Soviet propaganda became more vitriolic than ever before. With forebodings of a doom-laden 1984, the propaganda war heightened a sense of danger in the Soviet capital. Andropov's death changed the atmosphere as Chernenko began to modify the course, but shifting the machinery of the government toward accommodation took time, and only gradually did the portents of the day became less disquieting.

Chernenko wanted to mend his fences with the West, and he began with the Europeans. His first senior Western visitor was President François Mitterrand of France, whom Chernenko viewed as the architect of Moscow's recent debacle. As long as

Mitterrand's predecessor, the conservative Valéry Giscard d'Estaing, was in power, France had had a close relationship with Helmut Schmidt's government in Bonn, and together, Bonn and Paris had been able to influence or soften Washington's European policy. But Mitterrand, although a socialist, had aligned himself with Washington, thus undercutting Schmidt's position and letting the United States gain the initiative in Europe.

It was in this atmosphere that Chernenko endorsed a decision to boycott the 1984 Summer Olympics in Los Angeles. Since the American boycott of the Moscow Olympics four years earlier, there had been a temptation—it seemed almost irresistible in some quarters—to even the score. Yet key figures in the foreign policy establishment saw Soviet participation in Los Angeles as a way of easing tensions in Soviet-American relations. This was also Chernenko's view; moreover, he had been advised that spring that Reagan's reelection seemed likely, and he was therefore looking for a suitable opportunity to engage the American president well before November. But Washington seemed to believe that the Russians would come to Los Angeles under any circumstances, and it therefore ignored public and private Soviet objections about inadequate security arrangements at Los Angeles. The view of the U.S. Embassy, as I gathered from talking with American diplomats, was that the Russians were bluffing. By the time U.S. spokesmen vaguely approached the issue of "security" of Soviet athletes, which was Moscow's main concern, the decision had been made. The sports minister, Marat Gramov, hinted broadly in April that the boycott was a distinct possibility; Tass announced it on May 8.

While the level of Reagan administration rhetoric escalated over the boycott, the tone of the Soviet media became slightly more restrained. Chernenko had felt uncomfortable with Andropov's confrontational course, as had Gromyko. He had not favored the continuation of the Geneva talks after the first Pershings arrived in West Germany, but he questioned the wisdom of a policy so starkly confrontational that it could turn into a self-fulfilling prophecy. He was suspicious of the military, especially after the armed forces chiefs had thrown their weight against him in his first bid for the top position. He knew their power; in 1967, when Brezhnev had wanted to name Ustinov defense minister, the marshals simply refused to go along with the choice, and Brezhnev had to accept Marshal Andrei Grechko instead. Brezhnev had constant difficulties with Grechko on the questions of arms control, until Brezhnev and Chernenko came up with the idea of creating a special committee on strategic weapons composed of the ministers of defense and foreign affairs and the KGB chairman. The committee was created in 1973, and from that point on, the importance of the military chiefs had been reduced—but only slightly. The military still controlled the production of weapons, and many officials in Moscow blamed the Euromissile debacle on the unrestrained production of SS-20 missiles.

Like Brezhnev, Chernenko believed that there was a rough equilibirium between the forces of the United States and those of the Soviet Union—if not in the sense of exact numerical parity or symmetry of weapons systems, at least in the sense that neither could expect to destroy the other and emerge unscathed. He felt that the concept of mutually assured destruction operated as a restraint, irrespective of the willingness of the two sides to regulate their competition through accords. Finally, he felt that the existing power balance could not be changed quickly and decisively, that the Soviet-American arms competition was fundamentally a political conflict, and that the Russians should be pragmatic about it and wait for the end of Reagan's term in the White House. Like his mentor, Chernenko believed that the overriding need was to prevent accidental direct confrontation between the two nuclear superpowers. In his writings he had been an outspoken advocate of détente, emphasizing the importance of patient reaction to what he viewed as erratic American behavior. Although he was not an intellectual, he had acquired detailed knowledge of nuclear issues and the wisdom that came with the responsibility entrusted to him, first by Brezhnev and ultimately by the party. He was baffled by the Americans, especially by Secretary of Defense Caspar Weinberger and his public assertions that the Soviet Union was ahead in certain areas of weapons research and development. He had asked his personal assistant to have the accuracy of one of Weinberger's statements checked out in detail. When he received the answer, which was negative, Chernenko quipped, "The Americans lie more than Nikita Sergeyevich [Khrushchev] used to! I think that is a sign of weakness."

From the beginning he wanted to seize the initiative in arms control, expecting that by doing so he could inflict a worldwide political and moral defeat on the United States, or at a minimum, put the Reagan administration on the defensive, forcing it to justify its policies to the American people and their allies.

The change in Moscow's policy evolved speedily. After initial conciliatory noises, Chernenko proposed in late spring to open talks on space weapons with the United States in Geneva the following September. The Russians had studied and assessed Reagan's Strategic Defense Initiative and had concluded that it was another step in America's constant modernization program. This time, however, it was a step into an entirely new field of technology. While press accounts dealt with the explanations Reagan offered for his Star Wars plan, knowledgeable Soviet officials saw another purpose. They became convinced that the Americans were working on the miniaturization of new weapons, intending, if and when they succeeded in developing them, to place them into earth orbit. What was left unsaid, but was made amply clear in convoluted ways, was that the Russians were going to do the same.

Reagan's reply to Chernenko's proposal came in late July: The United States was willing to talk about space weapons provided that the Soviet Union returned to the negotiating table to discuss strategic and intermediate-range missiles. The Russians called a press conference to brand the message as a rejection. There were going to be no talks in Geneva in September. When I talked privately about this with Viktor Komplektov, deputy foreign minister, he outlined his concerns and then started joking about some technical aspects of dealing with the Reagan administration. Suddenly he stopped, his face turned gloomy, and he said, "I'm laughing, but this is a sad moment." His thinking echoed the prevailing view in Moscow, which could be summarized in this fashion: The Americans were pushing their rearmament program on the assumption that it would teach the Russians a lesson; they did not believe that the Russians had any real fight in them. But inability to see the issue of arms control detached from the overall Soviet-American rivalry blinded U.S. officials to the fact that the Russians were equally determined to keep up with the latest arms technology and not fall behind; more significant, senior Americans seemed incapable of looking beyond their short-term objectives at the long-range effects of arms competition, which if uncontrolled, could ultimately produce a calamity.

⦗⦗⦗ 4 ⦘⦘⦘

THIS line of reasoning was not confined to private conversations with officials who knew the issues and were allowed to discuss things with me. Lost in the unfolding propaganda exchanges during the early eighties was the extraordinary fact that the issue of arms control had gradually entered Soviet public debate. This struck me with the force of a revelation when I watched Marshal Nikolai Ogarkov conducting a press conference, carried live on Soviet television, to discuss the characteristics of various Soviet and American nuclear missiles and their numbers, providing large multicolor charts to illustrate his points. In the beginning of the seventies, even senior civilian officials did not know much about their country's strategic weaponry. Ogarkov himself, during SALT I negotiations, took an American delegate aside and reproached him for discussing Soviet weapons in front of the civilian members of the Soviet delegation, which included his nominal superior, a deputy foreign minister. That sort of information, Ogarkov said, was strictly the military's business.

In the eighties, however, not only were the numbers and properties of weapons discussed but, more important, their function and purpose were debated in public. It was a scrupulously one-sided debate, in which Moscow's past positions were criticized only obliquely and all blame for the existing difficulties was assigned to the "imperialists," and specifically to the United States. And yet it represented an important evolution of the society—an evolution that seeped into the consciousness of the elite gradually as more and more people acquired an intellectual understanding of nuclear issues. I suspected that this process had been, at least in part, accelerated by the Reagan administration's policies and pronouncements in the early eighties.

In the summer of 1984, the journal *Questions of Philosophy,* which is read by the party's ideological elite, carried an article arguing that the arms-control process was essential since "only collective security is possible" today. The article touched on a far more sensitive subject to back up its assertion—it questioned the concept of "class struggle," one of the sacred tenets of Marxism-Leninism. In orthodox Marxism-Leninism, all decisions must be weighed in the context of "class struggle," which will lead to the inevitable triumph of socialism in the world. The article, however, argued that the traditional "class" approach to international affairs must be replaced by a broader, "planetary," concept because of the existence of nuclear weapons. The article was written by Georgi Shahnazarov, who served as a personal adviser to Brezhnev and was later named deputy chief of a Central Committee department. "In the nuclear age," he continued, "war can no longer be considered as a means for achieving political objectives." Shahnazarov came to the following conclusion: "In general, one of the imperatives of the nuclear age can be formulated this way—there are no political objectives that could justify the use of means that could lead to a nuclear war." A similar argument was advanced in a public lecture by Radomir Bogdanov, an arms-control expert who was also deputy director of Arbatov's think tank; by historian Ivan Frolov in several articles; and by Anatoly Gromyko and Vladimir Lomeiko, the authors of a book entitled *New Thinking in the Nuclear Age.*

One of the leading rocket experts, Boris Raushenbakh, also touched on this question in a lecture he gave to the Soviet Writers' Union. Raushenbakh, who was the first to photograph the dark side of the moon, had worked for Sergei Korolyev in developing the Soviet space program (as well as Soviet strategic rocket forces, I presume); he was a member of the Academy of Sciences and a true renaissance man with wide-ranging interests. I had met him frequently, and I knew about his growing interest in and concern about the course of our civilization. Over the years, he and his colleagues had sent signals to other planets, messages designed to test the possible existence of other civilizations. They never received a reply. He had developed a theory on the basis of that experience; I am not sure that I understood it fully but the bottom line was that he had calculated that the span of life of a technological civilization was 120 years. He believed that the absence of replies to his signals to other planets was due to this short life span—that is, that other technological civilizations had existed but had self-destructed. In all these figures and calculations the implicit concern was about the role of nuclear weapons on earth, and that was what he talked about to the writers.

And that August, before we departed for vacation in the United States, I bought a new record by the country's most popular pop singer, Alla Pugachova, who articulated doomsday sentiments in the first antinuclear song I had ever heard in Russia. It was a lyrical piece in which Earth is depicted as a crystal ball that can easily be smashed. The refrain of the song says:

> Tell us, birds, the time has come.
> Our planet is a fragile glass.
> Virgin birch trees, rivers, and fields,
> all this, from above, is more delicate than glass.
> Can it be that we shall hear
> from all sides
> the farewell sound of crunching crystal?

5

THAT August the *Post* implemented its decision to expand the size of our Moscow bureau and sent Celestine Bohlen to us. I had met her briefly the previous year in Washington. She was intelligent, energetic, attractive, and a good writer. Moreover, she had a passion for politics and soon became a major asset to the bureau. She had lived in Moscow as a child when her father, Charles Bohlen, was the American ambassador. This last fact impressed the Russians. One of them, Valentin Berezhkov, had been Stalin's translator at Tehran when Bohlen acted as Roosevelt's Russian interpreter. So Celestine had instant access to Berezhkov, who now was the editor of a journal dealing with Soviet-American relations.

I had always liked the historical grain of Berezhkov's mind and his shrewd comments. He and his wife, Lera, had gone through a traumatic experience the previous year while Valentin was still with the Soviet embassy in Washington. Under circumstances that remained unclear, their teenage son wrote a letter to President Reagan asserting that he wanted to remain in the United

States. The publicity surrounding this incident caused a major embarrassment to the parents. Upon their return to Moscow, the son, Andrei, was sent to a high school in Tallin, where he did well, and eventually he entered Moscow University to study engineering.

Celestine was followed a week later by Robert Kaiser, his wife, Hannah, and their two daughters. Bob wrote one of the best books about Russia, *Russia: The People and the Power,* * after serving as the *Post*'s correspondent in Moscow in the early seventies. He was now to take my place for a month.

While all seemed serene, unexpected events again intervened. A couple of days before I departed from Moscow, we learned that Chernenko had been hospitalized. He had gone to Kislovodsk on holiday on July 15, but the weather there suddenly turned rainy and oppressively humid and stayed like that for about ten days. It was not salubrious weather for a man suffering from emphysema. He was taken from Kislovodsk to the Crimea, where the air is dry and warm, but his health did not improve. Then he was brought back to Moscow and hospitalized.

I felt uneasy as I left Moscow on vacation. Was I going to cover yet another state funeral? So many major Soviet figures had died during my watch that I felt like an expert funeral man. In early August Khrushchev's widow, Nina Petrovna, had died and was buried next to her husband in Novodyevichi Cemetery. The announcement of her death was made by the district party committee of Leninski District and the Housing Authority No. 19 for High-rise Buildings. It appeared in an evening newspaper. The former Kremlin first lady was identified by her maiden name— Nina Petrovna Kuharchuk, party member since 1920. The name Khrushchev was again relegated to oblivion.

*New York: Atheneum, 1976.

—————————————————— ‹‹‹ **6** ››› ——————————————————

GOING back for the fourth consecutive year in Moscow was more difficult than previous returns had been. We had vacationed on the shores of Lake Labelle, north of Montreal, in a cottage belonging to Mary and Serge Schmemann of the New York *Times*. I have always loved Canada, especially northern Canada, with its wistful tranquillity, its beautiful expanses of fields, forests, and lakes. I knew the country well, as I had covered Canada for the *Post* for a year and had crisscrossed it from one end to the other during two political campaigns.

From the Schmemann cottage we would drive along a country road on starlit September evenings to a small French Canadian restaurant, where we had exquisite dinners. In the middle of nowhere there was a restaurant with an ambience and cuisine surpassing anything Moscow was able to offer! When we came down to Washington, we saw old friends living in big, comfortable houses and enjoying off-duty weekends. I envied them. We drove by our own house to check on the birch tree we had planted before going to Moscow; it had shot up high into the air, its bark white, just like the birches you see in Russia. I was already looking forward to moving back into my own home. And yet my mind was in Moscow as I tried to reestablish my sense of connection with Russia and the stories and books I planned to write. I had not intended to stay in Moscow for the fourth year, but I had agreed to do it when my editors asked me to. I suppose I would not have agreed if Russia had not fascinated me, if I had not intuitively sensed that an additional investment on my part was necessary to round out my experiences of a Kremlin transition.

It rained as we drove along a gloomy and almost featureless

road from Sheremyetevo airport into the city. At least now, for the first time during my tour, I could be more relaxed. My job had been made easier by Bohlen's arrival.

The talk of Moscow was Chernenko and his health. The business of government continued to focus almost entirely on foreign affairs. Chernenko was moving to ease relations with the United States, and Reagan, facing reelection in November, was for the first time responding to Soviet overtures.

An important event had taken place while I was away. On September 5, Ogarkov was abruptly dismissed as Red Army chief of staff and replaced by Marshal Sergei Akhromeyev.

Ogarkov was a handsome, tall officer with an impressive military record. Unlike the old marshals, he was an intellectual who spoke English and was highly articulate, a forceful figure with a broader view of the military role and a sense of the balance between military and diplomatic interests—the prototype of a modern officer. His mind was sharp and incisive and deeply steeped in the history of warfare. He had intimate knowledge of strategic weapons, having served as the ranking military man in SALT negotiations with the United States. When, on one occasion, he referred to the Peloponnesian War, he did so to make a comparison with contemporary problems of strategy, not to show off the breadth of his knowledge. He was an Andropov loyalist and was vastly popular among younger senior officers, a fact that aroused the envy of other older ranking officers. He had become dedicated to the thesis that the basis of Soviet power was the Soviet economy, and that since the economy was showing structural weaknesses, it was mandatory to take corrective steps. This was the thrust of his published articles and books in the eighties. He was a straightforward man, prepared to assert his views.

Leslie Gelb, national security correspondent for the New York *Times,* who dealt with the Russians while he was a senior arms-control official in the Carter administration, told me how surprised and impressed he was on one occasion when Ogarkov, in the presence of senior Soviet political figures, engaged in assertive banter with an American official. At one point in the fall of 1979, when Lieutenant General Edward Rowney of the American delegation kept asserting that the Soviet "Backfire" bomber was an intercontinental aircraft, Ogarkov took over the conversation. "I'll make you a deal," Ogarkov told Rowney. "I'll give you a chance to fly it. You'll fill up the tank and I will give you a parachute to bail out when the plane does not reach the United States. I'll sign the deal right here!"

I too was surprised and impressed by Ogarkov's intellectual self-confidence and skill during one of his press conferences. I had planned to ask him for his views on the Middle East situation, where the deployment of American forces in Lebanon and adjacent waters and of Soviet forces in Syria had brought the armed forces of the two superpowers into perilous proximity—within fifty to sixty miles of each other. Given the explosiveness of the situation, I asked for his views on the conduct of both countries. But Leonid Zamyatin, who opened the press conference, chose to respond to my question with a diatribe against Washington's Middle East policy. When I got the floor again, I thanked Zamyatin but said I wanted to hear Ogarkov's views. The marshal offered a different point of view. He said the proximity of the forces of the two countries was not to his liking, that restraint was necessary on both sides, and that he preferred a political solution.

It was not possible to discover what had led to Ogarkov's dismissal. His name suddenly vanished; on September 20, it was missing from the obituary of Marshal Pavel Poluboyarev, who had died at the age of eighty-three on the previous day. All I learned was that he was transferred to Minsk to assume the command of a military theater that existed largely on paper. Various rumors circulated in Moscow. One version had it that Ogarkov was too forceful a figure in the leadership and had incurred the animosity of a number of top personalities, including Ustinov. It was said that Ogarkov had become too strong, that he had come into personal conflict with the old marshals on the issue of modernization of the chain of command (the antiaircraft and strategic rocket forces were outside the chain of command), that he had urged greater investments in technology and the creation of a rapid deployment force—all these elements, plus Chernenko's personal dislike of the marshal for his support of Andropov, were cited as reasons for his dismissal. Another version had it that Ogarkov had opposed Chernenko's planned rapprochement with Reagan, that there were disagreements over resources and strategic policy, and that he was peremptorily removed while hosting a visit by the Finnish chief of staff. The Finns learned about it while attending a Kirov Ballet performance in Leningrad; during an intermission, they received a courtesy note signed by the new chief of staff, expressing the hope that they were enjoying their stay in Leningrad and the Kirov performance.

But most of us were concentrating on the leader and his physical health. The signs were not encouraging. Chernenko addressed a convention of the Writers' Union, and the press printed the text of his long speech the next day, but a friendly writer who attended the convention told me that Chernenko had read only a portion of the speech. On television, he appeared to be thinner, and his slurred speech was hard to decipher. (After the convention, a new joke surfaced. Just as during Andropov's rule the wags called the Kremlin Andropolis, now it was renamed Ulan Constantinople, Chernenko's first name being Konstantin; the word *Ulan* was Mongolian for "red" and referred in a pejorative way to the leader's slightly Mongolian features.)

On the even of his seventy-third birthday, Chernenko was awarded the Order of Lenin; it was presented to him by Ustinov, who made no mention of the birthday but whose speech was full of praise that left Chernenko visibily touched. Chernenko was the only Soviet leader of his generation who had not served in World War II; he had attended a high party school in Moscow from 1943 to 1945 and had done his military service in the early thirties, serving as a private with the border guards in Central Asia. However much Soviet propaganda tried to fictionalize his service as that of a fearless horseback rider fighting Moslem "counterrevolutionaries," Chernenko was regarded by the officers corps with some contempt—a problem for a man who, in addition to being general secretary and president, was commander in chief of the armed forces by virtue of his position as chief of the Defense Council. So Ustinov's lavish praise was important to him, and when he replied to the speech his excitement made him an even poorer orator than he usually was.

His foreign policy pronouncements became more conciliatory. He clearly wanted to engage the Reagan administration in a dialogue. In mid-September, Gromyko had flown to the United Nations and subsequently held talks with Secretary of State George P. Shultz and the president. Then, in mid-October, Chernenko apparently decided to make a direct appeal to the Americans, to force the issue of nuclear arms into the U.S. presidential debate, to make sure—in the words of an adviser to Democratic presidential candidate Walter F. Mondale—that "his question gets asked" during the Reagan-Mondale television debates. I had suspected that the Russians would try to inject their argument into the U.S. presidential debate in one form or another.

⟨⟨⟨ 7 ⟩⟩⟩

CHERNENKO'S decision led to an invitation for me to interview him in his Kremlin office.

In early October, A. M. Rosenthal, the executive editor of the New York *Times,* arrived in Moscow to visit his son, who was a correspondent in the Associated Press bureau. Abe Rosenthal was a legend among foreign correspondents. He had won a Pulitzer Prize for his coverage of Poland and had done a superb job in India. I had a long conversation with him over dinner at the Schmemann apartment, and my impression was that he was indeed in Moscow to see his son, who was carrying on the family's journalistic tradition with distinction. But Abe was also an exceptionally competitive man, and I suspected that he had approached the Soviet ambassador in Washington, Anatoly Dobrynin, about an interview with Chernenko. What strengthened my suspicions was the fact that the *Times* bureau had scheduled a lavish reception for Rosenthal at the National Hotel, where he would meet several senior officials. If the Russians wanted to inject themselves into the American presidential campaign, Rosenthal offered an ideal opportunity.

I also suspected, however, that Rosenthal might have asked for a general interview, which would mean that he could raise unpleasant questions about domestic politics, Jewish emigration, and Sakharov. My own competitive instinct—fueled by the fierce rivalry between the *Post* and the *Times*—was aroused. The *Post,* I thought, could provide Chernenko with an alternative by submitting to him several questions dealing only with the issues Moscow was most interested in—Soviet-American relations and the star-crossed enterprise of arms control. I sent a message to Karen DeYoung, who was my foreign editor at the time, outlining my suspicions and proposing to send three questions to Chernenko, on the off chance that he would respond to them. There was nothing to be lost. I had previously written letters to Gromyko and other top leaders asking for interviews, but it had never entered my mind to ask to be received by the general secretary. A tsar does not receive resident correspondents; if he wants to talk, he invites the very top news executives or publishers. Only Khrushchev had received a resident correspondent for a conversation, and that was the veteran UPI bureau chief Henry Shapiro, who had spent nearly four decades in Moscow.

Karen endorsed my plan and I worked furiously to translate the questions into Russian and make sure that they reached either Vadim Pechenev or Viktor Pribitkov, Chernenko's two key personal assistants. This was the most difficult and complicated task, and it required the use of all the high-level contacts I could reach.

On October 16, a few days after Rosenthal left Moscow for New York without having seen Chernenko, the phone rang shortly before ten in the morning. As usual, I had worked late the night before and was still asleep. The caller was Alexander Sazonov of the Foreign Ministry. The general secretary, he said, had the answers to my questions and would receive me in his office at eleven o'clock. Could I be ready in thirty minutes? I am not sure exactly what I mumbled into the receiver, except that I asked Sazonov, incredulously, whether I had understood correctly that Chernenko would receive me for a conversation. "That's correct," he said. "Will you be ready in thirty minutes?"

Seldom had I woken up so quickly. While I took a cold shower, my wife helped get my clothes together. My mind was immobilized by the news. I tried to formulate additional questions but could not even remember the written ones I had submitted. I armed myself with a small voice-activated tape recorder, making sure that its batteries were working, and a pad and pen. Fully dressed, I sat near our living-room window. I noticed the first snow flurries of the winter.

A black government sedan arrived at the appointed hour and Sazonov got out of it and motioned for me to come down. The driver proceeded slowly. "We have time," Sazonov said. He was also excited; he had never been in the inner sanctum of Kremlin power. I liked Sazonov. He was an intelligent, soft-spoken man with a strong sense of humor and an almost complete lack of pretense. We had been together on several Foreign Ministry trips, and I always found him to be a decent and reasonable spokesman who argued his government's case well, using logic rather than emotion. Of course he strove to put across the official point of view; but it was also apparent to me that he never deliberately misled me. His balding dome made him look older than his age, as did his seriousness about his professional duties. In his off-hours, it seemed to me, he was a fine husband, concerned father, and generally good company. I enjoyed sparring verbally with him, but this was hardly the occasion. So I excused myself for not wanting to talk as we drove slowly down Kalinin Prospect and toward the Borovitsky Gate.

A plainclothesman halted us at the checkpoint and took the front seat. As we drove through the public part of the Kremlin, hundreds of foreign tourists were strolling around, taking photographs of the four churches and the tsar's bell and tsar's cannon (the last two offered an insight into the Russian character—both were so massive that they had never been used). Then we swung through a huge iron gate into the closed section of the Kremlin, located immediately behind the wall facing Red Square. Chernenko's office was inside the Old Senate Building, which houses the Council of Ministers. All the buildings in this section of the Kremlin are guarded by KGB soldiers in uniform. We entered the Senate building and checked our coats. Nobody asked for any identification cards—the presence of our escort was enough. Then we took the elevator to the third floor and went down the long corridor. "Where does the Politburo hold its meetings?" I asked the escort, a tall and muscular man in his late thirties who was wearing a gray business suit. He acted as if he had not heard the question, but as we turned a corner to the left at the end of the long corridor, he said, "Here," pointing at the doors. We passed another impressive door and came to another turn of the corridor, which swung to the right. A middle-aged man in the uniform of a KGB colonel stood in front of another nine- or ten-foot-high door. He merely nodded to the escort, opened the door, and we were in a huge antechamber of Chernenko's office.

We had arrived early. I saw Pechenev and Pribitkov and about ten other secretaries, all male, going about their work. There were no typewriters or any other office equipment in the room. Everybody was moving about very quietly, the way people move in a church. It was not entirely clear to me what they were doing, except that they were frequently on the phone. But they spoke so softly that I could not hear what they were saying. Waiting in the room were Andrei Alexandrov-Agentov, the intelligent and affable foreign policy adviser to all general secretaries since Brezhnev; Leonid Zamyatin; and Viktor Sukhadrev, the veteran Kremlin translator, who had no peers as a simultaneous Russian-English interpreter. I was surprised to see Sukhadrev because I had heard that he had been appointed ambassador to New Zealand. But from our conversation that morning I understood that he had no enthusiasm for the tranquillity of Wellington, despite the lofty position he was offered. (Subsequently Sukhadrev went to Ireland as ambassador.) I asked Alexandrov about a few bilateral issues, but my mind was elsewhere; I was still trying to formulate questions. Alexandrov warned me that he did not know how long I would stay with Chernenko because Syrian president Hafez Assad, who had arrived the previous day on an official visit, would come to see the leader at noon.

Meanwhile, Pechenev had disappeared into Chernenko's office and then reemerged to call in Alexandrov. At 10:55 Pechenev opened the doors and we were all led in. As we entered, Chernenko stood up from his desk, which was located behind a long conference table, and waited for me to approach him. He was about five feet eight; his complexion was ruddy and his handshake firm—he squeezed my hand like a steelworker. He did not shake hands with the others, nor did he pay any attention to them —treating them as if they were part of a chorus required on such occasions. "A visitor coming with the first snow is a good omen," he said, pointing at the snow flurries outside his window. Laughing broadly, he added, "According to an old Russian proverb, it means good luck."

An official photographer showed up from an adjacent room and began taking pictures. I noticed that the walls were covered with light yellow silk, while the moldings and trims were painted with gold leaf. Four huge windows, about twelve feet high, were partly covered by white silk curtains. I moved toward one window and discovered that they faced a carefully manicured inner courtyard. "Not that way," Chernenko said, taking my arm and leading me toward a picture of Lenin, the only picture in the room. "This picture is *na pamyat* (for remembrance)," he said, guiding me beneath it to his right. I looked at Chernenko carefully, for I had read in a newspaper the opinion of a physician who asserted that people with Chernenko's medical problem should have a bluish tinge around their lips; but there was none. He was a stocky, barrel-chested man with a broad face and thick white hair. He wore a dark blue business suit, a white shirt, and a blue tie with light blue stripes. I had the impression that, apart from his shallow breathing, he was physically strong. I wanted to feel him out, so I said, "Konstantin Ustinovich, I am not a head of state, I'm a journalist. I should be to your left." And I stepped behind him, took him by his shoulders and moved him to my right. He seemed pleased. His body was strong and muscular, the body of the Siberian farmer that he had been.

As we posed for the photographer, he said that he *really* wanted to resume arms talks with the United States. President Reagan merely talked about it but had done nothing so far to show that *he* really was interested. Nothing, he repeated for emphasis. The Americans talk about developing defensive systems, he proceeded, while the photographer clicked the camera, but at the same time budget figures show that they are engaged in a major buildup of offensive nuclear systems, which will last for the rest of this century. He mentioned several new U.S. strategic weapons systems. What was he to make of it all? He had been thinking about it—thinking why two great countries are not able to do something to secure peace. He thought about it at night, he said, and later, during the formal part of the interview, he returned to this theme, saying he was sure that Mr. Reagan or any other master of the White House undoubtedly had the same thoughts at night. "Only when you reach this office do you begin to understand certain things," he said, pointing at his desk. It was neat, with a stack of official papers and folders lined up on its left side, a fountain pen, and a cut-glass container filled with regular yellow pencils, all sharpened to perfection.

He looked at the photographer, then invited me to sit at the long table, which was covered with green baize. In front of him was a sheet of paper with my last name written on it in large letters. I placed my tiny tape recorder on the table and turned it on. He did not seem to notice. But suddenly he turned very formal, as though reciting from a prepared script. His breathing became heavy and his face assumed a stony expression; suddenly he looked like an ugly man. He wanted to see me personally to present his answers to my questions, he said. But he was doing so also "at the behest of my comrades"—a pointed indication that the answers represented an official viewpoint of the Soviet leadership. He turned now to Sukhadrev and awaited translation of his remarks. Alexandrov said there was no need for a translation, since I speak Russian. "I've noticed that," Chernenko said. "How come?" I explained to him that I had served in Moscow for a long time and that I was a Serb by background. He looked perplexed, mumbling to himself, "A Serb . . . a Serb," and I could see that he was searching his mind as he played with the pencil next to his clean pad. I felt slightly embarrassed by the long silence. Suddenly his face lit up, for he had finally located at least the general ethnic group for the Serbs. "That means you are a Slav?" he asked, not quite sure that he was correct. My affirmative reply pleased and relaxed him. "That's good," he said and the way he emphasized the word "good" seemed to confer a degree of acceptance that surprised me.

"Sukhadrev is without a job now," he said, laughing. Everybody joined in. He handed me the text of his written replies. Zamyatin reminded him that an English translation of the text was enclosed.

"You see, full service," Chernenko added, laughing again. The text was typed on very fine paper and bore his signature at the end. I could not take time to read the answers then and there, a fact that complicated the interview, but I decided to proceed with questions based on his remarks during the photographing session.

Chernenko outlined his arguments quietly; he seemed both deliberate and considerate, steering clear of ideological issues. His delivery was far better than in his public speeches, and he employed normal Russian phrases, in stark contrast to the stilted formality of his books and articles. His breathing was much less short and shallow than his wheeze in formal settings, and I thought that this might reflect the fact that, having reached the peak of power very late in life, he found the public and ceremonial part of the job alien and taxing.

He conducted the entire conversation without consulting his aides or any notes. But I was surprised how inadequate the staff preparation for the session was. Nobody, for instance, had objected to my placing the tape recorder on the table. After the session, while we were chatting in the antechamber, I heard Zamyatin ask the translator whether he had taken complete notes of the conversation. Sukhadrev replied, "Mr. Doder had the whole thing taped." Zamyatin looked surprised. Then he turned to me and said, "You can use the material. We will give you twenty-four hours before Tass releases the text of the interview. Is that fine with you?"

From the moment we sat down behind the baize-covered table, I had exactly twenty minutes with the Soviet leader. When the session ended and Chernenko moved over toward his desk, Alexandrov asked, "I assume we can count on the Washington *Post* to print the full text of the general secretary's remarks?"

It was an awkward moment for me. I was not in a position to make that commitment. I had not discussed any aspect of the interview in advance, either with my editors or with Soviet officials. In fact, the entire thing came up on such short notice that I could not—because of the time difference and the absence of direct dialing—get in touch with my editors in Washington. So I had to tell the leader of the other superpower that I could not guarantee that the full text of his remarks would be carried by the paper, although I was fairly sure, I added, that it would. Chernenko looked puzzled. What I said seemed to be outside the realm of his experience. Trying to reassure him, I added that I could guarantee that all his points would be printed as part of a long story I intended to write. That seemed to please him. "The longer the better." He laughed heartily.

While Alexandrov and Zamyatin were trying to end the chitchat, I asked for a signed photograph. A few days later Chernenko sent me an autographed color photograph of our meeting.

"Is the Washington *Post* an influential newspaper?" he said just before he escorted me out of the office.

I sat down in the antechamber to run quickly through my notes and make sure that I had properly grasped the essence of what Chernenko had said. It was clear to me that he had called me in to dramatize his message and achieve the greatest possible impact in the United States. And the message itself was interesting: He offered to resume arms-control talks at the first sign of a "genuine" American interest to sit at the negotiating table. He singled out several issues that he said would demonstrate such genuine interest, including ratification by the United States of already signed test-ban treaties. He expressed concern that a change in Reagan's pronouncement on nuclear arms was a "tactical" move before the forthcoming presidential elections. The Kremlin, he said, was not waiting for the outcome of the elections; it was prepared to deal with any American president who wanted to join him as a "partner in this sacred human task—for peace."

Sazonov and I were escorted back to the cloakroom by the same security man. I decided to take the stairs down, instead of the elevator, so that I could look the place over. "We can find our way out of here," I told the security man. "You don't really have to walk down with us." He laughed. "You know," he said firmly, "it's pretty hard to get into this building but sometimes it is even harder to get out of it."

The black sedan was waiting outside the entrance as we left the classical green-domed Senate building. We drove out through the Borovitsky Gate, the security man jumping out at the checkpoint and waving a friendly good-bye. Sazonov and I talked as we drove to my home. When I got pictures from Chernenko, he asked, could I give him one *na pamyat*? There was already a half an inch of snow on the streets.

It occurred to me later that Chernenko had looked remarkably strong and healthy that Tuesday morning, more so than on formal occasions earlier that fall. I wondered whether this was a reason for the complete suddenness of my interview, whether his closest aides, seeing that the boss was strong and fit that day, had decided to call me in on short notice. I have no answer to that question. On that Tuesday, I was elated, for I had an exclusive interview with the Kremlin tsar, news I knew would go around the world.

We transcribed the interview that afternoon. I played the tape for Bohlen, and also for my friends Malek of *Al Ahram* and Stanic of the Tanjug news agency. I owe a great debt of gratitude to Malek, who advised me to write down my personal impressions of Chernenko immediately and to recall all the details about the feel of the place. In the long run, that was more significant than the printed text of the interview. And it was Stanic who suggested that I phone the American ambassador, Arthur Hartman; neither Bohlen nor I had thought about doing so.

Since my story on Andropov's death, my relations with the U.S. Embassy had been strained; the smiles and friendly gestures were fewer. The embassy had produced a report suggesting that I had been tipped off by an important Soviet figure about the leader's death and that I subsequently went out to look for signs of emergency. This reaction was understandable, but I felt that I had lost access to what had been an oasis of understanding and friendliness. I obstinately sought to ignore this painful problem. It was necessary to keep the door open, even if it was not wide open. Now I had a chance to show courtesy toward the ambassador by giving him an advance summary of Chernenko's interview.

I phoned Hartman's residence and told his personal aide that I had something of importance to tell the ambassador. Hartman was taking a walk and was not available. I called the aide again a little later and told him that we had an important story, but since Hartman was not available, Bohlen would tell him details of the story later that evening, since she had been invited to a dinner by the Hartmans. He said that would be fine. For some reason, after I hung up, I felt that it was not proper to have someone else inform the ambassador about this important story, for he could interpret it as a slight. So I called the residence again and asked to speak to the Italian majordomo, Clemente, whom I knew well. I told Clemente that I had something important to tell the ambassador. Within a minute Art was on the phone. I told him about the interview and gave him Chernenko's main points.

The *Post* gave excellent display to the interview, carrying Chernenko's remarks in full. In the transmission process, however, a portion of his sentence asserting unequivocally that an improvement in Soviet-American relations was possible was inadvertently dropped from the text. I had included that remark in the main story—in fact the whole thrust of the report reflected that sentiment of Chernenko's—yet the specific phrase was missing from the official text. Early next morning, my phone kept ringing as Tass tried to clarify the omission. Indeed, the omission prompted the official news agency to release the text of the interview earlier than Zamyatin had said they would. Shortly after nine in the morning, Sazonov appeared at my apartment. I was baffled. Bohlen and I had worked into the early morning and were tired, too tired to make a final check of the text that had been transmitted earlier. In their Byzantine fashion, the Russians assumed that the omission was made in Washington by "anti-détente forces" in our newsroom—how else could one explain that the "key" sentence was missing? I tried to disabuse Sazonov of any such notion.

When we reached my office and checked the telex copies, I discovered to my great embarrassment that the mistake had indeed been made at our end. I immediately reached my home office by telex, but all the editors had left for the day. Sazonov mused about an official protest. "The key sentence!" he kept repeating. It occurred to me that the way out of the impasse was to write a story acknowledging that an omission had been made and then repeating the entire paragraph, including the "key" sentence. We would be making the point again, which meant that Chernenko would be getting additional mileage from our mistake. There was nothing else one could do. I asked Sazonov to sell this idea to Zamyatin and Alexandrov. He departed and phoned me shortly afterward. The compromise was accepted.

The interview had considerable impact, and various news organizations wanted to talk with me. But I decided against any interviews, letting Chernenko's remarks speak for themselves. That seemed to me a responsible step; it was certainly something the Russians appreciated. Apart from the propaganda aspect, the interview contained a message to the Reagan administration: Despite earlier vows not to return to the Geneva talks so long as Pershing Two and cruise missiles remained on European soil, Moscow was now abandoning that position and was eager to return to the negotiating table. Chernenko had been looking for a way to let this be known—and to do so with his dignity intact.

Chernenko's offer did not elicit an immediate positive reply from Washington that October. Eventually Chernenko took the American proposals of the previous summer—which Moscow had then denounced as a rejection of its proposal for space weapons talks—and turned them into his own. Reagan had no choice but to accept, for he was bringing the Russians back to the negotiating table on his own terms—he wanted to discuss curbs on strategic weapons and not just space arms. On November 22, an announcement was made simultaneously in Moscow and Washington that Gromyko and Shultz would meet in Geneva the following January to negotiate a resumption of talks about nuclear and space weapons. In Russia, the press play the announcement got was in inverse proportion to its significance—a one-paragraph story on page 5 of *Izvestia*. But Chernenko had managed to jettison the confrontational line of his predecessor and restore Brezhnev's old approach toward the United States.

⟨⟨ 8 ⟩⟩

APART from making a major personal imprint on foreign policy, Chernenko had done little beyond acting as a caretaker for a new generation of leaders. Many of his public activities were ceremonial duties, such as awarding decorations or giving pep talks, which he found increasingly difficult to deliver. When I analyzed what passed for his domestic initiatives, it became clear that all of them were rehashings of earlier schemes and none addressed the fundamental problems of the country—an excessively rigid centralized system, absence of initiative and motivation, and a sclerotic economy.*

Perhaps the most hilarious illustration of the poverty of ideas of the Chernenko leadership was given by one of his main sup-

*Continued disagreements within the elite surfaced in a public furor over an article in the journal *Questions of History* written by one of the leading advocates of reform, Yevgeny Ambartsumov, who called for more private enterprise in the economy; the author cited Lenin's New Economic Policy of 1921, which produced a brief revival of private enterprise to repair the major ravages of Bolshevism. Soon Ambartsumov and the journal were castigated publicly by the journal *Kommunist*, the main theoretical organ of the Central Committee. At a special meeting convened later in 1984, the editors of *Questions of History* were reported to have admitted "the justice of the criticism."

porters, Premier Nikolai Tikhonov. In late October Tikhonov announced a grandiose new program of land reclamation. Earlier in the year, Gorbachev had criticized such costly ventures (in a speech in Smolensk on June 25). The whole enterprise had the taste of stale medicine. Russian friends told me to read an article in the journal *Tekhnika Molodyozhi,* Number 11, published in 1979. I compared the article, written by Ivan Borodavchenko, with Tikhonov's speech; it turned out that the premier's speech writers had not only chosen a stale idea but had also lifted large chunks of material from the article, some almost word for word.

The October Plenum of the Central Committee endorsed the land-reclamation scheme as a novelty. What else did the plenum do? Chernenko made no changes in the Politburo or the Secretariat, and his reluctance to add new blood suggested that the balance of competing interests, personalities, and generations was set, if not altogether to his liking, at least in part to his advantage. The only man he seemed to be promoting was Vladimir Dolgikh, a young and vigorous nonvoting Politburo member who was once the leader of Chernenko's native Krasnoyarsk province. There was some talk in party circles that Dolgikh would be brought into the Politburo at the next plenum, but as winter set in and Chernenko's health worsened, then improved, then worsened again, the leader seemed more and more remote from the affairs of state.

As we approached the end of 1984, differences between Chernenko's coalition-against-change and Andropov's men became more evident. The December issue of the party's ideological journal, *Kommunist,* carried an article by Chernenko in which he insisted that any changes in the economy must follow the laws of socialism, a phrase he defined in the old dogmatic terms. In the process of change, he said, "the role of the party not only will not decline, but will increase."

Meanwhile Gorbachev, as the party's second secretary, was the keynote speaker at the December 10 ideological conference. But *Pravda* and other newspapers carried only portions of his speech, excerpts suggesting that he was in complete agreement with Chernenko's line. A week later the entire speech was published as a pamphlet with limited circulation. The parts that had not been published in the press revealed Gorbachev's true position. He argued that the economic slowdown started in "the seventies and the beginning of the eighties" and that it was to be explained "not only by the coincidence of a number of unfavorable factors but also by the fact that the need for change in some aspects of production relationships was not discovered in good time." The full text showed that Gorbachev remained very much the heir of Andropov; he described the state of the Soviet economy as "complex and dramatic" and talked about the need to use "such economic levers as price, cost, profit, credit, and certain others." He complained about the country's conservatism and inertia and attempts by unnamed exponents of Communist orthodoxy "to squeeze new phenomena into the Procrustean bed of moribund conceptions." What the country needed at this stage, he said, was "deep changes in the economy and the entire society." That was the only way to increase living standards, "the only way that socialism can advance to a new level of maturity."

In December, the balance of forces in the Politburo was sharply altered with the death of Marshal Dmitri Ustinov, who had been ill since late October. In mid-November we learned that he had suffered a stroke that had left him incapacitated. When he died, on December 20, the Soviet leadership lost the man who had been its "kingmaker" ever since the death of Mikhail Suslov in January 1982. Because of his personal prestige and experience, Ustinov had exerted a steadying influence during the last two Kremlin transitions. Now that role would fall on Gromyko, the senior and most experienced member of the Politburo, whose career spanned all Soviet leaders since Stalin.

Ironically, the death of Ustinov was announced by Gorbachev in Edinburgh. Gorbachev was on an official visit to Britain that had turned out to be a personal success for him; Prime Minister Margaret Thatcher, a strong Reagan supporter, said in a BBC interview after meeting the Soviet official: "I like Mr. Gorbachev. He is a man we can do business with." Moreover, Mrs. Thatcher voiced some fresh reservations about Reagan's Star Wars program. The death of Ustinov was a serious matter for Gorbachev, who arrived in Britain as crown prince of the Kremlin and who immediately cut his visit short and returned to Moscow to attend the deliberations on Ustinov's successor.

Chernenko now had the chance to appoint a young defense minister. There was some talk in Moscow that Grigori Romanov might be given the job if the leaders decided that it should go to a civilian, or that it would be given to one of the younger marshals if it was felt that the military should recapture the key cabinet position. Ultimately the decision was Chernenko's—and he did not take advantage of the opportunity. Instead he opted for a man of his own age, Marshal Sergei Sokolov, a colorless World War II front-line tank commander and a Brezhnev protégé who had been a deputy defense minister for seventeen years.

I observed that Chernenko was visibly shaken as he stood guard in the Hall of Columns behind the coffin of Ustinov. He was not present on the Lenin Mausoleum for the funeral. The weather in Moscow was frigid—it was minus 24 degrees centigrade at noon, and the windchill factor brought the temperature close to minus 35—not the kind of weather for people with lung problems. Gromyko, in effect, presided over the funeral; he stood there like a statue while all other top officials in the lineup were stamping their feet to keep out the chill; at seventy-five, he seemed a durable fixture in a world of transient Kremlin politicans.

—————————— ≪ **9** ≫ ——————————

WE celebrated the New Year at the Praga Restaurant with a group of friends from the American embassy. Such an evening of dancing and drinking provides one with a picture gallery of Soviet faces from which to interpret the country's mood: I can still see a tall man with a broad face and thinning blond hair who sent us a bottle of champagne when he heard us speak English; another bottle came from a neighboring table, a collective gesture of good-will. It always surprised me to discover, time and again, a deep well of good feeling about America at all levels of Soviet society, including the humblest. Whenever I drove my car from Moscow to Finland I tried to give rides to hitchhikers; since 1968 I had driven that road innumerable times and had many chances to talk with men and women, young and old—farmers, drifters, workers, all sorts of people. In addition to being curious, they invariably displayed sympathy toward the United States, even when they criticized our policies. What also struck me was the degree to which people outside the intellectual world of Moscow believed the Soviet government's version of events, even when the event —such as the invasion of Afghanistan—was explained away by grotesquely inadequate arguments that defied common sense. But the country lived a life of its own, its collective memory burdened by evocations of the past; even the capital was out of sync with America—the style and tone of its New Year's celebrations re-called an earlier era, almost an earlier century. The highlight of television programming on January 1, the first day of 1985, was a performance of Franz Lehar's *The Merry Widow.*

Most American correspondents went to Geneva to cover the Shultz-Gromyko meeting on January 7. Here was a chance, I thought, to put an end to the seemingly perpetual cycle of acrimony and tension. Geneva was almost as cold as Moscow, and we hung around the lobby of the Intercontinental Hotel during two days of news blackout. The talks ended successfully: The two superpowers agreed to resume substantive negotiations on strategic, medium-range, and space weapons. Having won its point as to the scope of the talks, Moscow could claim a diplomatic success and emphasize a new worry, Reagan's SDI program, while ignoring the fact that the Russians had returned to the bargaining table even though the United States had not removed its Pershing and cruise missiles from Europe as Andropov had demanded.

But the openly confrontational phase in Soviet-American relations—the most hostile in two decades—was over. Chernenko had made concessions, but he had brought his country back into dialogue with the United States. It was the most important achievement of his short rule.

CHAPTER NINE

GORBACHEV TRIUMPHANT

The Changing of the Kremlin Guard

THE FIRST TWO MONTHS OF **1985** were the most difficult and risky part of Mikhail Gorbachev's rise to supreme power. Power was within his reach, yet he had to dance up to it gingerly and without displaying a thirst for it. The old guard looked upon him with some suspicion, because of his youth and also because of his close association with Andropov. The entire country had seen Gorbachev's display of emotion during the formal obsequies for his mentor. He was the only member of the Politburo who joined the Andropov family in the Hall of Columns on the second day of the period of mourning. This bond carried obvious political benefits. He had inherited the institutional support of Andropov's coalition—the KGB, the officers corps, government technocrats, experts in numerous institutes, and a miscellany of intellectual and artistic figures, educational leaders, younger party members and industrial managers in the provinces. Yet the party bureaucracy was at the heart of the Soviet establishment, and it was dominated by the Brezhnevites.

In retrospect, December 1984 was surely thè turning point. Gorbachev's intelligence, poise, and composure during the visit to Britain commanded the attention of the elite and others in the country. He had accepted an element of risk by coming within the focus of the Western media, which guaranteed that any mistake would be not only publicized but also magnified. But he had impressed all those who met him, with both his ability and his personality.* In Britain, his success was accentuated by that of his wife—from the moment she stepped out of the plane at Heathrow, in a black fur-trimmed cossack coat that set off her reddish-tinted hair, her hosts and the British press were enthusiastic about her natural charm, unconventional beauty, intelligence, and engaging smile. Although a grandmother, she was trim and elegant, defying the stereotype that embarrasses many Soviet women—that of the good-natured, fat grandmother with gold teeth, felt boots, and a bright scarf tied under her chin. Together they stood in stark contrast to the dreary image of old guard officials; they were a couple who represented the new Soviet generation and who talked and behaved in a way the West could understand. Gorbachev's performance was more than his entrance onto the world stage; it also had a major impact at home, since it was shown on Soviet television. Andropov had brought him for the first time to the focus of the national consciousness in the summer of 1983. But now Gorbachev was on his own. My Soviet friends took great pride in the fact that a Soviet official could compete with the

*Over drinks at the Savoy Hotel, Gorbachev was introduced to John Harvey-Jones, chairman of the ICI, who wears his hair unfashionably long for the head of one of Britain's largest corporations. "How on earth does a man like you come to be chairman of ICI?" Gorbachev asked. "Parkinson's Law!" replied Harvey-Jones. "If you are referring to C. Northcote Parkinson, I've got news for you. He lives in Moscow now," Gorbachev replied.

American president in what has become Reagan's own trademark —showmanship, smooth public relations, charm, and grace.

Ustinov's death during Gorbachev's sojourn abroad had underscored the physical feebleness of the old guard and the pressing need to rejuvenate the leadership, a need that became even more urgent at the end of the month, when Chernenko's health began to weaken seriously.

Gorbachev had no illusions about the difficulty of his quest for the top leadership position. The party had already balked at naming him general secretary a year earlier, when they thwarted Andropov's designs and turned to Chernenko. But apart from this disappointment, his upward progression had been steady and swift. He had managed to maintain a precarious balance between his roles as Chernenko's deputy and as the heir of Andropov's legacy. Although his speeches stressed different themes, he had been a loyal number-two man. His major speech that December had given an indication of his impatience with the old guard when he complained about "inertia of thinking" that "as a rule generates inertia in practical matters." The party, he said, needed "inquiry and creativity, sensitivity to new phenomena and processes, and the decisive elimination of formalism, red tape, and idle talk." He cultivated the image of a man of strong convictions who believed in public service. Of course he wanted power, a political ally of his told me at the time, but he also had a sense of mission. Another official close to him quoted Gorbachev as saying to friends, "Can anyone believe that there is a person who would *want* to become general secretary at this time?" The remark may have reflected his acute appreciation of the country's problems—the fragility of the economy, the anticipated difficulties of national reconstruction, the imperative necessity to enter the computer age and to maintain strategic parity with the United States. The task was gargantuan.

With Chernenko hospitalized, the onset of 1985 provided an opportunity for politicking, building alliances and making deals, but we could not perceive any of this. Gorbachev avoided all publicity. When Senator Gary Hart of Colorado arrived in Moscow in January 1985 and specifically asked to meet him, Gorbachev politely declined, although he and Hart exchanged letters. "He had too much exposure with the British visit," one of his associates told me. "He doesn't need any more right now."

The first thing I heard upon returning from the Shultz-Gromyko talks in Geneva on January 10 was whispers that Chernenko was ill. He had last been seen in public on December 27. On December 28, Tass had announced a Warsaw Pact summit in Bulgaria for January 15, but now East European journalists said that the summit was called off. At the Foreign Ministry press club a few days later, an official confirmed this. The same evening, at a diplomatic reception, another official told me that Chernenko had been hospitalized for a respiratory ailment.

Throughout January and February a dome of smog hung over the bitterly cold city, making breathing difficult for a healthy person, let alone for a seventy-three-year-old man suffering from emphysema. I felt as if there was not enough oxygen in the air I was breathing. During such a deep-freeze period, life slowed down in general. The visible part of the Soviet political iceberg was foreign affairs, to the virtual exclusion of domestic issues. Looking in from the outside, it seemed at times that the Russians had achieved a fully automated domestic policy, that the country was indeed on "automatic pilot."

At that point a curious, and to many Russian officials disturbing, thing happened. With Chernenko fighting for his life, his staff began acting in his name. A stream of pronouncements attributed to the leader began to appear. On January 15, the press published Chernenko's foreword to the Polish edition of his book. Then came another foreword, addressed to French readers; a letter to a high-school senior in Calgary, Alberta; two letters to Scandinavian peace groups; and an "interview" with the Cable News Network (written replies to questions, handed to CNN's Stuart Loory by the

Foreign Ministry spokesman; the answers were unsigned). All of this was pure propaganda made up of trivialities and platitudes.*

Later, after Chernenko's death, a senior Kremlin official told me that many persons were concerned about the fact that "the boys around him played games with his speeches and articles. This should not be done to a leader. They put words into his mouth that were alien to him. In this last period you had all those forewords to his books, all that stuff, which was the work of scoundrels. Nobody could stop it, because they were acting on behalf of the leader, and you could not reach him because he was ill. And even if you reached him, you would not want to raise such unpleasant things with a sick man."

The country at that point was in effect an empire without an emperor. For more than one month the country's decision-making authority was in the hands of Chernenko's personal assistants Vadim Pechenev and Viktor Pribitkov, who were relatively young and relatively inexperienced men without any standing in the Kremlin establishment beyond the fact that they enjoyed the tsar's complete trust.†

The drift was almost palpable. In late January, the authorities censored a joint Soviet-Indian production, a documentary about Jawaharlal Nehru. The version screened on Soviet television eliminated the footage showing Nikita Khrushchev's meetings with Nehru and the late Soviet leader's triumphal tour of India. This was after Chernenko sanctioned the readmission of Vyacheslav Molotov, Stalin's deputy, to the Communist Party at the age of ninety-three. (Khrushchev had expelled Molotov from his party functions and the party itself). Then, a couple of weeks later,

---

*Two senior officials with direct access to the general secretary told me later that Chernenko's aides acted without his knowledge during the last weeks of his life; he was too ill to be consulted, they said.

†Both Pechenev and Pribitkov were promptly dismissed from their jobs upon Chernenko's death. Pechenev, who was appointed an editor of the journal *Politicheskoe Samoobrazovanie,* shortly afterward was even forced to resign his seat in the Supreme Soviet of the Russian Federation.

the authorities reversed themselves and rescreened the Nehru documentary, including the Khrushchev footage. And yet, in late January, censors approved the appearance of Stalin's picture on the cover of a major journal, albeit together with Roosevelt and Churchill.*

Also in late January rumors began to circulate throughout the city that Chernenko was dying and that either Viktor Grishin or Grigori Romanov was his designated successor.

Romanov, who held the requisite positions in the Politburo and the Secretariat, was a man of unquestioned administrative ability and ideological orthodoxy. Several Western ambassadors who had conversations with him while he was still the boss of Leningrad described him as a forceful figure with an unusually dogmatic mind. A Finnish politician who had seen him during a visit to Helsinki the previous autumn described him as crude and boorish and said he got roaring drunk during a state dinner. Yet his reputation in Russia was high. He was regarded as efficient and ruthless, and he had long-standing ties with the military-industrial complex. At sixty, he was relatively young—only six years older than Gorbachev. To add height to his five-foot-six frame he wore high heels. In Leningrad he had ruled like a potentate from the time of Catherine the Great, whose china he requisitioned from the Hermitage Museum for his daughter's wedding, a fact that became public knowledge after some of the irreplaceable china was broken in the revelry. He openly maintained a liaison with Ludmila Syenchina, a well-known pop singer who was thirty years his junior.

Romanov's stop-Gorbachev gambit involved supporting the candidacy of Grishin as yet another transitional figure. Grishin, the boss of Moscow, was known for his sartorial elegance, including a penchant for expensive Italian shoes. He also had a reputa-

*The picture, commemorating the fortieth anniversary of the Big Three meeting at Yalta, appeared on the cover of *Novoe Vremya*, February 1, 1985.

tion for corruption in running his city. In terms of tenure, he was the senior person on the Politburo. I could not determine to what extent Romanov and Grishin worked together. Kremlin insiders said later that Romanov's strategy was to create a deadlock in which he would become the compromise choice between Gorbachev and Grishin.

Like Gorbachev, Romanov kept himself out of the public eye. But we saw unmistakable signs of Grishin's bid in February and March. Gorbachev partisans were worried. "If he does not make it this time around," one source told me at the time, "his chances to do so in the future would rapidly diminish." Gorbachev himself decided his presence in Moscow was mandatory and canceled plans to represent the Kremlin at the congress of the French Communists in February and to meet with President Mitterrand.

A routine election campaign for the Supreme Soviet of the Russian Federation was under way, but apart from the speeches, the country's political life seemed at a standstill. In a one-party state and with only one slate of candidates, the election amounted to a mere civic exercise. Only Grishin made two speeches that February; all other Politburo members confined themselves to one mandatory campaign speech, in which they extolled Chernenko's leadership. Gorbachev went so far as to call Chernenko "the soul" of the Politburo.

<<< **2** >>>

WHEN my new foreign editor, Michael Getler, arrived in Moscow, it was difficult to arrange appointments with senior officials. Those we managed to see were prepared to talk only about such safe subjects as arms control and the forthcoming celebrations of the fortieth anniversary of the end of World War II. People were leery about discussing the Kremlin transition, but it was clear that the end of Chernenko's rule was near. The Foreign Ministry spokesman Vladimir Lomeiko assured Getler that Chernenko was on "winter vacation" outside Moscow. Other officials said privately that the leader was recuperating and that he occasionally went to the Kremlin to attend to business. A Politburo communiqué made specific mention of his presence at one regular meeting in February—the statement said he spoke about "agricultural questions." The previous day, however, Viktor Afanasiyev, editor in chief of *Pravda,* had said in a live television interview with Italian State Television that the leader was ill. A few days later Afanasiyev again made news by conceding to a group of visiting Japanese editors that Gorbachev's position could be described as that of "second general secretary." I had never heard such a description before. It was hard to evaluate what was happening behind the Kremlin walls, but the tensions were deep and intense.*

As if responding to renewed rumors about their leader's illness, Chernenko partisans passed the word that the leader had recovered and that he would meet the visiting Greek prime minister Andreas Papandreou. But the meeting was canceled at the last moment, and rumors flourished.

I had lunch during that period with Kemal Siddique, the astute ambassador of Singapore. "At this point, Chernenko's health is a sideshow," he said. "The main issue is the generational change,

---

*Although the world press quoted Afanasiyev as saying that Gorbachev was the party's "second general secretary," I learned two days later that he had never in fact specifically said so. Hiroshi Imai, my former neighbor who was a member of the Japanese delegation, told me that Afanasiyev had been describing Gorbachev's role in the Politburo. With Chernenko hospitalized, Gorbachev, as second secretary, chaired Politburo meetings. Imai, the only fluent Russian speaker in the Japanese group, asked Afanasiyev: "Could we then say that Gorbachev was in effect the party's second general secretary?" According to Imai, Afanasiyev replied with a shrug, "Well, if you want to." But, like virtually all other correspondents, I had already quoted Afanasiyev two days earlier as saying that Gorbachev was the party's "second general secretary," and I felt reluctant to make a correction. Here was a prime example of the congenital inability of correspondents to correct mistakes, which in effect creates "facts."

the process of self-renewal, which is something new for the Soviets, and they don't know how to deal with it. The appointment of Marshal Sergei Sokolov as defense minister shows that the current leadership is not yet ready to deal with it, but the process already has a momentum of its own, which cannot be arrested."

We were approaching February 22, the day of his election speech and the deadline when Chernenko would have to make a public appearance or face a serious erosion of his authority. The frozen vapor veil had dispersed and the sun hung low all day long in the southern skies, just above the rooftops. I drove out the government road toward the suburb of Uspenskoe several times to monitor the traffic of black limousines to and from the dacha enclaves and to look for signs of unusual activity. On cold winter days when the skies were clear and the sun hovered over the treetops, I came close to enjoying the Russian countryside the way my friends enjoyed it, and I thought I could understand the yearning of Russians living in foreign lands for this landscape. Halfway to Uspenskoe, on the left side, is Stalin's dacha, known as Dalynaya, which is well maintained but remains unoccupied. A high brick wall surrounds the compound, set in a forest of birch and pine. It seems as if Stalin's ghost resides there, for no one else ever uses this country home. I had passed by the dacha many times and each time I thought of the dictator's fearful grip on the nation, whose effects lingered into the present day.

Chernenko failed to appear at his Kremlin electoral rally. Grishin, who was presiding, told the nation that the leader stayed home "on the doctor's recommendation" but that he had asked him to convey his greetings to the voters of his district and the people of Moscow. For Soviet audiences, Grishin's remarks meant that Chernenko was seriously ill. To diplomats they signaled that another Kremlin transition was definitely under way.

Two days later, escorted by Grishin, a visibly frail Chernenko appeared in public to cast his ballot in the election. I saw him on television that evening. He looked pathetically weak, his eyes unfocused, his face blank. Earlier in the day the Foreign Ministry had alerted Western correspondents as to. the time they could observe Gorbachev casting his ballot at the polling station inside the ancient House of Architects. This in itself was unusual. In the past, we had been alerted only about the time and place of the leader's appearance. On that brilliantly sunny winter's day, Gorbachev took along with him his wife, Raisa, their daughter, Irina, a physician, and their granddaughter, Oksana. He seemed totally self-confident as Oksana dropped her grandfather's ballot into the box. "One more time," the delighted photographers shouted. But Gorbachev declined. "Even I have only one vote," he said, smiling.

Soviet television's special election coverage had no footage of Gorbachev or other Politburo members voting—only the macabre shots of Chernenko voting, accompanied by Grishin. The leader appeared to be suffering acute physical pain and was by all indications not fully aware of what was going on. The apparent purpose of this sad exercise was to present Grishin as Chernenko's anointed heir. The city's two evening papers published only the pictures of Chernenko and Tikhonov casting their ballots.

It was difficult to sort out such confusing signals. Senior officials dealing with foreign policy and security issues appeared concerned about the weakening of Moscow's position prior to the resumption of the Geneva talks. I sensed growing impatience with Chernenko. As one official put it derisively, the Kremlin leader "took it into his head to get sick [*umudrilsya zabolyet*] at such an inconvenient moment." The Foreign Ministry kept putting out proposals and debated U.S. arms-control positions, but these diversions hardly obscured the paralysis of the government.

—————————————— ‹‹‹ **3** ››› ——————————————

IN this mood of swirling confusion, Gromyko was the main steadying force. His role in the smooth transfer of power to a new generation was crucial. His hair was a bit grayer and a slight stoop was more noticeable, but he seemed as fit and alert as ever, a skillful diplomat now at the apex of his extraordinary career. He was not merely the specialist, the technician content to let others capture the glory and the power, but the most senior member of the leadership. His knowledge of the world and its leaders had earlier made him indispensable. His staying power, itself a tribute to his diplomatic finesse, had now become a major asset. Both the party and people knew him better than any other member of the leadership. One could not overestimate his prestige in the party. He had sat at Stalin's elbow at the Yalta and Potsdam summits in 1945, when Chernenko was a student at a party school in Moscow, Gorbachev was attending high school in Stavropol Krai, Premier Tikhonov was working as an engineer at a factory in Dnepropetrovsk, and Reagan, at the other end of the world, was pursuing his Hollywood career. Cordell Hull was secretary of state when Stalin appointed Gromyko, then thirty-four, ambassador to the United States.

All this was brought to public attention in the first months of 1985 by a new feature film, *Victory,* which detailed Russia's struggle against Nazi Germany. Scenes in the film showed Stalin and other key Kremlin officials making fateful decisions, and Gromyko was there, played by an actor who looked remarkably like the young and dapper Gromyko. In crucial meetings Stalin invariably turned to the young Gromyko for advice, or at least for his opinion. In fact the film somewhat enlarged Gromyko's role at the time— it seemed more like the role he played in his seventies.

Gromyko's image in the West is different. His dour, implacable exterior became the personification of Soviet diplomacy in the forties, when he was ambassador to the United States and then chief U.N. delegate. He became deputy foreign minister in 1948, then went to London for a two-year tour as ambassador, finally returning to the Stalinesque skyscraper that houses the Foreign Ministry. Since 1957, he had been its master. The early stages of his career rested not only on his competence but also on the fact that he had no political ambitions that could create jealousies and suspicions. He endured the whims of changing masters, including their sometimes humiliating jokes. He appeared unperturbed when Khrushchev once declared that his foreign minister was the sort of man who, if ordered to sit on a block of ice, would do so without question until ordered off (a remark that was made abroad and was not reported in the Soviet Union).

But that was a long time ago. His image at home was that of an intelligent, tough, and shrewd politician committed to a hard-line defense of Soviet interests. He rarely held press conferences, but when he did they were spectacular performances, carried live on Soviet television. He worked without notes but missed nothing, making no mistakes and never asking aides for facts and figures. Russians admired him for such performances; his style was that of a university professor gently and patiently lecturing to students and fielding their questions. In fact he had taught at Moscow's Institute of Economics before he turned to diplomacy in 1939. Few people knew that he was a trained economist with a doctorate in political economy.* His hard-line image at home—and in the West —was somewhat studied, presumably to protect himself from orthodox critics. Perhaps the most valuable part of *Breaking with Moscow* by Arkady Shevchenko, a Soviet diplomat who defected to the West, was his well-documented portrayal of Gromyko as

---

*His dissertation was entitled "The Role of Middle East Resources on the World's Strategic Balance."

a man of moderation within the Soviet context. Gromyko had risen to the peak of Kremlin authority through perseverance and ability, a career diplomat without a power base who eventually became head of state. He was always careful to assess the mood of his own country and the personalities who ran it. He had cultivated Brezhnev before the latter became general secretary and he had also established a close relationship with the younger man from Stavropol who was soon to become his boss.

But there was more to it. He acutely felt that generational conflict was the central rift in Soviet life in the eighties, a conflict that involved, as much as anything else, differing habits of mind. This was an enduring feature of Russian life, which had always been divided on generational lines over the social, political, and economic advantages or disadvantages of gradualism as opposed to quick reform. In Turgenev's masterpiece *Fathers and Sons,* Bazarov, the young medical student, who represents cynical and nihilist "sons," relentlessly criticizes the older generation for its failure to modernize the country, describing them as "reformers . . . who never accomplish anything." The poetry-loving "father," Nikolai Petrovich, is baffled by such criticism, for he has been kind to his peasant serfs, has "set up a model farm so that all over the province I am known as a *radical."* The novel did more than dramatize a new stage in the struggle against autocracy; it revealed a deep emotional division on the question of reform and change, a conflict that was to persist long after the cataclysmic end of tsardom. A person close to Gromyko told me that the veteran foreign minister had reflected on the generational conflict in the historical context and had reached the conclusion that the contemporary chasm between the generations was equally great, that the mind-set of the old guard was too conservative and too inflexible to permit needed reforms, and that younger men had to be given the chance to revitalize the system. But for all his wisdom, Gromyko reflected to some extent the attitudes of the old guard, who wanted Russia kept apart from contemporary Europe, isolated not only as a consequence of the Communist system they had imposed on it but also by the traditional sensibilities they sought to preserve among their people.

Yet when the moment came, Gromyko would side with the new generation. His role was crucial not only during the first two months of the year, when the infighting was at its most intensive, but, more important, at the decisive moments in March prior to and just after Chernenko's death. Gromyko's detractors would later charge—in private—that he did so for his own reasons, to gain the presidency and ensure for himself a burial ground in Red Square. He was seventy-six, an age when men often think about such things. But such criticism seems to me somewhat unfair. It is possible that Gromyko was anticipating the inevitable transfer of power to new people and decided to play with the winning crowd. But there was another, deeper reason. Gromyko knew how much damage the Kremlin had incurred because of weakness at the top during the protracted transition, and he was aware of the changes in the world, as well as in his own country. His son, Anatoly, and Vladimir Lomeiko, the foreign ministry spokesman, consulted the veteran foreign minister as they put together their book, *New Thinking in the Nuclear Age,* and it reflects Gromyko's own views. The book argues for a generally more cooperative approach in international relations in the shadow of the nuclear bomb; but it points out that even if the superpowers manage to avoid a nuclear holocaust, they may squander their resources on building new and more powerful weapons. This in turn would prevent them from seeking solutions to the growing and dangerous chasm between the developed northern nations and the poorer countries of the Southern Hemisphere, and to ecological mismanagement. What is required, the authors say, is "new thinking" that would allow East and West to compete in finding solutions to the problems of their societies, and to cooperate in the handling of global issues. By implication, the authors call for a "new thinking" in Soviet domestic affairs and a reassessment of domestic priorities.

The weather changed abruptly in early March and we had a series of welcome balmy spring days. Grishin again appeared with Chernenko at a Kremlin ceremony, where the dying Kremlin leader received a group of electoral officials. That was his last public function. There had been talk earlier that Gorbachev had been named to lead a parliamentary delegation on a visit to the United States, but he remained in Moscow, and Vladimir Shcherbitsky, the Ukrainian leader, took his place. Since Shcherbitsky was a member of the old guard, his departure for America furthered Gorbachev's interests; on the other hand, Vitali Vorotnikov, a member of Gorbachev's team, had departed for a visit to Yugoslavia.

Although his presence was required in Moscow, Gorbachev did make a trip he had made every year since he moved to Moscow. On March 2, his fifty-fourth birthday, he and his family flew to the Stavropol region to the village of Privolnoe, in the Red Guard district, where his mother, Maria Panteleyevna, lived, along with other Gorbachev relatives. After a festive family dinner, he returned the same evening to Moscow. The next day at a diplomatic reception I asked a highly placed official about the rumors that Grishin, or perhaps Romanov, would emerge victorious in the succession struggle. He scoffed at the idea. "These are persons with narrow experience. We are going to win, I'm sure." The "we" plainly referred to the Gorbachev camp; but, he added cautiously, "with such things there is uncertainty until the last moment."

On March 6, Chernenko's wife, Anna, hosted an annual reception for the women in Moscow's diplomatic community. Although her husband was gravely ill, she had to follow the implacable Kremlin protocol. Western participants described her as gracious and intelligent. She ushered them into the reception hall of the Kremlin guest house on Lenin Hills, where pink-draped tables were laden with crab and lobster, blini and caviar, fruit, wines, cognac, and vodka. After the banquet the women moved into the ballroom, where, despite the absence of their men, they took to the dance floor. Anna Chernenko joined in. Gorbachev's wife, Raisa, and Viktoria Brezhnev, the widow of a leader from the past, were among the Kremlin wives, but Andropov's widow, Tatyana, was not. Guests noted that Raisa Gorbachev remained on the sidelines and seemed careful not to upstage the more senior women. A few months earlier, on the London visit, she had captivated the gossip columnists with her chic wardrobe, appearing at a diplomatic reception in a cream satin two-piece dress, gold lamé sandals with chain straps, and pearl drop earrings; on this occasion she wore a dark suit.

Again the next day, the eve of International Women's Day, Chernenko failed to appear at the traditional Women's Day gala at the Bolshoi Theater.

The prospect of another Red Square state funeral—the third in less than three years—and another old tsar in the Kremlin—the fourth in three years—seemed to confound a weary nation. The shadow of death had been hanging over the Kremlin ever since Brezhnev was hospitalized in March 1982, never fully to recover his physical and mental vigor. For three years the office of general secretary had been occupied by dying men.

Officials now whispered that Chernenko was dying. Ironically, his public image had undergone a sharp change during the past months. His nationally televised appearances were painful to watch; the screen always showed him moving with difficulty, his eyes glazed, clearly in pain, yet struggling to perform his ceremonial duties, as was was expected of him. He no longer seemed a man who wanted to be general secretary. And the people began to feel sorry for him. They saw an old and sick man, bravely soldiering on in his post with a patriot's pride in the dignity of his country. In contrast to the widespread rejection that met him upon his election, he was accepted by the country in death, which finally came on March 10.

Bohlen and I had been working around the clock during the last few days. The change in the temperature, from extreme cold to springlike warmth, finally caught up with me and I came down with high temperature the day Chernenko died. Around three in the morning on March 11, I was awakened by a phone call from Washington. Ginny Hamill and Al Horne, my colleagues on the foreign desk of the *Post,* informed me that a member of the Soviet delegation led by Ukrainian leader Shcherbitsky had told a State Department escort in San Francisco that Chernenko had died. That was confirmed, they said, by a senior American diplomat in Geneva, where Vice President Bush was visiting. I rushed to the office, shaking from high fever yet wanting to do whatever possible at that late an hour. Moscow Radio, following the now established pattern, was playing classical music, Glinka and Rachmaninoff. I phoned Bohlen, and when she reached the office she reported that while driving over she felt for the first time that she was being followed by security agents. I also phoned my friend Stanic of Tanjug to inquire about Vorotnikov, the Politburo member who was visiting Yugoslavia. He checked his ticker and reported that Vorotnikov had interrupted his visit and returned to Moscow by air during the night, presumably to join leadership deliberations on the succession. Shcherbitsky also cut short his American journey, but his plane touched down in Moscow long after the succession decision was made.

The transition was unexpectedly smooth and swift, smoother and swifter than the two previous ones. Chernenko's death was announced on the morning of March 12 after about twelve hours of funeral dirges broadcast by radio and television. Four hours after the announcement, Gorbachev was elected general secretary of the Soviet Communist Party at an extraordinary session of the Central Committee. It was Gromyko who proposed his candidacy, in a speech designed to reassure the old guard. "Comrades," he said, looking at Gorbachev, "this man has a nice smile but he has got iron teeth." This remark, relayed to me by a Soviet politician present at the meeting and reported in the *Post,* was eliminated from the official text of Gromyko's remarks. (It was immediately picked up in the West. During the Geneva summit, a reporter shouted at Gorbachev during a photo opportunity, "Do you have iron teeth?" The Soviet leader replied, "No, fortunately I have all my own teeth.") Gromyko's speech was not carried in full in the press but was published almost a week later in the form of a pamphlet. It was a vote of confidence nobody in the hall could match—from the man who had come to symbolize in the eyes of the party the continuity of more than forty years of Soviet history. Gromyko was unusually eloquent and emotional in his speech, praising the youngest member of the leadership as an exceptionally gifted man. He added that he was in a position "to see it better than some other comrades," an indication that Gorbachev's election had not been as smooth as appeared on the surface. Another indication of old guard doubts about Gorbachev was Gromyko's repeated assertion that during Chernenko's illness Gorbachev was in fact running the Politburo and that he had performed the job "spectacularly"—in other words, that Gorbachev had been tested and had passed. A few months after his accession, Gorbachev loyalists would privately say that they believed Gromyko's role in the first three months of 1985—the crucial transition period —was the greatest service he had rendered to the Soviet state.

Dinmukhamed Kunaev, the Kazakh leader and a staunch Brezhnevite, also rose to endorse Gorbachev. "You should not think I am saying this because I'm speaking second, but I want to tell you that the eight hundred thousand Communists of Kazakhstan want this man," Kunaev said, pointing at Gorbachev.

The change of leadership came on the eve of Soviet-American talks in Geneva, and Gorbachev, in his acceptance speech, went out of his way to reassure the Reagan administration that Moscow's attitude remained unchanged and that the talks would open on schedule.

Earlier in the day, police had sealed off the center of Moscow in preparation for a state funeral. Some troops were also deployed. But the mood on that sunny March day was relaxed. When Gorbachev's election was announced, people cheered and congratulated one another. The transition was, at last, over. The new leader was, more than anything else, a man bred in the Communist organization of post-Stalin Russia. Nurtured in the Komsomol, the Stavropol party organization, and finally in the Secretariat in Moscow, he seemed a man who drew sustenance from the solidity of the party structure and the regularity of procedures. Communist rhetoric had been his native tongue for almost three decades. All this was reassuring to the old guard when it finally yielded the reins of power. I saw him as a classic true believer in the Soviet system, as any relatively young man would be after making the journey from a provincial office to the inner sanctum of the Kremlin in record time. But although he had absorbed much of the traditional party code, he was soon to show himself a different man.

Almost instantly Moscow wags came up with a new joke: Who supports Gorbachev in the Politburo? Nobody—he can walk all by himself.

But that was only a joke. Gorbachev in fact needed the support of many men and women, not only to run the country but to move it forward. The ruling establishment he inherited—even after Andropov's housecleaning—was old: The average age of the Politburo members was sixty-seven, of the top Cabinet officials, sixty-eight, of the Secretariat and also of the entire Central Committee, sixty-six. The system he inherited was almost perfectly designed to alienate men of ability and critical intelligence and deposit the business of government into the corrupt hands of a conservative bureaucracy. The great challenge Gorbachev faced was to harness all available talent and to fashion a new administration that could respond to the political realities of the end of the twentieth century and to the needs of the economy in a high-technology era.

CHAPTER TEN

A NEW BEGINNING

NOBODY KNEW QUITE WHAT TO EXPECT from the new leader. Mikhail Sergeyevich Gorbachev had been seen in the official lineups on Lenin Mausoleum and at various ceremonies, where he cut a dim figure as a younger man deferring to his seniors in settings dominated by the rigid rituals of Kremlin power. Except for his youth, there was very little that distinguished him from other Politburo members. But shortly after he assumed power, the country was in for a surprise.

He was five foot nine, stocky but not fat, and bald, with a red birthmark clearly visible on the front part of the dome, and graying sideburns that made him look older than his fifty-four years. He had fine dark brown eyes and wore steel-rimmed glasses. He was gentle in manner, smiled readily, and delivered off-the-cuff remarks in a soft voice with a distinct southern Russian intonation. But his actions soon revealed the toughness, adroitness, and intuition of a master, and he immediately seized power as if there was a natural despot in his soul. He emerged from the grayness of the old Kremlin leadership as a colorful and forceful figure, reminding me and my Soviet friends of Nikita Khrushchev, but a better-educated and more sophisticated version of Khrushchev. After a series of embarrassingly feeble old men at the top during the preceding four years, the sight of a youthful and energetic Kremlin chief symbolized the end of the interregnum and the uncertainties it bred. This fact in itself appeared to lift the country's spirits.

The transformation of Gorbachev from the youthful but still uncertain figure of his Politburo years into a confident and powerful national leader was so rapid and seemingly so effortless that it confounded his most ardent boosters. From the start, he appeared to be a man in a hurry who wanted the country to put behind it the traumatic years of leadership transition. Plunging into his job with zest after taking charge on March 12, 1985, he exuded an image of action and purpose wherever he went, urging the people to roll up their sleeves and remake the Soviet state. His activism, his instinct for maneuvering, and above all his speech-making ability came across clearly on national television. He was the first Soviet leader to be an instant television personality, bringing with him a casual tone, a mistrust of verbosity and sloganeering, a self-deprecating wit, and a sense of personal warmth. He seemed embarrassed by the banality of official rhetoric, and made it plain that his mind was not conventional even though it had been shaped in the bosom of the party. Like Khrushchev, Gorbachev was a surprising example of spontaneity, apparently a man who who lacked a doctrinaire belief in the sanctity of tradition. "What we need are revolutionary changes," he declared. His approach resembled Khrushchev's brand of populism. Gorbachev's populism, more than anything else, shaped his image. Temperamentally, he was a doer, more comfortable with empirical decisions based on common sense than with ideological prevarications about distant Communist goals. Already in April he spent two days in a Moscow neighborhood, visiting a factory, a hospital, a school, supermarkets, housing blocks, and even the apartment of a younger worker, for tea. In a televised speech he made remarks that echoed the average citizen's complaints about food shortages, shoddy consumer goods, and abysmally inadequate services. By May he was beginning to hit his stride. During a visit to Leningrad he made it clear that he was prepared to make difficult decisions, not empty promises. "One mustn't toy with the people," he said on May 17 *("S narodom nelzya zaigrivat")*. The next day, as he was bantering with a jostling crowd in the street, he asked for their support to "move the country forward." A woman in the crowd shouted, "Just get close to the people, and we'll not let you down." Hemmed in by the crowd, Gorbachev shot back, laughing, "Can I be any closer?"

Gorbachev was undoubtedly keenly aware of the importance of first impressions. Everything he did in his first months seemed designed to revive optimism and the impulse for change in the ruling establishment. The period of inactivity and transition had come to an end and he and his colleagues were ushering in a new period of action and forward movement. He seemed to see things in bright shades and to act with firm certitude. Was he a skilled politician? An accomplished public-relations man? Was he acting? Or was he, as I saw him during his initial period in office, a man driven by ambition and determination to harness the country's potential and carry out a national reconstruction?

The public aspects of his swift accession were unprecedented. A few hours after the announcement of Chernenko's death, Moscow Radio reported that Gorbachev had been elected general secretary. The next day the front pages of the newspapers featured his photograph and placed Chernenko's photograph and obituary on page 2. On each such occasion in the past, the dead leader's picture was featured on the front page, set off by thick black borders. Gorbachev also changed the Byzantine ritual of state funerals: For the first time army officers carried the dead leader's body on his final journey, while the new leader and other Politburo members walked behind them. These were immediate public demonstrations of a new Kremlin style.

What he did privately, however, was more significant. He called in the top newspaper editors and told them he did not want to be quoted endlessly and each day as a fountain of wisdom. "You can quote Marx and Lenin if you have to have quotations," he told one senior editor, emphasizing that he disliked empty phrases and patriotic exhortations. Next, he instructed senior officials of the Central Committee's propaganda department that he did not want image-makers to invent a heroic role for him in Stavropol during its Nazi occupation. "Let's not turn Stavropol into another Malaya Zemlya," he said, referring to a massive distortion by Brezhnev image-makers of the history of World War II, which made a marginal battle at Malaya Zemlya in which Brezhnev took part into a "turning point" of the war. Gorbachev also quietly ordered mandatory medical checkups for all senior officials, an unsettling move not only for scores of top figures who were past the retirement age but also for a far larger number of their associates and subordinates, who compose the vast web of patronage ties. He seemed to want to let it be known at the highest level that he needed healthy and vigorous people to run the country; in effect, that was a prelude to a major purge of the party bureaucracy.

I watched Gorbachev in Saint George's Hall during his inauguration, when he was presented to the world as the Kremlin's new master. He was accompanied by Gromyko, seventy-six, Tikhonov, eighty, Kuznetsov, eighty-three, and Ponomarev, eighty. The older men stood valiantly for more than an hour, shaking hands with various foreign potentates. I stayed after all other foreign visitors had departed and watched the leaders leaving the hall. Except for Gorbachev, all had difficulties walking; Tikhonov, his upper body twisting backward, his legs wobbly, had to be helped along by a security man to make sure that the premier did not collapse on the floor.

On that occasion I also witnessed the persistent rigidity of the vertical line of authority. The new leader, accompanied by Gromyko, Tikhonov, and Ponomarev, entered Saint George's Hall before the reception started, and Gorbachev invited Tikhonov and Gromyko—but not Ponomarev, an alternate member of the Politburo—to join him for a rest on a sofa in an alcove. All of them had just come from the long and elaborate funeral ceremonies, which were capped by a Red Square military parade they had watched standing atop Lenin Mausoleum. So I observed Ponomarev, a Communist Party member since 1919 who already held an important position in Moscow when Gorbachev was only a year old, standing like a schoolboy at the alcove's edge, furtively looking at his new boss in hopes of being invited to join him. But the invitation never came.

Gorbachev's new style was felt later that afternoon by foreign heads of government who met him privately. He only occasionally glanced at the documents lying before him and spoke freely with Mitterrand, Thatcher, and Kohl. While stressing to each the importance of bilateral relations, he criticized West European politicians for following America's lead without even a degree of prudent reservations. Gorbachev was harsher with Kohl than with the others, at one point chiding him for standing to attention before Reagan. When Bush returned to Washington, he privately described the new Soviet leader as an "impressive idea salesman."

The general Western impression of Gorbachev was positive. He appeared a smart and decisive man. And this was also the impression he left on the Soviet establishment. Soon the whole bureaucracy whispered about the new tsar's firmness of purpose and the fact that he did not mince words. He virtually threw out of his office the health minister, Sergei Burenkov, whom he had called in to inquire about the problem of alcoholism and how to deal with it. When Burenkov embarked on a long-winded bureaucratic summary of the problem, Gorbachev interrupted him. "Comrade Burenkov, we did not ask you to come here and tell us that alcoholism is bad. We know that. You'd better come later and tell us what we can do about it."

Of course there was a good deal of calculated posturing in all this. A new leader must show his appetite for exercising power from the first day so that the word will filter quietly through the ranks of party officials that he means business. Gorbachev was not feared like his mentor Andropov, whose stern and rigorous presence in the Kremlin had commanded instant respect and obedience. Gorbachev was a politician, determined to take charge and prepared to exploit situations and people while projecting imperturbable confidence in his own powers.

The purposes of these maneuvers became clear later in the year.

Gorbachev's most immediate and overriding objective was to restore the elite's confidence, which had sharply eroded during Brezhnev's last years, when the leadership had been unable to muster any sense of real urgency in the face of an obvious economic decline and growing signs of social disintegration, reflected in rampant alcoholism, increasing crime and corruption, and a decline in life expectancy for men. Brezhnev had failed to induce the elite to think in terms of challenge—either from within, arising from the discontent of the people, or from without, as American technological advances pushed Moscow into new and unexplored reaches of strategic competition. The party bureaucracy wallowed in cynicism, holding on to power for its own sake. Brezhnev alone was not to blame; but his illnesses, his personality and style, reinforced a curious uncertainty of purpose. In contrast, Gorbachev's actions from the very first day were designed to revive the elite's sense of optimism and direction, of moving toward a clearly stated goal—to improve the economy and raise the living standards of the Soviet people.

Another, larger objective for the new leader was to find a way of mobilizing broad support among the people for his policy of

275

national reconstruction. Already during Andropov's rule, the reformist elements had reached the conclusion that a national reconstruction could not be carried out by the party, the army, and the KGB—the three mainstays of the system—and that any meaningful changes required a much wider participation. As Andropov saw it, the government had to change the population's attitudes and traditional ways of doing things, to patiently explain its policies and generate a sense of social responsibility in a people whose social conduct vacillated between anarchy and blind obedience. His illness prevented Andropov from continuing his planned series of meetings with different elements of the society. Shortly after his death, a senior Central Committee figure characterized Andropov's approach as having produced "a significant change in the country's psychological mood," adding, "We all know that even the best policies of the leadership can produce no results if they are not supported from below."*

Gorbachev took up Andropov's approach with a greater vigor than his mentor could muster. The Russian word that best describes Gorbachev's first year in office is *perestroyka*. It means "reconstruction" or "rebuilding." Gorbachev himself has given the word a broader social connotation—it means, he has said, not only a "profound transformation" of the economy and "the entire system of social relations" but also "a major transformation of the mind." Indeed, as events unfolded, the word came to sum up a range of themes—openness, honesty, the need for more personal initiative, less talk, and more action.

From the start he sought to impress upon the country that changes were inevitable and were dictated by economic necessity. Why was he insisting on moving the country forward? He posed the rhetorical question with an affable smile as he spoke on May 17 at the Smolny Institute, which served as Lenin's headquar-

*Vadim Zagladin, "Continuity, Innovation, Dynamism," *Novoe Vremya,* February 24, 1984.

ters during the 1917 Bolshevik revolution. Why not enjoy life, resting and lying at anchor? No, comrades, he said, his face turning grave. "This is not the choice. We do *not* have such a choice." Just to maintain the existing living standards and defense needs, he continued, the country needed a minimal growth rate of 4 percent a year, instead of the current 3 percent.

Some of the figures he cited revealed inefficiency and waste the scope of which we could only suspect before. Certain power plants were so inefficient that, if their efficiency were raised not to Western levels but merely to the national Soviet average, the country would save twenty-two million tons of oil per year. "The idling time of power sets due to failure of equipment at atomic and thermal power stations leads to a loss in our country each year of fifteen thousand million kilowatt hours," he said. This amounted to the annual production of Dneprogas, one of the largest power plants in Russia. The computer industry was making "unsatisfactory" computers, he said, adding, "Let's be realistic about it." The country was wasting its resources on a massive scale—nearly one fourth of all drinking water, for instance, was lost outright because of faulty faucets. The people "simply do not care," he said. "We are swimming in resources but that wealth has corrupted us [*razv-ratilo nas*]." And what happens when you try to fix up your apartment? he asked the audience. "You will have to go to the *shabashnik* [a private contractor who operates semilegally]. And he is going to steal materials from a state company."

In speech after speech he hammered at the central theme of his program. The Soviet Union, he said, must bring its economy up to Western levels of efficiency and quality. To do that, to pull the country from its doldrums, there must be a thoroughgoing change in the way the economy is run, and the "very psychology of economic activity" must be altered. A novel notion that Khrushchev had raised in a boastful and nebulous way was formulated more succinctly by Gorbachev: Not slogans and propaganda but the quality of life in the Soviet Union ultimately constituted the image the country presented to the world. The challenge of raising living standards while maintaining adequate defenses—he put it in that order—would determine "the fate of socialism in the world."

He also flashed some sharp teeth in his Smolny speech. Since "we have no other option," he said, the adjustment will have to be made. Then, looking at the Leningrad party *aktiv,* a few thousand men and women who wield power in the region, he warned, "Those who do not intend to adjust and who are an obstacle to solving these new tasks must simply get out of the way." He paused and added for emphasis, "Get out of the way. Don't be a hindrance."

For the first time I noticed that audiences were hanging on a political leader's every word. Partly this was due to the hopeful prospects he sketched as he traveled to Leningrad, and to Kiev and Dnepropetrovsk, the Brezhnevite strongholds in the Ukraine. But apart from the allure of his message, there was Gorbachev's oratorical skill. He spoke without notes, smoothly and confidently. He engaged his audiences by making occasional self-deprecating jokes and by directing questions at them. And he benefited from a popular fatigue with a Kremlin of old men who clung to scraps of paper for the simplest announcement and who reduced governance to ritual and tiresome rhetoric.

And yet, at least initially, the people were cautious. They were not dancing in the streets. They had just begun to believe Andropov when Chernenko succeeded him, throwing a wet blanket on their raised hopes and expectations. The new leader's words were inspiring, but it could not automatically be assumed that they foreshadowed a real change in people's lives.

There was a good deal I could learn by keeping my eyes and ears open on the streets of Moscow. Women in queues waiting to buy daily necessities were grumbling as usual that spring, but there was also a note of optimism, a hope that *they* (the word always referred to the authorities) would finally do something about consumer goods and services. The average person wanted to believe in Gorbachev's pledges. Moreover, the age factor seemed to be a key ingredient in popular attitudes. The new leader was the youngest among the top leaders, the twenty-six men who belonged to the Politburo and the Secretariat, and he could well be at the helm at the start of the next millennium. To members of the younger generations Gorbachev's instincts seemed acutely contemporary. He appeared to reflect the disquietude of the postwar generation—he had been too young himself to take part in the war—and their longings for a better life. He even talked about "psychology," a word and discipline that had been taboo only a couple of decades earlier. In public speeches he denounced the *"pokazukha,"* or phony projects and Potemkin villages created to impress outsiders.

The queue is something more than the sum of the weary and irritable people it draws together; it is an entity per se, with its own logic and rules. Sentiments expressed at this level are an important indicator of the prevailing mood, for if there is a place to exercise a modicum of free speech, to let off steam in front of a crowd, the queue is this place—an impersonal forum where a common disgust at the hardships of daily existence justifies almost any criticism, any observation one might fling in a sardonic or humorous vein. And comments in the queues suggested that the people had extended the credit of their confidence to the young new leader.

The presence of a healthy younger man in the Kremlin also came as a relief to us correspondents. I finally felt free to travel extensively. For a long time—ever since Brezhnev was hospitalized in early 1982, and again under Andropov and Chernenko—I had been manacled to my Moscow office most of the time by the possibility of a major development in the Kremlin. As an onlooker analyzing the tragedy and comedy of Soviet life, I had not wanted to run the risk of missing a major transition development. I did manage to relax during brief trips to the West and occasional forays inside the Soviet Union during those years—I went to Buryatia, the Baltic Republics, the Ukraine, Siberia, Azerbaijan—but these were all very quick trips, and each took place shortly after a transition, when I needed to get out of the capital's oppressively tense atmosphere and to rest and sleep out of the telephone's reach. Now I could make more extensive trips around the country; this was the time to gauge its mood. So I traveled that spring and summer to Volgograd (formerly Stalingrad), to Crimea, Tadzhikistan, Kirgizia, and Uzbekistan.* In the course of these trips I again sensed Russia's vast spaces, the variety of her provinces and nationalities, the contradictions implicit in the endurance of Old Russia, barely covered by the new Communist veneer. The vastness and the complexity of the land made me more aware than I had been in Moscow of the difficulty of Gorbachev's mission.

I also went to Stavropol, Gorbachev's native region, to try to gain some understanding of the mind and instincts of the man who became the seventh undisputed Kremlin leader in Soviet history. This trip was not easy to arrange. The authorities assumed—correctly, I should add—that one of my objectives was to visit the village of Privolnoe, where Gorbachev was born in 1931, where he grew up, and where his mother and other relatives were still living. I also wanted to spend some time in the city of Stavropol, in which Gorbachev had spent his entire political career until he moved to Moscow in November 1978. My trip was canceled at the last moment, allegedly because there were no hotel rooms available, something the desk clerk at the Hotel Stavropol instantly denied when we reached her by phone. The permission was granted a week later, after I assured my contacts that I would not

*Volgograd provided an interesting insight into the new breed of local chieftains Gorbachev had placed in power. Vladimir Kalashnikov, Volgograd's first secretary, used to work for Gorbachev in Stavropol. Kalashnikov displayed what appeared to me a very high level of pragmatism by turning the fortieth anniversary of VE Day into a useful enterprise for Volgograd. Instead of building another magnificent monument, he asked the leaders of all Soviet republics to build and equip their own national restaurants in his new city.

make an attempt to visit Gorbachev's family village. "He"—and the way one official emphasized the word left no doubt as to whom he was talking about—"he doesn't want all sorts of people to go to the collective farm there and bother people."

2

GORBACHEV was born in the Stavropol backcountry, a land of kerosene lamps and outhouses during his boyhood, and his parents and grandparents were peasants. The village of Privolnoe, in the Krasnogvardeisk district about one hundred miles north-west of the city of Stavropol, was not even on the railway line. He was ten when Hitler's armies attacked Russia and eleven when Nazi troops occupied his native province. His father, Sergei, was drafted into the military and killed in the war. The Stavropol region was under Nazi occupation for about eight months, but the Germans concentrated their forces in the cities and along communication lines, leaving the countryside more or less alone.

His was a family of Russian farmers who had settled in Stavropol under the tsars. While details of his family background in the nineteenth century are not known, most Russian settlers in this border region were not serfs but free peasants who rendered military service to the empire in exchange for their privileged status. Like all peoples in border regions, Stavropol Russians tended to be strong nationalists and patriots. While he differs from the frontier stereotype by virtue of his education and responsibilities, Gorbachev remains a Russian to the core. Unlike those of his mentor, Andropov, Gorbachev's roots are purely Russian, and this was a vital element in his constitution and a source of his inner security. After he became the country's leader, he committed a public slip of the tongue in Kiev, the capital of the Ukraine, when he twice referred to the country he leads as "Russia," before correcting himself to say, "the Soviet Union, as we call it now, and as it in fact is." But the slip reflected his Russianness—most Russians think of the Soviet Union as Russia.

He tilled the soil, first with his father, later with his grandfather and alone. Toward the end of World War II, because of an acute shortage of male labor, he worked at Privolnoe's collective farm. In the mid-1940s, when the region was recovering from the harsh Nazi occupation and much of its social life was disrupted, Gorbachev's regular schooling may have been interrupted for a year or so. According to his official biography, he became an assistant to a harvesting-machine operator at the age of fifteen. Just how long he worked in that capacity is not known, but he must have been an outstanding worker—at eighteen he was awarded the Order of the Red Banner of Labor. It was this award that opened for Gorbachev a most important door—the next year he was recommended by local authorities for study at Moscow State University. He occasionally wore the decoration, particularly during his first year in Moscow. He was slightly older than other freshmen who entered the university's law school in 1950.

His choice of a legal education is interesting. The law school in those years was not the prime choice of upwardly mobile youths —Stalin's despotism recognized only one law and that was whatever the despot proclaimed the law to be. But Lenin had been a lawyer. Moreover, the law school was one of the few institutions of that period where students had to study different political cultures, constitutional law, and the history of ideas about the state. Gorbachev had to take Latin and to read authors as diverse as Rousseau, Hegel, Machiavelli, and Mill. In the long run, these studies equipped him for political leadership far better than engineering or economics would have done.

Members of the class of '55—the law school course is normally five years—remembered him thirty years later as an ambitious and hardworking student who was initially behind his city-reared classmates but moved to the top of the class after his sophomore year. In June 1985, they celebrated the thirtieth anniversary of their graduation at the Aragvi Restaurant and had sent an invitation to their most illustrious classmate. He did not attend the class reunion, but sent a warm letter, which was read at the celebration, excusing himself by citing pressures of his new job—there was "too much work" to be done. He recalled fondly the days when they were all attending school, adding that he had not changed at all: "I'm the same as I was back then."

He lived in the student housing complex near the Sokolniki Park and was known as an extrovert southerner who relished the *"ruski mat,"* as the rich compendium of curses and expletives is called in Russian. According to one classmate, his southern temperament came out in many ways, most notably in his gregariousness and in his love of language. The latter was still evident years later when, as Kremlin leader, he used vivid metaphors to make his point—as when he complained about Soviet-haters in the United States by saying "certain people in the United States are driving nails into this structure of our relationship, then cutting the [nail] heads off so the Soviets must use their teeth to pull them out."

His thirst for knowledge and culture was authentic. He and Raisa Maximovna Titorenko, a philosophy student he was dating, were known as avid theater-goers. Raya, as she was known at the time, was a strong and purposeful girl of unusual beauty who also came from the provinces, from Sterlitamak, a town near Ufa, in Bashkiria. They had a Komsomol wedding during their last year in Moscow, with friends shouting *"gorko, gorko,"* the traditional chant inviting the groom to kiss the bride for as long as the onlookers demand. Yet, my informant continued, it was clear even then that Gorbachev wanted to be a man of power. "He worked extremely hard but despite his high grades it was clear to us that he was more interested in public affairs than in law."

He became a Komsomol activist in his class, and he joined the party in 1952, less than a year before Stalin's death. In those years,

Gorbachev's clothes and manners showed him to be a "provincial," the sort Muscovite students looked down upon. At least in retrospect, the informant said, "he reminded me of a good provincial actor who arrives in the capital and is doing well, but who constantly feels an inner need to prove himself, to assert himself on and off the stage." Viktor Afanasiyev, *Pravda*'s editor in chief and a Gorbachev ally, made a similar point but said Gorbachev was a largely self-made man who had to fight for everything from the start. He had managed to be admitted to the university at a time when twenty-five students were competing for each slot, and he did so, Afanasiyev said in an interview, "without any connections—which means he was an able man." Without detracting from Gorbachev's talent and drive, it should be noted that Afanasiyev's remarks stretched the truth. In Stalin's Russia, an intelligent and ambitious collective-farm youth wanting to enter the university had a clear advantage over offspring of professional urban families. The editor's other remark was more to the point. Gorbachev was the first Soviet leader since Lenin to obtain a university education in a normal fashion and "not through correspondence courses or evening schools," a reference to the fact that academic degrees cited by other Kremlin leaders were less substantial, for they had obtained them as adults while holding high party offices.

Precious little information is available about Gorbachev's life between graduation in 1955, when he went back to his native province to become a Komsomol activist, and his return to Moscow in 1978, when he was made a secretary of the Central Committee. None of the published accounts mentions his service in the armed forces, a strange twist in the career pattern. That a promising young party member who completed law studies at the top of his class should decide not to seek a lucrative career in the capital but to return to a distant region is equally puzzling. (The population of the city of Stavropol at the time was 133,000.) It would appear logical only if Gorbachev at that time already harbored great ambitions. The path to power in the Soviet Union generally leads through regional party organizations and not through the Moscow bureaucracy.

His first years as a party activist in Stavropol coincided with the enormous social turmoil precipitated by Nikita Khrushchev's de-Stalinization policy, which was to start the process of definition of Gorbachev's political identity. Khrushchev's was the first political voice he listened to. Earlier, to be sure, there had been the voice of Stalin, but by the time Gorbachev joined the party Stalin's was the voice of a demigod who laid down the law. The exposure of Stalin's crimes had a deep impact on Gorbachev. One of his associates described him to me as "a child of the Twenty-second Party Congress," the most anti-Stalinist gathering ever convened by Khrushchev. It was the first congress young Gorbachev attended as a delegate from Stavropol. Whether by coincidence or not, Gorbachev picked another de-Stalinization landmark, February 25, as the opening date of his own congress—the Twenty-seventh Party Congress, over which he presided and which opened thirty years to the day after Khrushchev's "secret speech," in which he pilloried Stalin. Gorbachev's attitude on this thorny issue was revealed during his first month in office; he could not fake it. During Chernenko's last winter, Stalin had been fully rehabilitated as a military leader and diplomat. His deputy, Molotov, had been readmitted to the Communist Party at the age of ninety-three, and many influential Stalinists were making a forceful case for restoring the name Stalingrad to the city that was the site of the Stalingrad battle and that was renamed Volgograd by Khrushchev. Yet Gorbachev ruled against the name change.*

The Gorbachevs did not succumb to the boredom of provincial

---

*Kremlin insiders provided two different versions—one, that Chernenko had already approved the change and, the other, that Chernenko was inclined to do so but that the final decision had not been made. When I visited Volgograd, local officials told me that the change would be made in connection with the fortieth anniversary of the end of World War II and that the city had formally requested the change after it had been encouraged to do so.

life. He, already an up-and-coming provincial official, enrolled in the Stavropol Agricultural Institute's evening school in 1964, in what seems to have been a carefully calculated move to advance his political career. Raisa worked on her doctoral dissertation and took care of their daughter. Agriculture was one of the Soviet Union's most painful economic problems, but things were going well in Stavropol, a fertile, black-earth farming zone renowned for its grain and sheep. Its leader and Gorbachev's boss at the time, Fyodor Kulakov, received national recognition for his successes in the important grain-growing region.

In retrospect, it is clear that the Gorbachevs displayed a surprising degree of enlightenment and intellectual ambition. Raisa must have made her own contribution to it as they grew together intellectually. In 1967, Gorbachev completed his agricultural degree and Raisa, then thirty-four, finished her doctoral dissertation and submitted it to Moscow's Lenin Pedagogical Institute. An extensive summary of her doctoral thesis, entitled "Emergence of New Characteristics in the Daily Life of the Collective Farm Peasantry (Based on Sociological Investigations in the Stavropol Region)," is available at the Lenin Library. It shows the quality of her work to be well above average. Her methodology is surprising, as she used sociological techniques rarely applied in the Soviet Union of that day. Her thesis is based not only on official statistics, state archives, and government analyses but also on her own questionnaire, personal interviews, recollections by old peasants of customs and traditions, and personal inquiries at five collective farms. There is little doubt that her husband—who had to deal with the "difficulties and contradictions" involved in new patterns of rural life, the principal focus of Raisa's work—not only supported her research but also discussed it with her. Both read widely, and Raisa would later startle foreigners with her knowledge of literature—as she did during their visit to Britain in 1984, with questions about the plot structure of C. P. Snow and Iris Murdoch novels.

Another detail that illuminates the Gorbachevs' intellectual curiosity during that period was relayed to me by Michel Tatu, the astute political commentator and former Moscow correspondent of the Paris daily *Le Monde*. Tatu, who occasionally acted as Soviet affairs adviser to Mitterrand, met Gorbachev during his state visit to France in October 1985. The Soviet leader mentioned that he had visited Paris as a member of a Soviet delegation in 1966, and that a few years later, as a private citizen, he had made a five-thousand-kilometer auto trip through France with his wife. The couple ventured on a similar private visit to Italy. Such trips gave him a chance to take a personal look at the West, not as a member of an official Soviet delegation, shuttled mindlessly around during a short sojourn, but as a tourist intent on rummaging wherever his fancy took him. They also help explain Gorbachev's confident behavior on the international stage in the eighties.

In the mid-sixties, a Czechoslovak official, Zdenek Mlynar, whom Gorbachev had first known when they both attended Moscow State University and who had since become a leading reformist politician in Prague, visited Stavropol as a member of an official delegation and talked privately with Gorbachev. Mlynar's recollections are interesting since they show Gorbachev's mind as more practical than doctrinal. They discussed the prospects of reforming the socialist system. Mlynar says that Gorbachev regarded decentralization as the essential prerequisite for effective reforms in economic and political life, and that he considered Khrushchev's attempt to change things as having been in the nature of authoritarian intervention rather than a genuine devolution of power and responsibility to local governments.

Gorbachev's official biography does not mention any such details. It merely lists a progression of jobs in the Stavropol party organization, whose leader he became in 1970. He was thirty-nine years old. While his initial ascent up the hierarchical ladder was due to his intelligence and hard work, the appointment as first secretary of the Stavropol region could not have been made without the approval of two men who formerly held the same post—Kulakov and Mikhail Suslov—and who seem to have played an important role in Gorbachev's career. Kulakov had meanwhile moved to Moscow to become a Politburo member and Central Committee secretary in charge of agriculture. It seems that the ambitious young politician from Stavropol latched on to these two powerful figures in the Kremlin, who had personal links with the province. By then he had grasped the principles of the Soviet power structure, and especially the fact that political fortunes depended on patronage at the top.

Skimpy facts about that period suggest that Gorbachev had not yet acquired a sense of his own political direction. He seems to have vacillated between supporting the grandiose plans of the central authorities and implementing the pragmatic and effective measures he himself had developed. He favored giving larger private plots to farmers because of the high efficiency of private production, but that, of course, was something he could not do. But he had the courage to experiment with agricultural policies in his region, no doubt inspired to do so by his evaluation of the effects of excessive centralization and the absence of financial incentives. In the early seventies he introduced a bonus system based on production results without quotas and controls, and by the mid-seventies about 1,500 mechanized brigades in Stavropol operated under this decentralized system. According to press reports at the time, this system boosted harvest yields by 50 percent on irrigated lands and by 30 to 40 percent on nonirrigated territory. And yet, later in the seventies he initiated an experiment that was a complete reversal of this approach; it involved a greater degree of centralization, based on the concept of "agro-industrial complexes" with vast territories and mobile fleets of harvesters and transport vehicles. The so-called Ipatovo experiment eventually failed, but the promising results in its first year led many influential conservatives to point to it as the way for solving the country's food problems.

In retrospect, one could condemn the Gorbachev of the Stavropol period for being uncommitted—an ambitious and deft politician on the make who may have favored courses challenging the status quo but knew he had to put off direct collision with the conservative old guard. But courage and caution, personal charm and manipulative skills, ruthless determination and an inclination to flirt with liberal ideas all coexisted within him, enabling outsiders to find in Gorbachev whatever qualities they were looking for. It is conceivable that he acquired his agricultural education and then attempted to experiment with agricultural policies in Stavropol principally in order to advance his political career. It is also possible, however, that he was genuinely concerned about the grain imports, which had been increasing by leaps and bounds despite huge capital investments in Soviet agriculture. The Soviet Union depended on food imports, which meant that it depended on foreigners. This was undesirable for it left the country vulnerable and weak.

But one thing is clear: In the Soviet context he was a pragmatist, like his close friend Eduard Shevardnadze, from neighboring Georgia, who was equally convinced that changes were necessary. They had first met in the late fifties, when both were Komsomol leaders, and over the years they had become personal friends, visiting each other's home and discussing politics. This friendship apparently had, by degrees, an impact on Gorbachev's mind. The Georgian did not think in terms of absolutes or extremes; his whole cast of mind was un-Russian, for he possessed a sense of proportion and compromise and a keen appreciation of the chasm between the desirable and the possible. Shevardnadze was a superb organizer who saw the need to expand room for individual initiative in Georgia. When he became its leader, he quietly moved his republic away from highly centralized and inefficient agricultural practices. Shevardnadze's successes and the failure of the Ipatovo experiment seem to have finally persuaded Gorbachev of the inevitability of change and to have reinforced his distrust of comprehensive schemes.*

In the early seventies Gorbachev struck up another, far more important, friendship, which was to define both his career and his views.

Kulakov and Suslov had played important roles in Gorbachev's Stavropol career, but it was Andropov who launched him into a higher orbit, far higher than Gorbachev could have achieved on his own in the same time. Andropov had vacationed regularly in the northern Caucasus, and, following standard Soviet protocol, Gorbachev, the local first secretary, had personally greeted him whenever he arrived for vacation in Mineralnyye Vody or Kislovodsk. A shrewd judge of character, Andropov no doubt quickly identified the promising qualities of the young Stavropol chieftain and it is likely that their conversations became progressively more searching and candid as they walked in the woods of the north Caucasus. In spite of differences in temperament and age, they were in agreement on the key issues of policy. Andropov wanted to bring the energetic young man to Moscow, and the opportunity to do so presented itself when Kulakov suddenly died in the summer of 1978, leaving an opening in the leadership. Since Kulakov had been in charge of agriculture, Gorbachev, as an agricultural specialist and successful administrator of a major grain-growing region, seemed a natural choice to succeed him.

At the time when Gorbachev moved to Moscow in November 1978 to become a secretary of the Central Committee, the country

---

*While addressing a collective farm conference on December 20, 1978, shortly after he became the Central Committee secretary in charge of agriculture, Gorbachev voiced support for increasing the number of private plots and subsidiary farms. After he became Soviet leader in 1985, he sponsored a decree to distribute more than one million private plots to individuals each year. "We have been terribly afraid that this is something akin to private enterprise," he said, alluding to the long ideological struggle over private land holdings. "How can you call it private enterprise when a family has a garden? . . . Here we have to use our brains. Mathematically, comrades, our approach to this problem has been fundamentally weak. It is [still] very weak."

had just collected its best harvest in decades. From that year onward, it was to experience one disastrous harvest after another, and yet Gorbachev, who was responsible for agriculture, was not blamed for the failures. Like Reagan, Gorbachev seems a "Teflon" figure. Within one year he was a candidate Politburo member, and a year later he was a full member of that ruling council. He worked hard, getting to know people in the party bureaucracy, making no enemies, and retaining his image as an energetic man from Stavropol who posed no threat to other members of the leadership. He kept himself in the shadows, waiting for his chance. And it came when Andropov became general secretary.

⋘ 3 ⋙

STAVROPOL defined Gorbachev's mind and political instinct in a fundamental way. Having worked in Moscow for a mere six years before he became general secretary, he had not picked up all the views and bad habits of his predecessors. He knew how people were living outside the charmed confines of Central Committee and Kremlin life. Most high officials by tradition spend decades of their careers in Moscow, where they rarely see ordinary people except through the windows of their limousines. I suspect that Gorbachev's popular appeal, which is in part based on the breath of real life apparent in his speeches, must arise from his twenty-three years of service in Stavropol.

When I arrived in Stavropol in the summer of 1985 to search for clues about his life, I came across a great deal of pride in the native son but very little in the way of hard information. A local joke circulating at the time had the peculiar flavor of provincial southern Russia. An old woman, the story goes, was selling roasted sunflower seeds in Red Square when a furious policeman came up to her and told her to get lost. "You can't sell sunflower seeds in this sacred place," the policeman shouted. The old woman in peasant gear moved to the other side of the square and continued to offer her wares. The policeman, even more furious for having been so brazenly disobeyed, rushed over to her and began to book her. "You old hag, where are you from?" he demanded. "I'm from Stavropol, the village of Privolnoe . . ." The policeman quickly folded his pad, took the basket from her hands, and started shouting, "Here, folks, fine sunflower seeds, excellent quality! This nice grandma brought them from Stavropol. You have never seen such fine seeds!" My interlocutors told this story with chuckles and exclamations, as if they had pulled off a spectacular coup.

Stavropol looks like an old Russian town, with narrow streets lined with tall poplars, old merchant houses, a nineteenth-century market, and the more elegant one-story homes of tsarist officers. The Gorbachevs lived in one such home, painted green, on Dzerzhinski Street. The local KGB headquarters stands directly opposite the house. Gorbachev usually walked to work, since his office in Lenin Square was only a few hundred yards away. It was located inside a gleaming white five-story building in the shape of a rectangular box, which faces a large square with a statue of Lenin in the middle. Across from the party headquarters is one of the oldest buildings in town, which once housed the tsarist governors. In the summer of 1985 it was being completely rebuilt in baroque style to accommodate a local historical museum; workers were adding a second story to the old one-story mansion to make it look like a small Winter Palace.

I came away with a distinct impression that Stavropol's architecture had not been drastically sovietized, as had that of many other Russian cities, where impersonal streets and identical blocks of buildings conjure up the image of a collectivized future. (This may be because the city largely escaped destruction during World War II.) Nor had the landscape visible from atop the eighteenth-century fortress been clumsily exploited. Most people lived in single-family homes, or in small two- or three-story buildings. The city has a theater, a philharmonic orchestra, two newspapers, a radio station, a circus, a college, and a sheep institute. "You know," said a local construction engineer, "we have more than eight million sheep in Stavropol."

During Gorbachev's tenure as first secretary, Stavropol got a nicely designed glass-and-concrete airport terminal and a modern circus, which looks like a miniature of the new Moscow circus. There were several pleasant restaurants, without a bouncer at the door. Unlike northern Russians, who drink vodka, the Stavropol people seem to prefer wine. I shared several bottles of good local wine with a few residents, but they offered few insights into Gorbachev's career. That was odd, since regional first secretaries have immense power and considerable autonomy and many of them run their regions as personal fiefdoms. Gorbachev's career in Stavropol seems to have followed the classic pattern—a rise through the party ranks—but without rumors of corruption or stories about his clawing his way up in Byzantine power struggles. The only comments that suggested that Gorbachev was a man of much tougher fiber than was generally perceived were offered with knowing smiles: "The Muscovites had better wait a bit—they have yet to see the real Mikhail Sergeyevich!" Nobody suggested that he had been ambitious in any vulgar way, or that he had acted as a pompous provincial boss, but he was remembered as a forceful administrator who saw the strength of opposing arguments and telegraphed his own viewpoint, often unconsciously, by his body language or the way he summarized the problem. He was in daily touch with ordinary people—Stavropol was a place where it was impossible to live a life separate from the population—and everyone knew him. Later, as I listened to his speeches about devolution of responsibilities and financial autonomy, I had the feeling that Gorbachev had a clear idea of what life is like for an able provincial factory manager or administrator—and was aware that it is the less able managers who are comfortable with centralized planning and lack of responsibility.

But most of these observations, as well as those I heard in Moscow, were about a politician who had already risen to the top and played a role larger than life. As such, they tended to be hagiographical.

―――――――――――――― ≪ **4** ≫ ――――――――――――――

AFTER Gorbachev was thrust into the limelight in Moscow, many observers tended to focus on the new style he embodied. He was different in looks, mannerisms, and sophistication from his predecessors, who were rooted in more backward Russia. Gorbachev was a representative of the generation that came of age after World War II and began their careers after Stalin's death. He surrounded himself with men and women who had no links to the past and wanted a new beginning, realizing that although much had changed during forty years of peace, Soviet society continued to function in its established old ways. Hence there was more to the stylistic changes than mere public relations. Changes in style, of course, did not mean changes in Kremlin objectives, yet they were significant insofar as they might eventually influence substance.

A Central Committee member who had extensive dealings with him described Gorbachev to me as someone who possessed "that rare ability to be absolutely himself." This quality—and not any coaching—accounted for the effectiveness of his televised appearances. "Gorbachev is just himself; he does not worry about the cameras, and therefore he comes across. He is not playing a role, he does not worry about his looks. This is strange because with his birthmark [on his upper forehead] he could have grown up with some complexes. But he didn't. Maybe this is because he had hair when he was younger and it covered the birthmark."

The portrait painted by *Pravda* editor Viktor Afanasiyev, also a Central Committee member, was of an energetic man who possessed exceptional lucidity of mind and an ability to summarize divergent views and to put his finger on the heart of an issue. Afanasiyev, who said that he had worked with the leader on the drafting of a revised party program both in Moscow and at a dacha in the country, described him as being outgoing—"an extremely social man who loves jokes."

Yet another Kremlin insider gave a slightly more balanced picture. Gorbachev, he said, "is not a reflective person, but he has a restless and doubting mind. His memory is prodigious and so is his energy. He is a quick study." His sense of mission is absolutely authentic. From the start, he worked long hours; each day except Sunday we saw him drive to work at eight thirty-five and return home after seven.

There emerged from these discussions the impression of an enormously self-confident man who could be blunt without being offensive, clearly a man of power determined to exercise it in his own way. At the April 1985 Central Committee plenum, an example cited by one of my informants, he interrupted several speakers who advocated one or another idea. "He cut them off, very politely, addressing each speaker by his name and patronymic and excusing himself for interrupting. But then he proceeded to summarize the speaker's argument and recommendation and follow it up with questions—'But how can that be done?' or 'What do you think about another course of action?' The dialogues were conducted in front of everybody, and Gorbachev had all his emotions up front, sometimes being blunt, very blunt."

Foreigners who have met him have been favorably impressed. "I found myself talking to an absolutely modern man whom I could understand," said a Swiss socialist politician. Republican congressman Silvio Conte of Massachusetts, who saw Gorbachev with a group of American lawmakers, came away with the impression that the Kremlin had a different and even "Westernized" leader. Anthony Kershaw, the Conservative chairman of the British Parliament's foreign affairs committee, described him as a "politician rather than a dictator, though he could end up being both." After ninety minutes with him, Kershaw said Gorbachev was "in the same business as myself. He's flexible, a modern man, has a refined manner, seems in good health—which is always important for a politician in Russia—and makes points but doesn't hammer them." Henry A. Grunwald, editor in chief of *Time,* who, with Ray Cave and other *Time* executives, interviewed Gorbachev in late summer of 1985, described him as "well informed, urbane, energetic, tough, witty, and above all in possession of a disciplined intellect." Private assessments by senior American officials agreed with much of this but also described Gorbachev as too combative, scrappy, proud and opinionated, and impatient with those who offered elaborate and exceedingly well-documented suggestions.*

Yet for all his strength and confidence, Gorbachev sometimes displayed a typically Russian sense of insecurity and inadequacy in his dealings with foreigners. He sought to obscure these feelings by combativeness, and his agile mind and debating skills helped him do so. "Do you really think we are such simpletons?" he retorted during his Canadian visit when local politicians raised unpleasant questions about such matters as Afghanistan and human rights. During his London visit, he engaged in a game of one-upmanship with Trade Minister Paul Cannon. "If you send us

---

*The last point was corroborated by a senior Kremlin official in talking to me about Gromyko's elevation to the ceremonial position of president. The two men had established a close personal relationship. Moreover, Gromyko had been instrumental in guiding the last transition. But, the official said, there was an element of "natural irritation" between a younger chief and an older and highly experienced diplomat who tended to provide long and elaborate lectures, giving all shades of possibilities and nuances, before eventually making the point. Gorbachev could not treat Gromyko, a proud and sensitive man, as bluntly as he treated others.

a flea, we will put horseshoes on it," Gorbachev quipped at one point, quoting an old Russian tale whose moral is that if a foreigner thought he had done something well, the son of the Russian earth can always top it. Talking about arms control with an American congressional group, he suddenly said, "You are not talking to Tanzania or Uganda." In Paris, confronting a hostile question at a press conference, he waved his fist, saying, "Nobody talks like that to the Soviet Union."

5

THERE was nothing new in the leader's expressed determination at the outset of his rule to effect economic and other changes. From Lenin on, successive leaders, one after another, had insisted that things must improve. Even Chernenko pledged to continue Andropov's program, despite his known personal reservations.

This time there was a difference. The guideposts had already been set up by Andropov, and Gorbachev had to devise a rational and coherent plan of action. But that involved such intractable issues as prices, wages, fiscal incentives, and managerial authority, not to speak of complicated and multitiered relations between enterprises and the state. He had already developed skepticism about grandiose and comprehensive schemes and had decided to make incremental changes, building up a pattern that would eventually yield substantive improvements in the way Russians live. The debate over national reconstruction was to continue. He brought the reformist-minded economist Abel Aganbegian from Novosibirsk to Moscow and offered him the position of first deputy chairman of the State Planning Commission. Its longtime chairman, Nikolai Baibakov, one of the key opponents of reform, was pensioned off in October and replaced by a younger man, Nikolai Talyzin (Talyzin was made a candidate Politburo member as well). "Now you'll be able to *do* things," Gorbachev told Aganbegian. But the economist declined the offer, suggesting that he was "much more useful as a critic outside the administration, and you need that more as we are searching for our way." Gorbachev liked the answer. He had come to the conclusion, he told Aganbegian, that reform "must be a process" rather then a set of blueprints and administrative decrees. In the year leading up to the February 1986 party congress, he wanted to concentrate on getting new people into positions of authority. But he also wanted to attack major ailments of the society, and this was symbolized by his prompt attack on alcoholism.

Before 1985 the country had gone through repeated campaigns against alcohol, yet nothing had been done in two decades to arrest the growing problem. Already in the sixties, the writer Andrei Sinyavski had described alcoholism as "our most basic national vice." By the eighties, alcoholism had reached frightening proportions. The frenzied crush of bedraggled crowds at liquor stores was one of the most grisly sights I saw in Russia, and the number of young people in these crowds was alarming. Official statistics were equally frightening. The newspaper *Selskaya Zhizn* revealed in 1983 that a research program showed that the average age of chronic alcoholics had gone down by five to seven years during the previous decade. The study also showed that "90 percent [of alcoholics] were drawn into drinking before reaching the age of fifteen and one third before the age of ten." Alcoholism had a major adverse effect on labor and social discipline, and experts had come to the conclusion that it was also an important contributor to an unsettling demographic trend. This was reflected in the climb of mortality rates: an alarming decline in life expectancy for soviet men—from sixty-seven years in 1964 to under sixty-two years in 1980; and an equally alarming increase in infant mortality rates, about which the Russians have not been publishing information for more than a decade. Murray Feshbach, a leading American demographer, described this turn of events as "unique in the history of developed countries."* Soviet population growth dropped 50 percent between 1960 and 1980, to 0.8 percent annually, leading to an eventual shrinking of the labor force. Soviet specialists singled out alcohol consumption, along with high stress levels, poor hospital services, and richer diets, as the main causes of these problems. Russian nationalists, in particular, had begun a quiet campaign in the eighties against alcoholism, which they claimed was destroying "the essence of the nation."

Gorbachev moved to impose antialcoholism laws two months after his accession, restricting the number of sales outlets, shutting down a number of distilleries, and banning the sale of alcohol in public places except at certain hours. Nobody had expected such quick and drastic action, and the move involved political risks. On the one hand, imposing restrictions on something most Russians enjoyed was a way to demonstrate to everyone his determination and power. But failure to implement the new laws rigorously, on the other hand, would erode his authority.

There were several other substantive decisions that first spring and summer. One involved the forced retirement of more than a dozen senior military officers, including Marshal Vladimir Tolubko, the commander of the strategic forces; Admiral Sergei Gorshkov, the chief of naval operations; and General of the Army Alexei Yepishev, the chief of the political directorate of the armed forces. This change in the high command was something Gorbachev unexpectedly demanded and got in one fell swoop, a move none of his predecessors had been able to make so early in his term. By achieving it, the new leader indirectly assailed the military's title to shape the Kremlin's defense policy, which claimed from 11 to 13 percent of total GNP (compared with about 7 percent of GNP in the United States.) He seemed to want to ensure from the start that his pledge to raise the quality of life would not

---

*The Soviet death rate, which was 6.9 per 1,000 in 1964, jumped by 50 percent to 10.3 per 1,000 in 1980.

be derailed by an obstinately hungry military establishment.

All this was accompanied by shrewd political maneuvers that left all the threads of power in his hands. He acted more quickly and more boldly in consolidating his power than any of his predecessors. Within a month he elevated three close associates— Nikolai Ryzhkov, Yegor Ligachev, and KGB Chairman Viktor Chebrikov—to full membership in the Politburo, and appointed Viktor Nikonov as the new secretary of the Central Committee. Two months later he ousted from power his principal rival, Grigori Romanov, and appointed his old friend Shevardnadze foreign minister, elevating Gromyko to the presidency. Shevardnadze was also named full Politburo member. A few months later Ryzhkov replaced the eighty-year-old Nikolai Tikhonov as Soviet premier. Before the year's end, he ousted Viktor Grishin, another rival, from the Politburo and replaced him as chief of the Moscow Communist Party organization by Boris Yeltsyn, who was made an alternate Politburo member. Other top appointments included Georgi Razumovsky, in charge of personnel as head of the Central Committee's Organizational Department; Alexander Yakovlyev, former ambassador to Canada, as Gorbachev's closest foreign and domestic policy adviser; and Vsevolod Murakhovsky, a Gromyko protégé from Stavropol, as head of a new superministry of agriculture (the State Agroindustrial Committee, whose decisions "within the limits of its competence are binding on all ministries and departments," according to *Pravda.*)

The purge of upper echelons did not go without difficulty. It was relatively simple to remove Romanov, who had previously been cut off from his power base in Leningrad. The ouster of Grishin, however, was more complicated and ultimately required Gorbachev's direct personal intervention. Two other old guard Politburo members Gorbachev wanted out—Vladimir Shcherbitsky, the Ukrainian chief, and Dinmukhamed Kunaev, the boss of Kazakhstan—managed to survive the purge because of strong local support.

Grishin's ouster came after the Moscow Party Committee had already voted to reelect him. Gorbachev and his men had sent both public and private signals of displeasure with Grishin, assuming that the committee would take the hint. Gorbachev himself decided to attend the session to make sure that it was done. But the committee, packed by Grishin loyalists, ignored the signals and reelected their boss. In a dramatic hour that followed the vote, Gorbachev asked for the floor and read documents from the district attorney's office implicating Grishin in a criminal investigation of the city's housing construction authority. "After hearing this, comrades, do you want to reconsider your vote?" Gorbachev asked. The committee reversed itself.

But the purge had gone deep. The Soviet press, which became Gorbachev's tool for "psychological reconstruction," had become far more free-wheeling and critical—and the extent of the criticism was unprecedented. It probably culminated in an early 1986 article in *Pravda* that constituted a head-on assault on the party bureaucracy. Entitled "Purification," it purported to be a summary of letters from *Pravda* readers; but it echoed Milovan Djilas's *The New Class* in talking about an "entrenched, inert, immovable bureaucratic party" layer between the leadership and the working people, based on privileges.* Such public criticism gained in intensity as the party congress approached, and by the time it convened, Politburo member Gaidar Aliyev could tell a press conference that 82,000 *aparatchiks* had been replaced during the preceding twelve months, about 20 percent of the party bureaucracy. This was, according to a letter from an old Bolshevik pub-

*Pravda on February 13, 1986, also charged that many members of the party bureaucracy had "stopped being Communist long ago, [that] they only expected privileges from the party," that they had access to "special restaurants, special shops, special hospitals, and so on." The rest of the population had to wait in queues for their daily necessities. "Let the bosses go to a regular shop along with everyone else and stand in line as other people do. Then, perhaps, the lines everybody is so fed up with will be liquidated. But it is unlikely that those who enjoy special perks will renounce their privileges voluntarily. What we need is a law and a thorough purge of the *aparat.*"

lished in *Pravda,* "not a purge but purification" of the party.

The press also reflected Gorbachev's intentions on the economic front. That was most eloquently symbolized by the fact that the economist Tatyana Zaslavskaya, the author of the controversial 1983 "Novosibirsk Report," was now given front-page space in major national newspapers to argue forcefully for a radical overhaul of the economy. She also advanced the once heretical notion of interest groups and inevitable clashes of interests in socialist countries.*

Within his first twelve months in office, Gorbachev's policies held out the prospect of a significant modernization of Soviet society during the last decades of this century. But in addition to overcoming the enormous reservoir of inertia and resistance to change at home, he also had to contend with challenges abroad.

<<< **6** >>>

H E had come to the general secretary's office long after Soviet-American détente had collapsed. Under Andropov, relations had deteriorated further into confrontation. Diplomacy for both sides had become an exercise in public relations, and for all practical purposes the break in communication was almost complete. But then Chernenko switched Moscow's position, and the two superpowers restored their dialogue, although it was clearly going to be a different type of dialogue. One of the first things Gorbachev did

---

*The Kremlin's Marxist-Leninist dogma, Zaslavskaya wrote in the daily *Sovyetskaya Rosiya,* holds that "in a socialist society there are no and cannot be any groups that are interested in retaining outdated relations, and therefore that there is no place for social conflicts." The facts, she asserted, "do not bear out this point of view." She also reported the findings of a study showing that 90 percent of managers and 84 percent of workers in the Soviet Union believe that "they could work much more effectively under different economic conditions."

upon his accession was to signal that he intended to continue his predecessor's course.

This initial move was predictable. Gorbachev had spent his entire career in local and national politics and had begun on-the-job training in international issues only during Andropov's rule. Domestic issues were still at the top of Gorbachev's agenda. But foreign affairs impinged directly and painfully on his domestic policies—especially the increasingly exasperating question of the arms race. Defense policy had always claimed a disproportionately large chunk of GNP. Reagan's SDI program had begun to weigh heavily on the minds of Kremlin officials, who feared that the Americans would move even farther ahead in technology, that the military programs would have nonmilitary spinoffs, and that the Russians would be left ever farther behind in the technological race, not only by the United States but also by smaller countries such as Japan. This meant that substantial new investments were needed in Russia's military industry. Hence Gorbachev had to focus promptly on foreign affairs.

We don't know Gorbachev's views on foreign affairs during the turbulent years 1983 and 1984. Andropov had drawn him into Soviet-American relations, and Andropov's view was that Moscow should deemphasize its preoccupation with a bipolar world. Andropov saw his predecessor's policy as having caught the Kremlin in a web of constantly shifting U.S. strategic concepts and in a numbers game which forced the Russians to constantly catch up and match the United States. This was the American game, and it had a detrimental effect on Soviet military planning and programs. The same view was held by senior military figures.* When Andropov fell ill, it was Gorbachev who implemented tough decisions that led to the collapse of the Geneva talks in late 1983. As

---

*Colonel General Nikolai Chervov was quite explicit about it in an interview during which he told my colleague Jim Hoagland and me that Moscow would no longer "ape" U.S. weapons programs and specifically Reagan's SDI program.

Chernenko's number-two man a year later, Gorbachev had to carry out an entirely different policy toward the United States, one that led to the resumption of the Geneva talks. Whatever his former personal views, Gorbachev, once in power, was nobody's disciple in foreign affairs. His experience in the Politburo had taught him that he must not count on lasting cooperation from any major capitalist power, and that he was assured of American hostility. But he needed a pause in Soviet-American military rivalry. One of his main reasons for going to Geneva for a summit meeting with Reagan in November 1985 was to gain a sense of whether the arms race could be limited. In addition to using the opportunity to press his case before the West Europeans and Japanese, Gorbachev wanted to weigh Reagan's intentions for the future and incorporate them into Moscow's practical assessments and economic plans for the rest of this century. What the summit accomplished is significant only if set against the background of five years of acrimony and hostility. The two men, after an unprecedented degree of personal togetherness, retreated from ugly rhetoric. Their five hours of privacy gave off a glow of civility. Neither side could comfortably return to the invective that had previously marked the relations between the two superpowers during Reagan's presidency. While they failed to reach any agreement on the basic arms issues before them, they made the first step toward restarting the dialogue. A month or so later, on New Year's Day, the two leaders exchanged televised greetings and wished each other's people a year of peace. It was the first time an American president had spoken directly to the Russian people since Richard Nixon did so in 1972. Moscow also allowed a handful of refusenik families to leave and released Anatoly Shcharansky, the Jewish activist who had been imprisoned since 1977.

By the time the Twenty-seventh Party Congress convened on February 25, 1986, the first phase of Gorbachev's Kremlin stewardship had come to an end. Politically, he had been largely successful. He had a calmer international climate. He had managed to put new men into leading positions in the country. He had changed the mood of the establishment and restored its sense of direction.

Returning to Moscow after an absence of six months, I was immediately confronted by the most conspicuous change. I went to a restaurant with a friend, who had forewarned me to take along a flask of vodka to drink with our dinner. I thought that was wholly unnecessary since the waiters of that particular establishment had known me for a long time and were always able to come up with delicacies not listed on the menu. Alas, my waiter friends told me, the antialcoholism campaign had become more effective than even they had thought possible. We had mineral water with our caviar.

Another symbol of change, to me at least, appeared in the shape of Viktor Grishin, the once mighty boss of Moscow who used to move about the city in the midst of a fleet of black limousines and was always surrounded by scores of aides. I ran into him just before the party congress on a narrow snowbound side street just off Kalinin Prospect. A lonely man in a black woolen coat with a Karakul collar and Karakul hat, he walked cautiously, like an old pensioner. I found it hard to believe that, only a year ago, this man had aspired to become the tsar. "The son of a bitch is still able to walk," a Soviet friend of mine commented. We decided to follow him as he struggled on foot through noontime throngs of Muscovites. Many turned their heads when they recognized him.

But Gorbachev was beginning to discover that it was easier to run a political campaign—or a political purge—than to change the policies of a hidebound regime. The next phase promised to be more difficult. The task before him is, to use his own word, "titanic."

——≪ CHAPTER ELEVEN ≫——

GRAND AIMS
AND REALITY

FROM THE KREMLIN, the preceding months of feverish activity must have had a very purposeful look indeed. When the Twenty-seventh Communist Party Congress concluded on March 6, 1986, and endorsed his program, Mikhail Gorbachev could contemplate with satisfaction not only the formal consolidation of his power but the mandate for change that it gave him.

So far he had been lucky—everything had broken right for him. That the congress itself came so early in his tenure was particularly fortunate, for it allowed him to install his own Central Committee rather than work with the men and policies of his predecessors. Party congresses somewhat resemble party conventions in the West. However, in a one-party system they are, at least theoretically, far more significant, for the congress elects the policy-making Central Committee, which in turn elects the new Politburo and Secretariat. Gorbachev and his team thus received a formal mandate for their program for the rest of the eighties.

"Stop for an instant, as they say, and you fall behind a mile," he told the delegates inside the Kremlin Palace of Congresses as he outlined the historic challenge before the country. A combination of inefficient and archaic economic, social, and political institutions threatened to deny his country entry into the age of high technology and consequently to limit its role as a major world power. While the situation cried out for change, his predecessors had thought about "how to improve the economy without changing anything." Gorbachev was quoting the nineteenth-century satirical writer Saltykov-Shchedrin, who spoke of Russian officials of his day as persons incapable of taking timely and decisive action.

Gorbachev was determined to act and to act forcefully. He also must have been aware that he was treading a familiar path. The quest for change is not new in Russia, and many rulers, from tsars to general secretaries, have tried to reform things. One has only to look back to see similar problems, similar dilemmas and preoccupations, recurring throughout Russian history. In each instance, the state was the agent of change—and so it remains.

But there were two new elements in his approach. First, the entire Gorbachev enterprise was almost exclusively inspired and justified by economic necessity, rather than by dreams of Russian prestige or a glorious Communist future. The second element was a psychological insight. Gorbachev seemed more aware than any of his predecessors had been that the very obduracy of the Russian people in clinging to their way of life constituted the most formidable barrier to change, one that had humbled tsars and party chiefs. To succeed, he must alter the way Russians live and think. It was this second aspect of his task that he considered the more daunting and consequently the problem requiring his greatest attention. On July 2, 1985, when he had to explain why he had not assumed the presidency, a largely ceremonial position in the Soviet hierarchy, he declared he had to "concentrate as much as possible" on internal issues. He had defined as his highest priority "organizational tasks—to activate all units in the political system and to mobilize the masses" for his national reconstruction program. Therefore he had been trying to conduct a dialogue with the people, calling for a transformation of national values and purposes. Before any structural tinkering with the system, Gorbachev felt, a major effort was necessary to change the psychological attitude of the population toward their work and society. A majority in the elite had grasped Gorbachev's central point—as a senior Kremlin official put it—that the country had either to accept the challenge of national reconstruction or accept defeat. But the country at large had not grasped this point, and so Gorbachev dramatized it, plunging into the crowds and delivering sermons about redoubled effort and initiative. Speaking to the workers in the industrial city of Tolyatti, in southern Russia, in April 1986, he put it bluntly: "We have to begin, first of all, with changes in our attitudes and psychology," he said, "with the style and method of work. I have to tell you frankly that if we do not change ourselves, I am deeply convinced, there will be no changes in the economy and our social life." And changes "in our attitudes and psychology" had to occur at all levels, including the government and the Politburo.*

No Soviet leader had ever told his people that they might fail. Gorbachev designed these words to galvanize the population into action, to generate a sense of responsibility for the fate of the country. In the same speech he talked a great deal about the need for "an atmosphere of openness and honesty" in industrial enterprises—about the necessity to stop falsifying reports and turning criticism into "farce." He wanted to impress upon the people that democratization involved taking personal responsibility. In this respect he resembled Lenin more than any of his other predecessors, for after Lenin had consolidated his power, he regarded as

*Pravda, April 9, 1986.

308

his most important function that of being a public educator—he is still generally referred to as the "great teacher."

Gorbachev also sought to reduce Russia's reliance on Western technology and innovation. In his view, the country must draw its purpose and vigor from the energies released and the objectives pursued inside the Soviet Union. But how to free national vitality? More and more, in the inner councils, he insisted that both economic and military strength were necessary to guarantee national security in the long run. One legacy of the Brezhnev years—the achievement of strategic parity with the United States—was a key ingredient in this thinking. The belief in Gorbachev's circle was that no significant changes in the strategic balance would occur for the rest of this century, that the Russians would be able to maintain an essential equivalence in strategic weapons irrespective of American attempts to gain superiority. This confidence gave him a sense of security while reinforcing his focus on internal problems. Although he publicly exaggerated the threat of Western technological advances in order to mobilize the people, the real strategic threat to the Soviet Union, in his mind, was an inefficient economy incapable of fully entering the age of high technology. Yet he knew that what was economically desirable had to be tempered by what was politically possible. Although he talked about "radical reforms," he had not yet defined them. His rhetoric was intended to dramatize the need for change and thereby create a climate conducive to it. In practice, however, he was cautious, deliberate, eschewing a headlong plunge into the unknown. Changes would have to be made carefully, and he would have to manipulate various elements in the party to bring them about.

Yet the strategic thrust of his ideas is clear. The Soviet Union achieved nuclear parity with the United States at a staggering cost, involving not merely huge expenditures on weapons production but also a structural deformation of the economy. The country today has in effect two almost separate economies: the military, which claims all the resources and talents available to keep it galloping in the arms race; and the civilian, which is still unable to meet the basic needs of its people. Gorbachev's problem is how to create a modern and unified economy without endangering his country's security.

His performance during his first year in office was a triumph of politics. He proved himself adept in balancing political interests. At the congress, he took the middle ground between his ideological chief, Yegor Ligachev, whose pronouncements have a distinctly conservative tinge, and his protégé, Boris Yeltsin, the Moscow party chief, who was the most outspoken advocate of radical changes. The sight of these two men, both of them close to the leader, seemed to reassure the elite that future reforms would be prudent, that nothing would be done precipitously, that Gorbachev would indeed loosen the system but not go so far as to provoke a political cataclysm. But while Ligachev was there to calm the fears of conservatives, it was Yeltsin who seemed to reflect Gorbachev's views more closely, assailing the party bureaucracy without mincing words and calling for a reform of the country's leading political institutions, including the *aparat* of the Central Committee, whose members, he said, have "simply forgotten what real party work is."

At the party congress Gorbachev brought a number of new people into the top leadership. Lev Zaikov was made a full member of the Politburo while Yuri Solvoyov and Nikolai Slyunkov were made candidate members. But it is in the Secretariat where real changes took place. Among the new secretaries of the Central Committee were Anatoly Dobrynin, the former veteran ambassador to Washington, and four Gorbachev protégés—Alexander Yakovlyev, Georgi Razumovsky, Vadim Medvedev, and Alexandra Biryukova. Biryukova was the first woman to join the top leadership since Yekatarina Furtseva, who served in Khrushchev's Politburo.

The Twenty-seventh Party Congress was the most open meeting of Soviet Communists in post-Stalinist Russia. Perhaps this was because the younger members had no responsibility for past mistakes, no need to look for excuses—they started with a clean slate. And the older members, one senior official told me between sessions, wanted to go through "an open moral purification in order to avoid entering a new phase of our life with hidden old sins and mistakes." The new leaders were better educated than their predecessors, and they saw the outside world from the viewpoint of relatively junior officials who had not been involved in the shaping of foreign policy, but they knew the domestic scene well, because nearly all of them had made their careers in the provinces. Thus they fully understood the economic and social nature of the economic and social crisis into which the society had plunged in the early 1980s.

Yeltsyn seemed to be a spokesman for the new generation when, after his blistering attack on the party bureaucracy, he said: "Delegates may well ask why I did not say all this in my speech at the Twenty-sixth Party Congress [in 1981]. Well, I can answer and answer frankly—I obviously did not have enough courage or political experience at the time."

His rhetorical question and answer expressed a sentiment that was widespread among Gorbachev's supporters. From the same rostrum thirty years earlier, Khrushchev had posed a similar question, saying "some comrades may ask" why he and other members of the leadership had not stood up against Stalin's murderous policy and "why they are doing so now." But Khrushchev did not give a straight answer. Instead, Khrushchev dwelled on Stalin's enormous power and sickly suspiciousness, which "choked a person morally and physically" and created a situation "where one could not express one's own will." Yeltsyn's answer was honest, and it rang true in the ears of the average citizen.

Yeltsyn's speech brought the congress to life. Observing the proceedings on closed-circuit television, one felt at times that the changes in the political system had been profound indeed and that the pattern of "clique politics" had given way to a far more complex system of interests and arrangements. Khrushchev's Twentieth Party Congress thirty years earlier was a watershed event since it did away with the Stalinist system of mass terror and exposed the almost unimaginable grip a lone tyrant had on a great country. But Khrushchev's was a personal and emotional struggle against morally reprehensible aspects of Stalinism, and he used it to consolidate his power against his enemies—Molotov, Malenkov, Kaganovich, and other Stalin confederates.

There was never any question about Gorbachev's preeminence at the Twenty-seventh Party Congress. He dominated it conspicuously. Unlike Khrushchev, Gorbachev did not have to make a "secret speech" or denounce his predecessors—the course of events during the previous six years had by itself condemned the old guard. Yet there were some jarring notes, making it clear that doubts existed within the establishment about the scope and the pace of change. But the political struggle at the congress focused on policies and ideas rather than personalities. Gorbachev himself indicated that by referring only obliquely to figures in the party who held that "any change in the economic mechanism constitutes a deviation from socialism." The guerrilla warfare between reformists and conservatives was, of course, inherent in the situation. What seemed new to me was the fact that officials did not pretend that everything was running smoothly and without conflicts. Nor did they, in private conversations with me, hide the fact that they had yet to discover a coherent policy for the resolution of problems.

I had spoken earlier with Fyodor Burlatsky, a prominent commentator and political scientist, who has been among the leading thinkers in the establishment and an outspoken advocate of democratization. What sort of changes are contemplated? He said that this question "has been the subject of serious discussion and *even political struggle"*—he emphasized these words—"because we have a number of conservatively inclined people, many of whom fear possible destabilizing effects and point to the [1980–

1981] Polish crisis." But, Burlatsky continued, "the resistance extends far deeper. The majority of workers are not interested; they are afraid of competition." The picture he painted was one of inherent disorder and inertness among the great mass of people, which would make any large-scale social reorganization extremely difficult without strong, coercive pressure from above. As Burlatsky put it, "the strongest political will" is needed to push the program of reforms.

For what Gorbachev is attempting to do amounts to a second de-Stalinization, and a more complicated and risky process than the one carried out by Khrushchev. Khrushchev began his struggle against Stalin's ghost thirty years earlier, and his revelations about Stalin's crimes—the title of his "secret speech" was "The Cult of Personality and Its Consequences"—discredited the use of mass terror. When Khrushchev broadened his struggle against other "consequences" of Stalinism, he was deposed. Gorbachev has started a broad and well-organized assault against the political and economic "consequences" of Stalinism that have survived until present, and this means attacking the system itself.

Hostile critics could point out almost immediately after the conclusion of the congress that although Gorbachev displayed impressive political skills, he had not yet translated them into policy. Indeed, at the center of his vision of economic change there seemed to be an ill-defined core. Gorbachev has made vague references to the concepts of supply and demand, devolution of managerial authority, realistic prices, and modernization of the banking and financial systems. He has also talked about workers' participation in the decision-making process at the workplace. All these economic tools are to be applied "within the socialist context"—but how that is to be done remains unclear.

In particular, nothing specific was said at the Congress about the pricing system, which many experts understand is the key to meaningful reforms. Changing it would open the way for using economic levers throughout the economy—and would begin to take the government out of the business of subsidizing virtually everything. Yet it is clear that any move in this direction would confront a vast reservoir of resistance at all levels. Most people eagerly favor economic changes as long as they do not affect the low costs of housing, heating, food, transportation, medical care, education, and other services—all of which are subsidized by the state. Economist Abel Aganbegian, a Gorbachev adviser, has made it clear that eventually the pricing system will be reformed, at least in part. Briefing journalists, he said he advocates the termination of government subsidies across the board, except in certain welfare areas such as child support, assistance to the elderly, and medical services, and in the publishing industry. But such changes should not be expected anytime soon. Only in agriculture, he said, can modest reforms of the pricing system be expected in the near future.*

Senior officials told me privately that the reform timetable had to be slow and gradual, that the coming five years would see only cautious changes and experimentation to prepare the ground for "radical" steps in the nineties.

⫷ 2 ⫸

GORBACHEV'S ideas were based upon the conviction that the Soviet system is a superior form of social organization and that socialism as an economic system contains vast untapped possibilities. Its failure to develop its true potential was due to the

---

*Aganbegian indicated that the government intends to allow the peasants to sell most of their grain and produce at whatever prices they can obtain, except for a small amount to be sold at fixed prices to the state. This suggests that the state intends to buy additional produce and grain from the peasants at higher prices to stimulate production.

fact that it had relied—wrongly, his advisers say—on the principle of coercion. The coercive aspect had deformed the system, although it made it perform well during a series of crises—the civil war, industrialization, World War II, and postwar reconstruction. "We thought that we could go on forever like this," one high official conceded privately. It was difficult for the old guard to grasp that during the past forty years of peace things had changed and that force, while effective in earlier periods, was no longer an efficient stimulus in the high-tech age. What is required now is a judicious application of basic economic laws to free hidden potentials of the system. "We also reached another conclusion, a conclusion that shocked many of us, I might add," he continued. "That conclusion is that we cannot develop our economy without democratizing our society."

Gorbachev, in his main report to the congress, asserted that future development "is inconceivable and impossible without a further development of all the aspects and manifestations of socialist democracy."

What precisely was meant by "democratization" remains somewhat unclear, although the thrust of Gorbachev's policies suggests a degree of liberalization. He has shown interest in the arts, phoning theater director Oleg Yefremov to tell him that he enjoyed his new Chekhov production and adding, "I know that you have had some problems. But you should not worry, just carry on without worrying about the future." Since Gorbachev's accession, no movies have been banned, and all films previously banned by the censors have been released. Changes have also been apparent in the press, which has become more open and lively. It carried a call for an end to literary censorship by Yevgeny Yevtushenko, the establishment poet; such a demand could be advanced only with the tacit backing of the top leadership. There have been other significant departures in public life, perhaps best symbolized by the first live television broadcast of

a Soviet space launch and by the public outcry against the poisonous practice of anonymous letters—the common form of denunciation, since all are investigated by the police.

The new leadership has also showed itself far more adept than
earlier regimes in its public relations on the international scene,
shrewdly exploiting the Western mass media. Gorbachev himself
has no problems conducting press conferences and interviews
with foreign journalists. His televised performances are done
skillfully and carry conviction. For the first time a member of the
Politburo, Gaidar Aliyev, was assigned to brief the press about the
proceedings at the party congress.

All these developments are not merely manifestations of the
new style. These are signs of real change. And they suggest a
trend toward convergence between East and West—the trend first
forecast in 1968 by the nuclear physicist Andrei Sakharov. To
succeed, Gorbachev has not only to struggle against the inertness
of the Soviet society but also to modernize the party's ideological
and political image. In his own words, the party has to "blend the
grandeur of our aims with our real capabilities." The result of this
"blending" has been a scaling-down of the Kremlin's messianic
ambitions, a retreat from Bolshevik utopianism, a more realistic
assessment of international relations, and an important adjustment of dogma.

<<< **3** >>>

NOTHING better illuminates the scope of the Kremlin's ideological adjustments than Gorbachev's revised program of the Soviet Communist Party.

Political scientist Fyodor Burlatsky had pointed out in an article
the confusing aspect of the party's pretensions. Under Brezhnev,
the Kremlin proclaimed itself to be in the phase of "developed

socialism." Yet, Burlatsky said, no one ever established social objectives and standards for such a society. The party was guided by the "Communist ideal," which, as successive Kremlin leaders said publicly, was something to be achieved in the distant future. Consequently, Burlatsky argued, Soviet society was without a map and a compass to chart its present course. In the eighties, Andropov had begun revising Khrushchev's utopian we-will-over-take-America-by-1980 program, some of whose provisions, in Andropov's words, had clearly been "divorced from reality." But his successor, Chernenko, reverted to the Brezhnev policy. In outlining his attitude toward the party program, Chernenko asserted that the party had to retain "everything that has been earlier accomplished," adding the standard conservative cry, "This is how it was in the past. This will always remain so in the future."*

Once he became leader, Gorbachev moved quickly to distance himself from Brezhnev's policies and Chernenko's revisions. He was now in control of the party, and it was his program that was eventually adopted at the party congress. The first sign of this was his decision to quietly abandon the description of the Soviet Union as being in the phase of "developed socialism." Entire libraries had been written on this subject under Brezhnev and again under Chernenko. Andropov had delivered the first blow at the concept when in June 1983 he declared: "The party has determined that Soviet society finds itself at the beginning of this historically long period." Gorbachev simply eliminated the word "developed," thereby changing the party's image of itself.

To a Western reader, such changes might seem merely a bewildering scholastic exercise, but in the discourse of Soviet Marxism they cut deep. One could compare them with the difficult theologi-

---

*Gorbachev, while serving as Chernenko's number-two man, defined continuity somewhat differently in a speech to the Stavropol voters in February 1985. He saw it as an effort "to consolidate and to develop positive trends, and to bolster and augment everything new and progressive that has become part of our social life recently." He further defined the word "recently" as coinciding precisely with the fifteen months of Andropov's rule.

cal debates over the Immaculate Conception, in which every word was defined precisely after endless discussion.

But there were other and perhaps more important changes. Khrushchev's program, adopted in 1961, saw the second half of the twentieth century as a period of "struggle" between imperialism, led by the United States, and communism and socialism, led by the Soviet Union. This struggle was to lead to "the downfall of imperialism" and ultimately to "the triumph of socialism and communism on a worldwide scale." Gorbachev's revised program dropped the concept of "struggle" between the two systems. The current period was described as one of "historic competition," and the promised "downfall of imperialism" was not mentioned. Instead of the expected "triumph" of communism, there was a more ambiguous phrase holding out hopes that "mankind's movement toward socialism and communism" cannot be reversed.

In essence, these phrases seem designed to convey the notion that the Russians now want to pursue their national interests in a way that is compatible with maintaining peace, that the Soviet Union wants to behave like any other country of its power and size—and that communism's "manifest destiny" is to improve the quality of life in the Soviet Union rather than to work to overthrow bourgeois societies. The last point was buttressed by a toning-down of Lenin's dream of revolutionizing and reordering the world. Gorbachev explicitly asserted that Moscow was no longer in the business of "stimulating revolutions" in other parts of the world. The blanket explanation for the retreat from Lenin's declaration of war against bourgeois societies everywhere is that such a conflict would be suicidal in the world of nuclear arms. Gorbachev also abandoned Khrushchev's ideological rationale for the policy of "peaceful coexistence" with the West. This policy, in Khrushchev's definition, was "a special kind of class warfare." For Gorbachev it is just what it says—peaceful coexistence. We must move, he said, toward an interdependent, even integral, world, "groping in the dark, as it were." Moreover, the Kremlin no longer insisted that the Soviet model of socialism is the only correct one. There are, Gorbachev said, "endless variations of socialism but they have one general objective." The objective was "socialism and peace."

――――――― ⟪⟪ **4** ⟫⟫ ―――――――

GORBACHEV'S honeymoon with the Soviet people, after lasting for more than a year, was interrupted in the early morning hours of April 26, 1986, when a sudden surge of power touched off a disastrous explosion at the Chernobyl nuclear plant in the Ukraine. His hesitant response to the crisis briefly tarnished his reputation for decisiveness and openness.

The Russians at first refused to admit to the disaster, which spewed radiation over the rest of Europe; then they acknowledged it grudgingly. It was the old, old Russian story of refusing to promptly confront an unpleasant reality, of stonewalling while hoping the disaster would somehow vanish by itself. Not until nine days after the accident, following the visit to Chernobyl by Ryzhkov and Ligachev, did a coherent information operation snap into action. Eighteen days after the accident, Gorbachev went on national television to discuss the disaster. A probable explanation for the delay has been suggested: Soviet scientists had warned that for the first two weeks, as rescue teams sought to contain the disaster, there was a distinct possibility that another of the three nuclear reactors might explode, creating an even more dangerous situation. Only after the Chernobyl explosion was contained, according to this argument, was Gorbachev able to address the nation with confidence.

Although the televised speech was unprecedented in the Soviet context, it seemed to come too late to publicly demonstrate Gorbachev's leadership. To be sure, it is difficult to assess his handling of the situation and its impact on the Soviet public since no other event in recent Soviet history supplies a precedent against which both can be gauged. Yet it is precisely a political leader's reaction to the unexpected that constitutes a major test of his leadership. By the standards Gorbachev had set for himself, he fell short in the test of Chernobyl.

The disaster brought him face to face with the realities of the system, especially its weak information network and the reluctance of professional managers to challenge party bosses. In the months after Chernobyl, Gorbachev managed to recover from most of its domestic political consequences, but his prestige was at least temporarily affected, especially in the intellectual community. Perhaps for this reason Gorbachev has gone out of his way to mobilize the country's intellectuals behind his program. It may be too early to talk about a new cultural thaw, yet something was definitely beginning to change in the spring of 1986, something that reflected the sense of new possibilities that Gorbachev has released in the Soviet cultural world by signaling a readiness for a more open debate. One of the signals was the departure of Culture Minister Pyotr Demichev. New figures known to be liberal have come to the leadership of several creative-arts unions. Elem Klimov, an accomplished movie director who in the past had difficulties with the state censors, was appointed the chief of the Filmmakers' Union; Vladimir Karpov, who was imprisoned during Stalin's last years and who is an admirer of Boris Pasternak, was elected head of the Writers' Union. The Writers' Union Congress in late June was marked by unprecedented candor and debate. Moreover the works of Nikolai Gumilev, a poet who was executed as a counterrevolutionary in 1921, have begun appearing in literary journals, and several literary commissions have been created to prepare for publications works by such controversial authors as the Russian émigré novelist Vladimir Nabokov, who was not formerly recognized in the Soviet Union, and the poet Osip Mandelstam, who died in a Stalinist labor camp. For the first time Joyce's *Ulysses* was being translated for publication in Moscow.

Gorbachev himself has changed before the nation's eyes in the course of 1985 and early 1986 and is likely to continue to change. What we saw in the summer of 1986 was a more skillful and assertive leader—confident enough to press for an arms control summit with Ronald Reagan. He gave off vibrations of control and competence, a reassuring figure who represented the coming generations. His style and pronouncements provided a sharp contrast to the dullness and anti-intellectualism of Brezhnev and Chernenko. He had matured. His generally successful performance seemed to have given him a sense of his own political identity, reinforced by his new understanding of the use of power and its limitations, and perhaps even more by his growing mastery of political and diplomatic skills. He was a modern politician. He resisted attempts by the party bureaucracy to turn him into a tsar, cut off from the substance of politics by Kremlin rituals—the endless presentation of honors, the incessant quotation of the general secretary's remarks by every conceivable speech-giver and editorial-writer, the larger-than-life portraits throughout a land that stretches over two continents. Brezhnev and Chernenko relished that role, as did the old guard, to whom it represented the weakness of the leader and the participation of the establishment in a hierarchical order of clearly defined rights and privileges. Like his models, Lenin and his mentor, Andropov, Gorbachev was interested in the effective use of political power rather than the rituals of leadership. "Why should one keep quoting Mikhail Sergeyevich!" Gorbachev exclaimed, interrupting a speaker at the congress who had repeatedly referred to the leader's speeches.

So how realistic are the hopes in the West that Gorbachev's accession to power foreshadows a basic transformation of Soviet life? What will come of the expectations he has been raising in his own country? To what extent will his plans be stymied by his ideological and political legacy? Do conditions exist that will allow him to carry out his vision?

Russians themselves are asking such questions, as doubts linger at all levels of society. Typical was the reaction of a couple whom I have known for eighteen years. The husband, a prominent non-Communist intellectual, professed to feel the same hopes and expectations that he felt as a young man following Khrushchev's de-Stalinization. "Fresh winds are blowing; we are breathing easier," he said. His wife, also an intellectual, contended that nothing was changing. "Gorbachev, Gorbachev! Just more of the same," she said. A family argument erupted in front of me.

Undoubtedly, the process of change in the Soviet Union will continue as Gorbachev defines his policies. Undoubtedly, new men and women will be coming to the fore if the momentum for change is maintained.

Yet the problems are enormous and perhaps insurmountable. His country's geography, history, and tradition have put it in a curious position between East and West, and it has never made the choice between these two civilizations. Its exceptionally conservative society cannot easily be manipulated; in the past it has responded mostly to force. In this context, Gorbachev appears almost a tragic figure. He has set out to modernize his country, but the challenge he has presented may prove to be too exacting and too ambitious. He started out as a serious reformer, but he could become an autocrat if the inherited problems prove intractable and if his people exhaust the energy and commitment of the new Kremlin management team.

But, as I have repeatedly attempted to show, the quest for change has occupied the foreground in the eighties; almost imperceptibly the country has been taking on a new shape. Gorbachev's Russia, in short, is on the verge of becoming a complex and rich society potentially capable of generating a new vitality if the leadership finds the strength to jettison the utopian ideological assumptions and Stalinist practices that are holding it back. Observed from this angle, Gorbachev seems the most enlightened Soviet ruler to date, a modern man who might eventually place a personal imprint on his age.

GLOSSARY

As this book is intended for general readers as well as specialists, it may be helpful to clarify a few basic institutions of the Soviet political system.

• *The general secretary of the Communist Party of the Soviet Union* is the country's leader.

• The country's president, or titular head of state, holds a largely honorific position. His formal title is *president of the Presidium of the Supreme Soviet* (parliament).

• The *Politburo* is the real decision-making center of power. It is chaired by the general secretary, who is also a Politburo member. The Politburo normally has about a dozen full members with voting privileges, and six or seven candidate (nonvoting) members.

• The *Secretariat of the Communist Party Central Committee* is another key center of authority. It is chaired by the general secretary and includes nine secretaries of the Central Committee, each in charge of a different aspect of the country's life. Some Politburo members are also secretaries of the Central

Committee, a combination of jobs that makes them preeminent in the hierarchy. The Secretariat shapes issues for Politburo decisions.

• The *Central Committee* is composed of about 300 members and about 170 candidate (nonvoting) members, who are top officials from throughout the country. Theoretically, it is the main policy-making body, but it meets only two or three times a year and almost invariably endorses the leader's decisions.

• The *Council of Defense* is the military high command. The general secretary automatically becomes its chairman. Other members include top military and political officials.

• The *Soviet government,* which is also known as the *Council of Ministers,* is the executive arm of the Communist Party. It is headed by the *Premier,* who is always a full Politburo member.

• The *Supreme Soviet* is a two-chamber parliament. One chamber, the *Council of the Union,* includes deputies from each province (*oblast*). The other, the *Council of the Nationalities,* includes representatives from the fifteen national republics. The Supreme Soviet meets twice a year for sessions that normally last two days; it performs a largely rubber-stamp function. The *Presidium of the Supreme Soviet* consists of forty-four members and is chaired by the country's head of state. It meets more frequently to give legal form to the party's decisions.

INDEX

ABOUT THE AUTHOR

DUSKO DODER, Moscow bureau chief of the Washington *Post* from 1981 to 1985, has reported extensively on Soviet and East European affairs since 1968. A graduate of Washington University, St. Louis, and recipient of two advanced degrees at Columbia University, he served as Moscow correspondent for United Press International from 1968 to 1970 before joining the Washington *Post,* where he also served as chief of the paper's East European bureau. Doder's dispatches from Moscow were awarded the 1982 Overseas Press Club Citation for Excellence and Georgetown University's 1984 Edward Weintal Prize for Diplomatic Reporting.

Mr. Doder is now on the *Post* staff in Washington, where he lives with his wife and son.